The Novel
and the Police

The Novel
and the Police

D. A. Miller

University of California Press
BERKELEY   LOS ANGELES
LONDON

University of California Press
Berkeley and Los Angeles, California
University of California Press, Ltd.
London, England
© 1988 by
The Regents of the University of California
Printed in the United States of America

Library of Congress Cataloging-in-Publication Data

Miller, D. A., 1948–
    The novel and the police.

    Includes index.
    1. English fiction—19th century—History and
criticism.   2. Police in literature.   3. Social control
in literature.   4. Collins, Wilkie, 1824–1889—Political
and social views.   5. Dickens, Charles, 1812–1870.   Bleak
House.   6. Trollope, Anthony, 1815–1882.   Barchester
Towers.   I. Title.
PR878.P59M55   1988b   823'.8'09355   87-25470
ISBN 0-520-06746-0 (alk. paper)

The author acknowledges permission to reprint the
essays in this volume as follows:

"The Novel and the Police," from *Glyph: Johns
Hopkins Textual Studies* 8 (Baltimore: Johns Hopkins
University Press, 1981), pp. 127–47.

"From *roman policier* to *roman-police*: Wilkie Collins's
The Moonstone," from *Novel* 13, no. 2 (Winter 1980):
153–70.

"Discipline in Different Voices: Bureaucracy, Police,
Family, and *Bleak House*," from *Representations* 1
(February 1983): 59–89. Copyright © 1983 by The
Regents of the University of California.

"The Novel as Usual: Trollope's *Barchester Towers*,"
from *Sex, Politics, and Science in the Nineteenth-Century
Novel: Selected Papers from the English Institute, 1983–
84*, ed. Ruth Bernard Yeazell (Baltimore: Johns
Hopkins University Press, 1986), pp. 1–38.

"*Cage aux folles*: Sensation and Gender in Wilkie
Collins's *The Woman in White*," from *The Nineteenth-
Century British Novel*, ed. Jeremy Hawthorn (London:
Edward Arnold, 1986), pp. 95–124.

"Secret Subjects, Open Secrets," from *The Dickens
Studies Annual* 14 (New York: AMS Press, 1985),
pp. 17–38.

Contents

Foreword: "But Officer . . ."   vii

ONE
The Novel and the Police   1

TWO
From *roman policier* to *roman-police*:
Wilkie Collins's *The Moonstone*   33

THREE
Discipline in Different Voices:
Bureaucracy, Police, Family, and *Bleak House*   58

FOUR
The Novel as Usual:
Trollope's *Barchester Towers*   107

FIVE
Cage aux folles: Sensation and Gender
in Wilkie Collins's *The Woman in White*   146

SIX
Secret Subjects, Open Secrets   192

Index   221

Foreword: "But Officer . . ."

*Even the blandest (or bluffest) "scholarly work" fears getting into
trouble: less with the adversaries whose particular attacks it keeps busy
anticipating than through what, but for the spectacle of this very activity, might be perceived as an overall lack of* authorization. *It is as
though, unless the work at once assumed its most densely professional
form, it would somehow get unplugged from whatever power station (the
academy, the specialization) enables it to speak. Nothing expresses—
or allays—this separation anxiety better than the protocol requiring
an introduction to "situate" the work within its institutional and discursive matrix. The same nervous ritual that attests a positive dread
of being asocial—of failing to furnish the proper authorities with one's
papers, and vice versa—places these possibilities at an infinite remove
from a writing whose thorough assimilation, courted from the start,
makes it too readable to need to be read much further. If only for this
reason, the moment when "explanations are in order" may rightly give
rise to the desire to withhold them (like Balzac's Vautrin, whose last
words to the police as they open his closets and seize his effects are "Vous
ne saurez rien") long enough, at any rate, to draw attention to what
is most compelling in the demand for them.*

And the police? In entrusting the arresting character of my
title to a term whose mere mention arouses some anxiety (not
necessarily least in the law-abiding), I admit to melodramatiz-
ing—even at the risk of seeming to misname—the main con-

cern of my work. This work centers not on the police, in the modern institutional shape they acquire in Western liberal culture during the nineteenth century, but on the ramification within the same culture of less visible, less visibly violent modes of "social control." A power that, like the police, theatrically displays its repressiveness becomes of interest here only in its relation to an extralegal series of "micro-powers" disseminating and dissembling their effects in the wings of that spectacle. Michel Foucault has called this series *discipline*, and its most pertinent general propagations include: (1) an ideal of unseen but all-seeing surveillance, which, though partly realized in several, often interconnected institutions, is identified with none; (2) a regime of the norm, in which normalizing perceptions, prescriptions, and sanctions are diffused in discourses and practices throughout the social fabric; and (3) various technologies of the self and its sexuality, which administer the subject's own contribution to the intensive and continuous "pastoral" care that liberal society proposes to take of each and every one of its charges.[1] To label all this "the police" thus anticipates moving the question of policing out of the streets, as it were,

---

1. It might go without saying, but as he used to joke, it goes better with saying, that I largely find the conceptual bearings of this study in the thought of Michel Foucault, from whose personal counsel I also had opportunity to profit. Yet in announcing my project as "a Foucaldian reading of the Novel," I mean to signal, besides an intellectual debt, an intellectual gamble for which that debt is the capital. For perhaps the most notable reticence in Foucault's work concerns precisely the reading of literary texts and literary institutions, which, though often and suggestively cited in passing, are never given a role to play within the disciplinary processes under consideration. As Foucault once put it in an interview with Roger-Pol Droit (published posthumously in *Le Monde*, September 6, 1986, p. 12), "Pour moi, la littérature était à chaque fois l'objet d'un constat, pas celui d'une analyse ni d'une réduction ni d'une intégration au champ même de l'analyse" (On every occasion I made literature the object of a report, not of an analysis and not of a reduction to, or an integration into, the very field of analysis).

into the closet—I mean, into the private and domestic sphere on which the very identity of the liberal subject depends. Though ordinarily off-limits to the police, this sphere is nonetheless, I argue, a highly active site for the production and circulation of a complex power whose characteristically minor, fluid, and "implicit" operations distract our attention from the unprecedented density of its regulation. Were an apology required for the histrionics of, for instance, my title, it would be this: that only an ostentation of style and argument can provide the "flash" of increased visibility needed to render modern discipline a problem in its own right far more fundamental than any it invents to attach its subjects.

Yet it by no means inevitably follows that this extended understanding of policing is suitably promoted through a study of some novels by Dickens, Trollope, and Wilkie Collins. Few of course would dispute that, with Dickens, the English novel for the first time features a massive thematization of social discipline, or that, in direct and undisguised response to Dickens, Trollope and Collins develop the two most important inflections of this thematization in the "realist" and "sensation" traditions respectively.[2] The difficulty lies less in justifying the individual names chosen to bear the burden of the case than in understanding why the Victorian novel, however exemplified, should be particularly worthy to register such a case in the first place. The use of a fictional representation might seem to trivialize a disciplinary function that would be better illustrated in discourses whose practical orientation is immediately conse-

2. A roughly similar triangulation might be shown to determine the corpus of nineteenth-century French fiction, where Balzac decisively sets forth the disciplinary themes and plots that, always in allusion to his achievement, will be rehearsed either hyperbolically by the feuilletonistes (Sue, du Terrail) or litotically by the realists (Flaubert, Maupassant, Zola). The first essay in this volume locates what for merely practical reasons I have confined myself to treating as the English instance within the broader context of the Western European novel.

quential. And the use of an outmoded representation suggests the academician's familiar retreat from the contemporary issues that, sniperlike, he targets only from the safe ground of an obsolescence. Yet perhaps no openly fictional form has ever sought to "make a difference" in the world more than the Victorian novel, whose cultural hegemony and diffusion well qualified it to become the primary spiritual exercise of an entire age. As I hope to show, the point of the exercise, relentlessly and often literally brought home as much in the novel's characteristic forms and conditions of reception as in its themes, is to confirm the novel-reader in his identity as "liberal subject," a term with which I allude not just to the subject whose private life, mental or domestic, is felt to provide constant inarguable evidence of his constitutive "freedom," but also to, broadly speaking, the political regime that sets store by this subject. Such confirmation is thoroughly imaginary, to be sure, but so too, I will eventually be suggesting, is the identity of the liberal subject, who seems to recognize himself most fully only when he forgets or disavows his functional implication in a system of carceral restraints or disciplinary injunctions. I further assume that the traditional novel—the novel that many people define their modernity by no longer reading—remains a vital consideration in our culture: not in the pious and misleading sense that, for instance, "Masterpiece Theatre" has dramatized all but one of the novels I mainly discuss, but because the office that the traditional novel once performed has not disappeared along with it. The "death of the novel" (of that novel, at any rate) has really meant the explosion everywhere of the novelistic, no longer bound in three-deckers, but freely scattered across a far greater range of cultural experience. To speak of the relation of the Victorian novel to the age of which it was, *faute de mieux*, the mass culture, is thus to recognize a central episode in the genealogy of our present.

It has become easy to show how the various decorums that determine a work of literature, from within as well as from without, are exceeded by the disseminal operations of language, narrative, or desire—so easy that the demonstration now proceeds as predictably as any other ritual. Whenever a text makes confident claims to cognition, these will soon be rendered undecidable, and whatever ideological projects it advances will in the course of their elaboration be disrupted, "internally distanciated." Full, focused psychological subjects will be emptied out and decentered as invariably as desire will resurface at the very site of its apparent containment. So common have arguments along these lines become that, even if it were true that literature exercises a destabilizing function in our culture, the current consensus that it does so does not. Yet the point of remarking what one might call (doing violence to wide differences of approach, but not to the orthodoxy in which they have come to cohere) the "subversion hypothesis" of recent literary studies cannot be to dispute the evidence of such subversion, which may well be literature's most definitive, powerful, and seductive effect. It is rather a matter of seeing how this effect tends to function within the overbearing cultural "mythologies" that will already have appropriated it.

Thus, in the case of the nineteenth-century novel, it is at present widely held that (1) though the project of this novel is to produce a stable, centered subject in a stable, centered world, (2) this project is inevitably doomed to failure. Whether the failure is greeted with philosophical resignation (to the fact that meaning can never be pinned down), political relief (that a work's suspect ideological messages don't finally hang together), or erotic celebration (of a desire that erupts when and where it is least wanted), it always gives evidence of a process that, while inherent in "the text," nonetheless remains curiously outside and deconstructive of what this text mundanely "wants to say." Even the most rigorous intentions to the contrary haven't prevented such an account of the novel from reinforcing the familiar mythological opposition between "literature" (which is compensated for its lack of power by an ability to penetrate power's ruses) and "society" (which, albeit oppressively powerful, never quite *knows* its own strength). Not only does this account help preserve for literature—as the very concept of literariness—an almost or even frankly ontological distance from the worldly discourses with which literature could otherwise be seen to collaborate. It also helps preserve the very models of social and psychological centering that, as though they had entranced even the activity of demystifying them, are tirelessly rehearsed within it. Aside from their in-dubitable nostalgia value, moreover, these models are largely irrelevant to a social order that is busy attaining the condition of (just for instance) the money by which it is obsessed as well as driven: its lack of particularity, the mobility of its exchange, its infinitely removed finality.

Accordingly, this book attempts to redress the "positive" achievement of nineteenth-century fiction. Just as I will argue that the theme of the police is an "alibi" for a station-house that now is everywhere, even or especially in the novel one reads at home, so I will imply the complementary claim that the nov-el's critical relation to society, much advertised in the novel and its literary criticism, masks the extent to which modern social organization has made even "scandal" a systematic function of its routine self-maintenance.[3] From this perspective, the enter-

3. Consider, from Dickens's *Bleak House*, Esther's account of her last visit, with Ada and Richard, to the Court of Chancery: "We found such an unusual crowd in the Court of Chancery that it was full to the door and we could neither see nor hear what was passing within. It appeared to be something droll, for occasionally there was a laugh, and a cry of 'Si-lence!' It appeared to be something interesting, for everyone was pushing and striving to get nearer. It appeared to be something that made the professional gentlemen very merry, for there were several young coun-sellors in wigs and whiskers on the outside of the crowd, and when one of them told the others about it, they put their hands in their pockets, and quite doubled themselves up with laughter, and went stamping about the pavement in the hall. . . . Our suspense was short; for a break up soon took place in the crowd, and the people came streaming out looking flushed and hot, and bringing a quantity of bad air with them.

prise of the traditional novel would no longer (or not just) be the doomed attempt to produce a stable subject in a stable world, but would instead (or in addition) be the more successful task of forming—by means of that very "failure"—a subject habituated to psychic displacements, evacuations, reinvestments, in a social order whose totalizing power circulates all the more easily for being pulverized.

Almost from the start, *The Novel and the Police* aspired to what is still unclear it has been granted: the fully contradictory status of a "book of essays," whole enough, at moments, to cohere in an identifiable set of concerns, but partial enough, at other or even the same moments, to frustrate the totalization

---

Still they were all exceedingly amused, and were more like people coming out from a Farce or a Juggler than from a court of Justice. We stood aside, watching for any countenance we knew; and presently great bundles of paper began to be carried out—bundles in bags, bundles too large to be got into any bags, immense masses of papers of all shapes, which the bearers staggered under, and threw down for the time being, anyhow, on the Hall pavement, while they went back to bring out more. Even these clerks were laughing. We glanced at the papers, and seeing Jarndyce and Jarndyce everywhere, asked an official-looking person who was standing in the midst of them, whether the cause was over. 'Yes,' he said; 'it was all up with it at last!' and burst out laughing too" (*Bleak House* [Oxford: Oxford University Press, 1948], p. 865). As it reaches its conclusion, what one reader has called Dickens's "carnivalization of bureaucracy" becomes nothing more—or less—than a carnivalization *by* bureaucracy. Esther is in no laughing mood; rather it is the professional gentlemen, the counsellors, and the clerks who "double themselves up" in amusement and who are willing to produce and receive the whole performance as Farce. Accordingly, Dickens's satire on the court cannot be described as simply a repetition of social tragedy as literary farce, since it is farce itself that must be repeated (and as what, if not the laughable, farcical protest against ever being anything but farce). This fact must cast a long shadow on the novel's efforts to satirize the court in ways not already foreseen and put to good use by the requirements of bureaucratic operation.

that could here betoken only the unresisted triumph of the subject matter—of "the police," that is, who (as Raskolnikov
needlessly points out to Porfiry Petrovich in *Crime and Punishment*) "turn everything to account." Under the circumstances,
might not a possibly saving grace abide in the dissonance that
results when—stupidly or not—one lets stand the arrogant
hermetic presumption of each essay that all the others alongside
it do not exist or do not proceed under the same annihilating
presumption; or when—lazily or not—one neglects to homog-
enize the various moments of a discourse that may thus be
caught in the several acts of revising (dismissing, forgetting,
blinding) what is consequently no longer quite "itself"? Or, on
the contrary, would not the effects of this uneven, not to say
arrested development play precisely into the ideology of the liberal subject who, never fixed in any of the determinations that
he may provisionally entertain, is always free to remake himself; and whose now-fashionable lack of anguish or embarrassment before heterogeneity depends on an imperial state (of "affairs") that has already unified the world in a total system? Such
are the ambiguities that the form of this book seeks to make
legible, though with a view less to "having it either way" than
to having it neither. Almost as though I were thus claiming to
embrace an *exemplary* double bind (that of a particular historical
moment or formation), I have inscribed whatever maneuver-
ability this writing supposes within a resistance both to disciplinary order and to an already venerable means of displacing
and further developing this order: the notion of our simple
"liberation" from it.

I am happy to be able to thank the John Simon Guggenheim
Memorial Foundation for a fellowship in 1983–84, when I
wrote parts of this book. It lies beyond my skill, however, to
acknowledge the precious interlocution of those whom, in the
course of writing, I came to consider my secret sharers, without
appearing either to repay them (with a more aggressive shade

of meaning: pay them back) or to render their generosity my own in recognizing it. At any rate, I take a less ponderous pleasure in inviting the following friends to concelebrate (as at a party) the term of a labor that, I like to think, need no longer detain me: Travis Amos, Marston Anderson, Mitchell Breitwieser, Peter Brooks, Carol T. Christ, Christopher Craft, Catherine Gallagher, Stephen Greenblatt, Lizbeth Hasse, Neil Hertz, Audrey Jaffe, Franco Moretti, Paul Morrison, Laura Mullen, Caroline Newman, Mary Ann O'Farrell, Eve Kosofsky Sedgwick, Garrett Stewart, David Suchoff, Steph Zlott, and Alex Zwerdling. I do not imagine needing to invite Ann Bermingham, to whom I dedicate "a work that escapes the both of us."

ONE

The Novel and the Police

I

The frequent appearance of policemen in novels is too evident
to need detecting. Yet oddly enough, the ostensive thematic of
regulation thereby engendered has never impugned our belief
that "of all literary genres, the novel remains the most free, the
most *lawless*."[1] Though the phrase comes from Gide, the notion
it expresses has dominated nearly every conception of the form.
If a certain puritanical tradition, for instance, is profoundly suspicious of the novel, this is because the novel is felt to celebrate
and encourage misconduct, rather than censure and repress it. A
libertarian criticism may revalue this misconduct as human freedom, but it otherwise produces a remarkably similar version of
the novel, which, in league with rebel forces, would bespeak and
inspire various projects of insurrection. This evasive or escapist
novel persists even in formalist accounts of the genre as constantly needing to subvert and make strange its inherited prescriptions. All these views commonly imply what Roger Caillois
has called "the contradiction between the idea of the police and
the nature of the novel."[2] For when the novel is conceived of as a

1. André Gide, *Les faux-monnayeurs*, in *Oeuvres complètes*, ed. L. Martin-
   Chauffier, 15 vols. (Paris: Nouvelle Revue Française, 1932–39), 12:268.
   "De tous les genres littéraires . . . le roman reste le plus libre, le plus
   lawless."
2. Roger Caillois, *Puissances du roman* (Marseilles: Sagittaire, 1942), p.
   140.

successful act of truancy, no other role for the police is possible
than that of a patrol which ineptly stands guard over a border
fated to be transgressed. In what follows, I shall be considering
what such views necessarily dismiss: the possibility of a radical
entanglement between the nature of the novel and the practice of
the police. In particular, I shall want to address two questions
deriving from this entanglement. How do the police systematically function as a topic in the "world" of the novel? And how
does the novel—as a set of representational techniques—systematically participate in a general economy of policing power?
Registering the emergence of the modern police as well as modern disciplinary power in general, the novel of the nineteenth
century seemed to me a good field in which these questions
might first be posed. Practically, the "nineteenth-century
novel" here will mean these names: Dickens, Collins, Trollope,
Eliot, Balzac, Stendhal, Zola; and these traditions: Newgate fiction, sensation fiction, detective fiction, realist fiction. Theoretically, it will derive its ultimate coherence from the strategies
of the "policing function" that my intention is to trace.

II

One reason for mistrusting the view that contraposes the notions of novel and police is that the novel itself does most to
promote such a view. Crucially, the novel organizes its world
in a way that already restricts the pertinence of the police. Regularly including the topic of the police, the novel no less regularly sets it against other topics of surpassing interest—so that
the centrality of what it puts at the center is established by
holding the police to their place on the periphery. At times,
the limitations placed by the novel on the power of the police
are coolly taken for granted, as in the long tradition of portraying the police as incompetent or powerless. At others, more
tellingly, the marginality is dramatized as a gradual process of

marginalization, in which police work becomes less and less relevant to what the novel is "really" about.

Even in the special case of detective fiction, where police detectives often hold center stage, the police never quite emerge from the ghetto in which the novel generally confines them. I don't simply refer to the fact that the work of detection is frequently transferred from the police to a private or amateur agent. Whether the investigation is conducted by police or private detectives, its sheer intrusiveness posits a world whose normality has been hitherto defined as a matter of *not needing* the police or policelike detectives. The investigation repairs this normality, not only by solving the crime, but also, far more important, by withdrawing from what had been, for an aberrant moment, its "scene." Along with the criminal, criminology itself is deported elsewhere.

In the economy of the "mainstream" novel, a more obviously circumscribed police apparatus functions somewhat analogously to define the field that exceeds its range. Its very limitations bear witness to the existence of other domains, formally lawless, outside and beyond its powers of supervision and detection. Characteristically locating its story in an everyday middle-class world, the novel takes frequent and explicit notice that this is an area that for the most part the law does not cover or supervise. Yet when the law falls short in the novel, the world is never reduced to anarchy as a result. In the same move whereby the police are contained in a marginal pocket of the representation, the work of the police is superseded by the operations of another, informal, and extralegal principle of organization and control.

Central among the ideological effects that such a pattern produces is the notion of *delinquency*. For the official police share their ghetto with an official criminality: the population of petty, repeated offenders, whose conspicuousness licenses it to enact, together with the police, a normative scenario of crime and punishment. To confine the actions of the police to a delinquent milieu has inevitably the result of consolidating the milieu itself, which not only stages a normative version of crime and punishment, but contains it as well in a world radically divorced from our own. Throughout the nineteenth-century novel, the confinement of the police allusively reinforces this ideology of delinquency. We may see it exemplarily surface in a novel such as *Oliver Twist* (1838). Though the novel is plainly written as a humane attack on the institutions that help produce the delinquent milieu, the very terms of the attack strengthen the perception of delinquency that upholds the phenomenon.

A large part of the moral shock *Oliver Twist* seeks to induce has to do with the *coherence* of delinquency, as a structured milieu or network. The logic of Oliver's "career," for instance, establishes workhouse, apprenticeship, and membership in Fagin's gang as versions of a single experience of incarceration. Other delinquent careers are similarly full of superficial movement in which nothing really changes. The Artful Dodger's fate links Fagin's gang with prison and deportation, and Noah Claypole discards the uniform of a charity boy for the more picturesque attire of Fagin's gang with as much ease as he later betrays the gang to become a police informer. Nor is it fortuitous that Fagin recruits his gang from institutions such as workhouses and groups such as apprentices, or that Mr. and Mrs. Bumble become paupers "in that very same workhouse in which they had once lorded it over others."[3] The world of delinquency encompasses not only the delinquents themselves, but also the persons and institutions supposed to reform them or prevent them from forming. The policemen in the novel—the Bow Street runners Duff and Blathers—belong to this

---

3. Charles Dickens, *Oliver Twist* (Oxford: Oxford University Press, 1949), p. 414. In the case of works cited more than once, page references to the edition first noted will be thereafter given parenthetically in the text.

world, too. The story they tell about a man named Chickweed *who robbed himself* nicely illustrates the unity of both sides of the law in the delinquent context, the same unity that has allowed cop Blathers to call robber Chickweed "one of the family" (227). Police and offenders are conjoined in a single system for the formation and re-formation of delinquents. More than an obvious phonetic linkage connects the police magistrate Mr. Fang with Fagin himself, who avidly reads the *Police Gazette* and regularly delivers certain gang members to the police.

In proportion as Dickens stresses the coherence and systematic nature of delinquency, he makes it an *enclosed* world from which it is all but impossible to escape. Characters may move from more to less advantageous positions in the system, but they never depart from it altogether—what is worse, they apparently never want to. With the exception of Oliver, characters are either appallingly comfortable with their roles or pathetically resigned to them. An elsewhere or an otherwise cannot be conceived, much less desired and sought out. The closed-circuit character of delinquency is, of course, a sign of Dickens's progressive attitude, his willingness to see coercive system where it was traditional only to see bad morals. Yet one should recognize how closing the circuit results in an "outside" as well as an "inside," an "outside" precisely determined as *outside the circuit*. At the same time as the novel exposes the network that ties together the workhouse, Fagin's gang, and the police *within* the world of delinquency, it also draws a circle around it, and in that gesture, holds the line of a *cordon sanitaire*. Perhaps the novel offers its most literal image of holding the line in the gesture of *shrinking* that accompanies Nancy's contact with the "outside." "The poorest women fall back," as Nancy makes her way along the crowded pavement, and even Rose Maylie is shown "involuntarily falling from her strange companion" (302). When Nancy herself, anticipating her meeting with Rose, "thought of the wide contrast which the small room would in another moment contain, she felt burdened with the sense of her own deep shame, and shrunk as though she could scarcely bear the presence of her with whom she had sought this interview" (301). Much of the proof of Nancy's ultimate goodness lies in her awed recognition of the impermeable boundaries that separate her from Rose Maylie. It is this, as much as her love for Bill Sikes (the two things are not ultimately very different), that brings her to say to Rose's offers of help: "I wish to go back. . . . I must go back" (304). Righteously "exposed" in the novel, the world of delinquency is also actively occulted: made cryptic by virtue of its cryptlike isolation.

Outside and surrounding the world of delinquency lies the middle-class world of private life, presided over by Oliver's benefactors Mr. Brownlow, Mr. Losberne, and the Maylies. What repeatedly and rhapsodically characterizes this world is the contrast that opposes it to the world of delinquency. Thus, at Mr. Brownlow's, "everything was so quiet, and neat, and orderly; everybody was kind and gentle; that *after the noise and turbulence in the midst of which* [Oliver] *had always lived*, it seemed like Heaven itself"; and at the Maylies' country cottage, "Oliver, *whose days had been spent among squalid crowds, and in the midst of noise and brawling*, seemed to enter on a new existence" (94, 238; italics added). No doubt, the contrast serves the ends of Dickens's moral and political outrage: the middle-class standards in effect, say, at Mr. Brownlow's dramatically enhance our appreciation of the miseries of delinquency. However, the outrage is limited in the contrast, too, since these miseries in turn help secure a proper (relieved, grateful) appreciation of *the standards themselves*. It is systematically unclear which kind of appreciation *Oliver Twist* does most to foster. Much as delinquency is circumscribed by middle-class private life, the indignation to which delinquency gives rise is bounded by gratitude for the class habits and securities that make indignation possible.

The "alternative" character of the middle-class community depends significantly on the fact that it is kept free, not just from noise and squalor, but also from the police. When this freedom is momentarily violated by Duff and Blathers, who want to know Oliver's story, Mr. Losberne persuades Rose and Mrs. Maylie not to cooperate with them:

> "The more I think of it," said the doctor, "the more I see that it will occasion endless trouble and difficulty if we put these men in possession of the boy's real story. I am certain it will not be believed; and even if they can do nothing to him in the end, still the dragging it forward, and giving publicity to all the doubts that will be cast upon it, must interfere, materially, with your benevolent plan of rescuing him from misery." (225)

The police are felt to obstruct an alternative power of regulation, such as the plan of rescue implies. Not to cooperate with the police, therefore, is part of a strategy of surreptitiously assuming and revising their functions. Losberne himself, for instance, soon forces his way into a suspect dwelling in the best policial manner. In a more central and extensive pattern, Oliver's diabolical half-brother Monks is subject to a replicated version of a whole legal and police apparatus. There is no wish to prosecute Monks legally because, as Mr. Brownlow says, "there must be circumstances in Oliver's little history which it would be painful to drag before the public eye" (352). Instead Brownlow proposes "to extort the secret" from Monks (351). Accordingly, Monks is "kidnapped in the street" by two of Brownlow's men and submitted to a long cross-examination in which he is overwhelmed by the "accumulated charges" (372, 378). The Bumbles are brought in to testify against him, and the "trial" concludes with his agreement to render up Oliver's patrimony and sign a written admission that he stole it.

We would call this vigilantism, except that no ultimate conflict of purpose or interest divides it from the legal and police apparatus that it supplants. Such division as does surface between the law and its supplement seems to articulate a deeper congruency, as though the text were positing something like a doctrine of "separation of powers," whereby each in its own sphere rendered assistance to the other, in the coherence of a single policing action. Thus, while the law gets rid of Fagin and his gang, the amateur supplement gets rid of Monks. Monks's final fate is instructive in this light. Retired with his portion to the New World, "he once more fell into his old courses, and, after undergoing a long confinement for some fresh act of fraud and knavery, at length sunk under an attack of his old disorder, and died in prison" (412). The two systems of regulation beautifully support one another. Only when the embarrassment that an initial appeal to the law would have created has been circumvented, does the law come to claim its own; and in so doing, it punishes on behalf of the vigilantes. A similar complicitousness obtains in the fate of the Bumbles. Although the reason for dealing with Monks privately has been to keep the secret of Oliver's parentage, it is hard to know on what basis the Bumbles are "deprived of their position" at the end, since this would imply a disclosure of their involvement in Monks's scheme to the proper authorities. Even if the confusion is inadvertent, it attests to the tacit concurrence the text assumes between the law and its supplement.

The two systems come together, then, in the connivance of class rule, but more of society is covered by the rule than outsiders such as Fagin or monsters such as Monks. Perhaps finally more interesting than the quasi-legal procedures applied to Monks are the disciplinary techniques imposed on Oliver himself. From his first moment at Mr. Brownlow's, Oliver is subject to incessant examination:

"Oliver what? Oliver White, eh?"

"No, sir, Twist, Oliver Twist."

"Queer name!" said the old gentleman. "What made you tell the magistrate that your name was White?"

"I never told him so, sir," returned Oliver in amazement.

This sounded so like a falsehood, that the old gentleman looked somewhat sternly in Oliver's face. It was impossible to doubt him; there was truth in every one of its thin and sharpened lineaments. (81)

However "impossible" Oliver is to doubt, Brownlow is capable of making "inquiries" to "confirm" his "statement" (96). The object of both interrogation and inquiry is to produce and possess a *full account* of Oliver. "Let me hear your story," Brownlow demands of Oliver, "where you come from; who brought you up; and how you got into the company in which I found you" (96). With a similar intent, when Oliver later disappears, he advertises for "such information as will lead to the discovery of the said Oliver Twist, or tend to throw any light upon his previous history" (123). It is clear what kind of narrative Oliver's "story" is supposed to be: the continuous line of an evolution. Not unlike the novel itself, Brownlow is seeking to articulate an original "story" over the heterogeneous and lacunary data provided in the "plot." It is also clear what Oliver's story, so constructed, is going to do: it will entitle him to what his Standard English already anticipates, a full integration into middle-class respectability. Another side to this entitlement, however, is alluded to in Brownlow's advertisement, which concludes with "a full description of Oliver's dress, person, appearance, and disappearance" (123). The "full description" allows Oliver to be identified and (what comes to the same thing here) *traced*. And if, as Brownlow thinks possible, Oliver has "absconded," then he will be traced *against his will*. To constitute Oliver as an object of knowledge is thus to assume power over him as well. One remembers that the police, too, wanted to know Oliver's story.

The same ideals of continuity and repleteness that determine the major articulations of this story govern the minor ones as well. The "new existence" Oliver enters into at the Maylies' cottage consists predominantly in a routine and a timetable:

Every morning he went to a white-headed old gentleman, who lived near the little church: who taught him to read better, and to write: and who spoke so kindly, and took such pains, that Oliver could never try enough to please him. Then, he would walk with Mrs. Maylie and Rose, and hear them talk of books; or perhaps sit near them, in some shady place, and listen whilst the young lady read: which he could have done, until it grew too dark to see the letters. Then, he had his own lesson for the next day to prepare; and at this, he would work hard, in a little room which looked into the garden, till evening came slowly on, when the ladies would walk out again, and he with them: listening with such pleasure to all they said: and so happy if they wanted a flower that he could climb to reach, or had forgotten anything he could run to fetch: that he could never be quick enough about it. When it became quite dark, and they returned home, the young lady would sit down to the piano, and play some pleasant air, or sing, in a low and gentle voice, some old song which it pleased her aunt to hear. There would be no candles lighted at such times as these; and Oliver would sit by one of the windows, listening to the sweet music, in a perfect rapture. (238)

This "iterative" tense continues to determine the presentation of the idyll, whose serenity depends crucially on its legato: on its not leaving a moment blank, or out of consecutive order. "No wonder," the text concludes, that at the end of a very short time, "Oliver had become completely domesticated with the old lady and her niece" (239). No wonder indeed, when the techniques that structure Oliver's time are precisely those of a domesticating pedagogy. Despite the half-lights and soft kindly tones, *as well as by means of them*, a technology of discipline constitutes this happy family as a field of power relations. Recalling that Blathers called Chickweed "one of the family," conjoining those who work the police apparatus and those whom it works over, we might propose a sense—only discreetly broached by the text—in which the family itself is "one of the family" of disciplinary institutions.

III

Oliver Twist suggests that the story of the Novel is essentially the story of an active regulation. Such a story apparently requires a double plot: regulation is secured in a minor way along the lines of an official police force, and in a major way in the working-through of an amateur supplement. As an example of high-realist fiction, Trollope's *The Eustace Diamonds* (1873) reverses the overt representational priorities of *Oliver Twist*. Trollope is much more concerned to explore his high-bourgeois world than he is to portray delinquency, which he seems prepared to take for granted. Thus, by way of shorthand, the novel will illustrate both the generality and the continuity of the doubly regulatory enterprise I've been discussing in Dickens. What needs regulation in *The Eustace Diamonds*, of course, is Lizzie's initial appropriation of the diamonds. The very status of the "theft" is open to question. Lizzie cannot clearly be said to "steal" what is already in her possession, and her assertion that her late husband gave her the diamonds cannot be proved or disproved. Although the family lawyer, Mr. Camperdown, is sure that "Lizzie Eustace had stolen the diamonds, as a pickpocket steals a watch," his opinion is no more a legal one than that of the reader, who knows, Trollope says, that Mr. Camperdown is "right."[4] In fact, according to the formal legal opinion solicited from Mr. Dove, the Eustace family may not reclaim the diamonds as heirlooms while there are some grounds on which Lizzie might claim them herself as "paraphernalia."

Part of what places Lizzie's theft in the interstices of the law is her position as Lady Eustace. It is not just that John Eustace refuses to prosecute on account of the consequent scandal, or that Lizzie is invited and visited by the best society. The law does not cover a lady's action here for the same reason that Mr. Camperdown is ignorant of the claim for paraphernalia:

Up to this moment, though he had been called upon to arrange great dealings in reference to widows, he had never as yet heard of a claim made by a widow for paraphernalia. But then the widows with whom he had been called upon to deal, had been ladies quite content to ac-

4. Anthony Trollope, *The Eustace Diamonds*, 2 vols. in 1 (Oxford: Oxford University Press, 1973), 1:252.

cept the good things settled upon them by the liberal prudence of their friends and husbands—not greedy, blood-sucking harpies such as this Lady Eustace. (1:254)

If, as Dove's opinion shows, the legal precedents about heirlooms do not clearly define the status of Lizzie's possession of the diamonds, it is because a similar question has not previously arisen. In the world Lizzie inhabits, the general trustworthiness of widows of peers has been such that it didn't need to arise. Nor—a fortiori—have the police been much accustomed to enter this world. As Scotland Yard itself acknowledges, at a later turn in the story, "had it been an affair simply of thieves, such as thieves ordinarily are, everthing would have been discovered long since;—but when lords and ladies with titles come to be mixed up with such an affair,—folk in whose house a policeman can't have his will at searching and browbeating,—how is a detective to detect anything?" (2:155).

The property whose proper ownership is put in doubt is the novel's titular instance of the impropriety that comes to rule the conduct of Lizzie, characterize her parasitical friends (Lord George, Mrs. Carbuncle, Reverend Emilius), and contaminate the otherwise decent Frank Greystock. Significantly, Lizzie's legally ambiguous retention of the diamonds opens up a series of thefts that—in certain aspects at least—resemble and prolong the initial impropriety. First, the notoriety of the diamonds in her possession attracts the attentions of professional thieves, who attempt to steal the diamonds at Carlisle, but (Lizzie's affidavit to the contrary) fail to obtain them. Their failure in turn generates a later attempt in London, in which the diamonds are successfully abstracted. In part, Trollope is no doubt using the series to suggest the "dissemination" of lawlessness. But if one theft leads to another, this is finally so that theft itself can lead to *arrest* within the circuit of the law. Subsequent thefts do not simply repeat the initial impropriety, but revise it as well, recasting it into what are legally more legible terms.

The plot of the novel "passes on," as it were, the initial offense until it reaches a place within the law's jurisdiction.

Thus, the last theft is very different from the first. It involves a breaking and entering by two professional thieves (Smiler and Cann), working in collaboration with Lizzie's maid (Patience Crabstick) and at the behest of a "Jew jeweller" (Mr. Benjamin), who exports the stolen diamonds and has them recut. In short, theft finally comes to lodge in the world of delinquency: within the practice of a power that binds thieves and police together in the same degree as it isolates the economy they form from the rest of the world represented in the novel. In the circulation of this economy, nothing is less surprising than that Lizzie's maid should pass from a liaison with one of the thieves to a marriage with one of the thief-takers, or that the other thief should be easily persuaded to turn Crown's evidence. Even in terms of the common idiom they speak, police and thieves are all closer to one another than they are to Frank Greystock and Lord Fawn. Yet if theft now has the transparent clarity of pickpocketing a watch, it also has some of the inconsequence. As it is moved down to a sphere where it can be legally named, investigated, and prosecuted, it becomes—in every respect but the magnitude of the stolen goods—a *petty theft*: committed by petty thieves and policed by petit-bourgeois detectives, all of whom are confined to the peripheral world of a subplot. The impropriety which gave rise to the narrative is arrested on so different a terrain from the novel's main ground that, even after the police investigation has solved its "pretty little mystery," the larger question of Lizzie herself must remain:

Miss Crabstick and Mr. Cann were in comfortable quarters, and were prepared to tell all that they could tell. Mr. Smiler was in durance, and Mr. Benjamin was at Vienna, in the hands of the Austrian police, who were prepared to give him up to those who desired his society in England, on the completion of certain legal formalities. That Mr. Benjamin and Mr. Smiler would be prosecuted, the latter for the robbery and the former for conspiracy to rob, and for receiving stolen goods, was a matter of course. But what was to be done with Lady Eustace? That, at the present moment, was the prevailing trouble with the police. (2:261)

Ultimately, however, it is a trouble *only* with the police. Though Lizzie is never punished by the law, never even has to appear at Benjamin and Smiler's trial, she does not quite get off the hook. For the novel elaborates a far more extensive and imposing principle of social control in what Trollope calls the "world." The coercive force of the "world" shows up best in the case of Lord Fawn, who, if asked what his prevailing motive was in all he did or intended to do, "would have declared that it was above all things necessary that he should put himself right in the eye of the British public" (2:247). Under this principle, Fawn first tries to break off his engagement to Lizzie, when it looks as though the world will disapprove of her holding on to the Eustace diamonds. Later when, in the person of Lady Glencora Palliser, the world takes up Lizzie and considers her a wronged woman, Fawn is once again willing to marry her. The coercion exercised by public opinion in the novel is purely mental, but that apparently suffices. The social order that prevents Frank Greystock from dueling with Fawn—"public opinion is now so much opposed to that kind of thing, that it is out of the question"—allows him to predict with confidence, "the world will punish him" (1:216). As Stendhal might say, society has moved from red to black: from the direct and quasi-instantaneous ceremonies of physical punishment to the prolonged mental mortifications of a diffuse social discipline. Trollope's obvious point in the novel about the instability of public opinion (taking up Lizzie to drop her in the end) should not obscure its role as a policing force. Lizzie may fear the legal consequences of her perjury at Carlisle, but what she actually suffers is the social humiliation of its being publicly known. It is enough to exile her to an untouchable *bohème* in which there is nothing to do but marry the disreputable Reverend Emilius. The Duke of Omnium, whose interest in Lizzie had extended to the thought of visiting her, is at the end quite fatigued with his fascination. "I am afraid, you know," he declares to Glencora, "that your friend hasn't what I call a good time before her" (2:375).

The understatement is profoundly consistent with the nature of discipline. What most sharply differentiates the legal economy of police power from the "amateur" economy of its supplement is precisely the latter's policy of *discretion*. It would be false to see Trollope or Dickens engaged in crudely "repressing" the policing function carried on in everyday life, since, as we have seen, the world they create exemplifies such a function. Yet it would be equally misleading to see *Oliver Twist* or *The Eustace Diamonds* advertising such a function. Though both novels draw abundant analogies between the official police apparatus and its supplementary discipline, they qualify the sameness that such analogies invite us to construe with an extreme sense of difference. When in *The Eustace Diamonds*, for example, Lizzie's gardener Andy Gowran is brought before Lord Fawn to attest to her misbehavior with Frank Greystock, he sees this situation in the legal terms of a trial: "This was a lord of Parliament, and a government lord, and might probably have the power of hanging such a one as Andy Gowran were he to commit perjury, or say anything which the lord might choose to call perjury" (2:175). But the naive exaggeration of the perception ironically repudiates the metaphor it calls into play. The metaphor is more tellingly repudiated a second time, when Fawn refuses to solicit what Gowran has to say. "He could not bring himself to inquire minutely as to poor Lizzie's flirting among the rocks. He was weak, and foolish, and, in many respects, ignorant,—but he was a gentleman" (2:177). "Gentlemanliness" is thus promoted as a kind of social security, defending the privacy of private life from its invasion by policelike practices of surveillance. Yet there is a curious gratuitousness in Fawn's principled refusal to hear Gowran. Though Gowran never makes his full disclosure to Fawn, the latter can hardly be in any doubt about its content. That he already knows what Gowran has to tell is precisely the *reason* for his shamed unwillingness to hear it. Octave Mannoni, following Freud, would speak here of a mechanism of *disavowal* (*Verleugnung*): "Je sais bien, mais quand même . . ."—"Of course I know, but still. . . ."[5] By means of disavowal, one can make an admission while remaining comfortably blind to its consequences. The mechanism allows Fawn to preserve his knowledge about Lizzie together with the fantasy of his distance from the process of securing it. In more general terms, the discretion of social discipline in the Novel seems to rely on a strategy of *disavowing the police*: acknowledging its affinity with police practices by way of insisting on the fantasy of its otherness. Rendered discreet by disavowal, discipline is also thereby rendered more effective—including among its effects that "freedom" or "lawlessness" for which critics of the Novel (perpetuating the ruse) have often mistaken it. Inobtrusively supplying the place of the police in places where the police cannot be, the mechanisms of discipline seem to entail a relative *relaxation* of policing power. No doubt this manner of passing off the regulation of everyday life is the best manner of passing it on.

IV

What has been standing at the back of my argument up to now, and what I hope will allow me to carry it some steps further, is the general history of the rise of disciplinary power,

5. See Octave Mannoni, "Je sais bien, mais quand même . . . ," in his *Clefs pour l'imaginaire* (Paris: Seuil, 1969), pp. 9–33.

such as provided by Michel Foucault in *Surveiller et punir*.[6] There Foucault documents and describes the new type of power that begins to permeate Western societies from the end of the eighteenth century. This new type of power ("new" perhaps only in its newly dominant role) cannot be identified with an institution or a state apparatus, though these may certainly employ or underwrite it. The efficacy of discipline lies precisely in the fact that it is only a *mode* of power, "comprising a whole set of instruments, techniques, procedures, levels of application, targets" (215). The mobility it enjoys as a technology allows precisely for its wide diffusion, which extends from obviously disciplinary institutions (such as the prison) to institutions officially determined by "other" functions (such as the school) down to the tiniest practices of everyday social life. This mobile power is also a modest one. Maintained well below the level of emergence of "the great apparatuses and the great political struggles" (223), its modalities are humble, its procedures minor. It is most characteristically exercised on "little things." While it thus harkens back to an earlier theology of the detail, the detail is now significant "not so much for the meaning that it conceals within it as for the hold it provides for the power that wishes to seize it" (140). The sheer pettiness of discipline's coercions tends to keep them from scrutiny, and the diffusion of discipline's operations precludes locating them in an attackable center. Disciplinary power constitutively mobilizes a tactic of tact: it is the policing power that never passes for such, but is either invisible or visible only under cover of other, nobler or simply blander intentionalities (to educate, to cure, to produce, to defend). Traditional power founded its authority in the spectacle of its force, and those on whom this power was exercised could, conversely, remain in the shade. By contrast, disciplin-

6. Michel Foucault, *Surveiller et punir* (Paris: Gallimard, 1975). Foucault will be cited in the English translation of Alan Sheridan, *Discipline and Punish* (New York: Pantheon, 1977).

ary power tends to remain invisible, while imposing on those whom it subjects "a principle of compulsory visibility" (187). As in Jeremy Bentham's plan for the Panopticon, a circular prison disposed about a central watchtower, surveillance is exercised on fully visible "prisoners" by unseen "guards." What this machinery of surveillance is set up to monitor is the elaborate regulation (timetables, exercises, and so on) that discipline simultaneously deploys to occupy its subjects. The aim of such regulation is to enforce not so much a norm as the normality of normativeness itself. Rather than in rendering all its subjects uniformly "normal," discipline is interested in putting in place a perceptual grid in which a division between the normal and the deviant inherently imposes itself. Concomitantly, discipline attenuates the role of actual supervisors by enlisting the consciousness of its subjects in the work of supervision. The Panopticon, where it matters less that the inmates may at any moment be watched than that they know this, only begins to suggest the extent to which disciplinary order relies on a subjectivity that, through a rich array of spiritual management techniques, it compels to endless self-examination. Throughout the nineteenth century, discipline, on the plan of hierarchical surveillance, normalization, and the development of a subjectivity supportive of both, progressively "reforms" the major institutions of society: prison, school, factory, barracks, hospital.

And the novel? May we not pose the question of the novel—whose literary hegemony is achieved precisely in the nineteenth century—in the context of the age of discipline? I have been implying, of course, that discipline provides the novel with its essential "content." A case might be made, moreover, drawing on a more somber tradition than the one exemplified in the fundamentally "comic" novels thus far considered, that this content is by no means always discreet. The novel frequently places its protagonists under a social surveillance whose explicit coerciveness has nothing to do with the euphoria of Oliver Twist's holiday in the country or the genteel understatement of Trollope's "world." In Stendhal's *Le rouge et le noir* (1830), for instance, the seminary Julien Sorel attends at Besançon is openly shown to encompass a full range of disciplinary practices. Constant supervision is secured either by Abbé Castanède's secret police or through Abbé Pirard's "moyens de surveillance."[7] Exercises such as saying the rosary, singing canticles to the Sacred Heart, "etc., etc.," are regulated according to a timetable punctuated by the monastic bell. Normalizing sanctions extend from examinations to the most trivial bodily movements, such as eating a hard-boiled egg. Part of what makes Julien's career so depressing is that he never really finds his way out of the seminary. The Hôtel de la Mole only reduplicates its machinery in less obvious ways: as Julien is obliged to note, "Tout se sait, ici comme au séminaire!" (Everything gets known, here just as much as in the seminary; 465). And the notorious drawback of being in prison is that the prisoner may not close the door on the multilateral disciplinary attempts to interpret and appropriate his crime. One scarcely needs to put great pressure on the text to see all this. The mechanisms of discipline are as indiscreet in Stendhal's presentation as his disapproval of them is explicit.

Something like that disapproval is the hallmark of all the novels which, abandoning the strategy of treating discipline with discretion, make discipline a conspicuous practice. If such novels typically tell the story of how their heroes come to be destroyed by the forces of social regulation and standardization, they inevitably tell it *with regret*. Just as Stendhal's sympathies are with Julien rather than with the directors of the seminary or the bourgeois jury that condemns him, characters like Dorothea Brooke and Tertius Lydgate seem far more admirable to George Eliot than the citizens of *Middlemarch* (1873) who en-

---

7. Stendhal, *Le rouge et le noir*, in *Romans et nouvelles*, ed. Henri Martineau, 2 vols. (Paris: Bibliothèque de la Pléiade, 1952–55), 1:406.

mesh them in their "petty mediums." The explicitly thematized *censure* of discipline seems to provide surer ground for retaining the opposition between the novel and the police that our readings of Dickens and Trollope put in question. The specific liabilities we have seen in that opposition when its terms were an official police and an amateur supplement cease to pertain when *both* modes of policing are opposed to the transcendent, censorious perspective taken by the novel. No longer arising from within the world of the novel, the opposition could now less vulnerably play between the world of the novel and the act of portraying it.

Yet we have already seen how the "disavowal" of the police by its disciplinary supplement allows the latter to exercise policing power at other, less visible levels and in other, more effective modes. Similarly, the novel's own repudiation of policing power can be seen not to depart from, but to extend the pattern of this discreet *Aufhebung*. Whenever the novel censures policing power, it has already reinvented it, in *the very practice of novelistic representation*. A usefully broad example of this occurs in Zola's *Nana* (1880). The prostitutes in the novel, one recalls, are in mortal terror of the police. So great is their fear of the law and the prefecture that some remain paralyzed at the doors of the cafés when a police raid sweeps the avenue they walk. Nana herself "avait toujours tremblé devant la loi, cette puissance inconnue, cette vengeance des hommes qui pouvaient la supprimer" (had always trembled before the law, that unknown authority, that male vengeance which had the power to do away with her).[8] Even amid her luxury, she "avait conservé une épouvante de la police, n'aimant pas à en entendre parler, pas plus que de la mort" (had never got over a fear of the police, whom she no more wanted to hear mentioned than she would

---

8. Emile Zola, *Nana*, in *Les Rougon-Macquart*, ed. Armand Lanoux and Henri Mitterand, 5 vols. (Paris: Bibliothèque de la Pléiade, 1960–67), 2:1315.

death; 1374). The greatest anxiety is apparently inspired by the prospect of being "mise en carte": put on a police list entailing obligatory medical examination. Zola permits us no illusions about the policing of prostitution. When not seeking simply to terrorize, the *agents de moeurs* underhandedly trade their protection for sexual favors, as the experience of Nana's friend Satin shows. Yet the police procedures that are censured in the story reappear less corruptibly in Zola's method of telling it. What is *Nana* but an extended *mise-en-carte* of a prostitute: an elaborately researched "examination" sustained at the highest level by the latest scientific notions of pathology and at the lowest by the numerous "fiches" on which data is accumulated? In a larger social dimension, and with a similar prophylactic intention, Zola wants to register the Parisian *fille* no less than the police. *Nana* is the title of a file, referring both to the prostitute who resists the record and to the novel whose representational practice has already overcome this resistance.

To the extent that the genre of the novel *belongs* to the disciplinary field that it portrays, our attention needs to go beyond the policing forces represented in the novel to focus on what Foucault might call the "micro-politics" of novelistic convention. By way of broaching this micro-politics, I would like to consider a crucial episode in its genealogy, where the police and the narrative devices that usurp their power are most in evidence: namely, the encounter between Fouché's secret police and the omniscient narrator in Balzac's *Une ténébreuse affaire* (1841). While it is an exaggeration to say that Fouché "invented" the modern police, the greater organization and extent of the police machine over which he presided were considerable enough to make it substantially new.[9] The increased importance of the *secret* police was a particularly significant aspect of

9. See Leon Radzinowicz, "Certain Political Aspects of the Police of France," in his *A History of English Criminal Law*, 4 vols. (London: Stevens and Sons, 1948–68), 3:539–74 (appendix 8); and Caillois, p. 81.

⌐this newness. Disguises and dissimulation began to encroach upon uniforms and naked force as dominant modes of police action. Alongside the "old" virtue of speed and the "old" routine of pursuit, the "new" methods of detective investigation arose into prominence. The contrast between old and new policial "styles" is precisely the burden of the comparison between Balzac's two agents, Peyrade and Corentin.

Le premier pouvait couper lui-même une tête, mais le second était capable d'entortiller, dans les filets de la calomnie et de l'intrigue, l'innocence, la beauté, la vertu, de les noyer, ou de les empoisonner froidement. L'homme rubicond aurait consolé sa victime par des lazzis, l'autre n'aurait pas même souri. Le premier avait quarante-cinq ans, il devait aimer la bonne chère et les femmes. Ces sortes d'hommes ont tous des passions qui les rendent esclaves de leur métier. Mais le jeune homme était sans passions et sans vices. S'il était espion, il appartenait à la diplomatie, et travaillait pour l'art pur. Il concevait, l'autre exécutait; il était l'idée, l'autre était la forme.

(If the former could decapitate someone with his own hands, the latter was capable of entangling innocence, beauty, virtue in networks of calumny and intrigue, of coolly drowning or poisoning them. While the florid-faced man would have consoled his victim with jests, his cohort would not even have smiled. Peyrade was forty-five and evidently liked women and good food. The passions of all such men keep them slaves to their trade. But the young Corentin was devoid of both passion and vice. He may have been a spy, but he was also a diplomat, who worked simply for the sake of his art. He drew up the plans that his companion executed; he provided the concept to which the other gave form.)[10]

The differences announce the passage from a dominantly corporal and spectacular punishment to a hidden and devious discipline: from a police whose practice is best exemplified in the act of capital execution, occupying a single moment in time at

10. Honoré de Balzac, *Une ténébreuse affaire* (Paris: Collection Folio, 1973), p. 37.

a single point of space, to a police defined in terms of the spatial extension of its networks and the temporal deployment of its intrigues. Not unlike the novel, the new police has charge of a "world" and a "plot."

Both men, of course, are privileged seers. Like Balzac's doctors and lawyers, his *agents de police* are privy to what goes on behind the "scènes de la vie privée," and they thus resemble the novelist whose activity is also conceived as a penetration of social surfaces. Nonetheless, the text pointedly distinguishes the vision of each. Peyrade's eyes present a powerful image: "Ces deux yeux fureteurs et perspicaces, d'un bleu glacial et glacé, pouvaient être pris pour le modèle de ce fameux oeil, le redoubtable emblème de la police, inventé pendant la Révolution" (Prying, perspicacious, glazed in glacial blue, these eyes might have been taken for the original of that notorious and formidable Eye which served as the emblem of the police under the Revolution; 36). But what is impressive as an emblem is less effective than what it emblematizes. Openly displaying their prying acuteness, Peyrade's eyes virtually constitute a warning against their own powers. Not surprisingly, the eyes of the more effective Corentin are simply "impénétrables": "leur regard était aussi discret que devait l'être sa bouche mince et serré" (their gaze was as guarded as his thin, tight-lipped mouth; 37). Yet of course the "impenetrable" powers of vision ascribed to him have already been penetrated by the narration that renders them. Much as the eyes of Peyrade advertise a power that is better served in the inscrutable Corentin, the eyes of both glance at the superiority of the narration that has improved upon the perspicacity of the one and the impenetrability of the other. On the side of perspicacity, Balzac's omniscient narration assumes a fully panoptic view of the world it places under surveillance. Nothing worth knowing escapes its notation, and its complete knowledge includes the knowledge that it is always right. This infallible super-vision is frequently dramatized in Balzac's descriptions as an irresistible process of detection. Thus, from the worn creases of Peyrade's breeches, the text infers that he has a desk job; from his manner of taking snuff, that he must be an official. One thing inevitably "indicates," "betrays," "conceals" a defining something else. On the side of impenetrability, this panoptic vision constitutes its own immunity from being seen in turn. For it intrinsically deprives us of the outside position from which it might be "placed." There is no other perspective on the world than its own, because the world entirely coincides with that perspective. We are always situated inside the narrator's viewpoint, and even to speak of a "narrator" at all is to misunderstand a technique that, never identified with a *person*, institutes a faceless and multilateral regard.

Flaubert famously declared that "l'auteur, dans son oeuvre, doit être comme Dieu dans l'univers, présent partout et visible nulle part" (the author in his work should be like God in His universe, everywhere present but nowhere visible).[11] But God is not the only such unseen over-seer. In an early detective novel, *Monsieur Lecoq* (1869), Emile Gaboriau calls the police "cette puissance mystérieuse . . . qu'on ne voit ni n'entend, et qui néanmoins entend et voit tout" (that mysterious authority which, though neither seen nor heard itself, nonetheless sees and hears everything else).[12] It doesn't finally matter whether we gloss panoptical narration as a kind of providence or as a kind of police, since the police are only—as Gaboriau also called them—a "Providence au petit pied" (234), a "little providence" fully analogous to the great. What matters is that the faceless gaze becomes an ideal of the power of regulation. Power, of course, might seem precisely what the convention of omniscient narration foregoes. Omniscient narration may typically know all, but it can hardly *do* all. "Poor Dorothea," "poor

---

11. Gustave Flaubert, in a letter to Louise Colet (9 December 1852), *Extraits de la correspondance; ou, Préface à la vie d'écrivain*, ed. Geneviève Bollème (Paris: Seuil, 1963), p. 95.

12. Emile Gaboriau, *Monsieur Lecoq: L'enquête* (Paris: Garnier, 1978), p. 18.

Lydgate," "poor Rosamond," the narrator of *Middlemarch* frequently exclaims, and the lament is credible only in an arrangement that keeps the function of narration separate from the causalities operating in the narrative. The *knowledge* commanded in omniscient narration is thus opposed to the *power* that inheres in the circumstances of the novelistic world. Yet by now the gesture of disowning power should seem to define the basic move of a familiar power play, in which the name of power is given over to one agency in order that the function of power may be less visibly retained by another. Impotent to intervene in the "facts," the narration nevertheless controls the discursive framework in which they are perceived as such. One thinks, for example, of the typologies to which novelists like Balzac or Zola subject their characters, or of the more general normalizing function which automatically divides characters into good and bad, normal and deviant. The panopticism of the novel thus coincides with what Mikhail Bakhtin has called its "monologism": the working of an implied master-voice whose accents have already unified the world in a single interpretative center. Accordingly, in the monological novel, "every struggle of two voices for possession of and dominance in the world in which they appear is decided in advance—it is a sham struggle."[13]

Yet to speak of sham struggles is also to imply the necessity for shamming them. The master-voice of monologism never simply soliloquizes. It continually needs to confirm its authority by qualifying, canceling, endorsing, subsuming all the other voices it lets speak. No doubt the need stands behind the great prominence the nineteenth-century novel gives to *style indirect libre*, in which, respeaking a character's thoughts or speeches, the narration simultaneously subverts their authority and secures its own. The resistance that monologism requires

13. Mikhail Bakhtin, *Problems of Dostoevsky's Poetics*, trans. R. W. Rostel (Ann Arbor, Mich.: Ardis, 1973), p. 168.

to confirm itself, however, is most basically offered by the narrative itself. For the "birth of narrative" marks an apparent *gap* in the novel's system of knowledge. The thoroughness with which *Père Goriot* (1834) masters every inch of space belonging to the Pension Vauquer, for example, lapses abruptly when it comes to the pensioners themselves. Instead of making assertions, the narration now poses questions, and in place of exhaustive catalogues, it provides us with teasingly elliptical portraits. Exactly at the point of interrogation, the exposition ceases and the narrative proper—what Balzac calls the drama—begins. Yet the "origin" of narrative in a cognitive gap also indicates to what end narrative will be directed. Substituting a temporal mode of mastery for a spatial one, Balzac's "drama" will achieve the same full knowledge of character that has already been acquired of habitat.

The feat is possible because nineteenth-century narrative is generally conceived as a *genesis*: a linear, cumulative time of evolution. Such a genesis secures duration against the dispersive tendencies that are literally "brought into line" by it. Once on this line, character or event may be successively placed and coherently evaluated. It should be recalled that, in *Oliver Twist*, both the police and Mr. Brownlow sought to construct for Oliver a story organized in just this way. The ideal of genetic time prevails in nineteenth-century fiction even where it appears to be discredited. A novel like *Middlemarch* forcefully dismisses the notion of a "key" which would align "all the mythical systems and erratic mythical fragments in the world" with "a tradition originally revealed,"[14] but when it comes to its own will-to-power, the novel presents its characters in a similar genetic scheme. The moral lesson George Eliot seeks to impose depends on our ability to correlate the end of a character's career with what was there in germ at the beginning—in Lydgate's "spots of commonness," for instance, or in Bulstrode's past.

14. George Eliot, *Middlemarch* (Baltimore: Penguin, 1965), p. 46.

Structured as a genesis, the narrative that seems to resist a novel's control thereby becomes a technique for achieving it. As it forwards a story of social discipline, the narrative also advances the novel's omniscient word. It is frequently hard to distinguish the omniscience from the social control it parallels, since the latter too is often a matter of "mere" knowledge. Lizzie Eustace poses a threat to Trollopian society precisely because she is unknown. Lord Fawn "knew nothing about her, and had not taken the slightest trouble to make inquiry" (1:78). "You don't know her, mama," Mrs. Hittaway tells Lady Fawn (1:81). "Of the manner in which the diamonds had been placed in [Lizzie's] hands, no one knew more than she chose to tell" (1:15). What mainly happens in *The Eustace Diamonds* is that the world comes to know Lizzie better. Paradoxically, what gives both the world and the narration that idealizes its powers a hold on Lizzie is her own undisciplined desires. These generate the narrative by which she is brought under control. Leo Bersani has argued that the realist novel exhibits a "fear" of desire, whose primal disruptiveness it anxiously represses.[15] Yet power can scarcely be exercised *except* on what resists it, and—shifting Bersani's emphasis somewhat—one might claim that the novel rather than fearing desire *solicits* it. Through the very intensity of the counterpressure it mounts, desire brings the desiring subject into a maximally close "fit" with the power he or she means to resist. Thus, Lizzie's desires are at once the effect of the power she withstands and the cause of its intensified operation.

Insistently, the novel shows disciplinary power to inhere in the very resistance to it. At the macroscopic level, the demonstration is carried in the attempt of the protagonist to break away from the social control that thereby reclaims him. At the microscopic level, it is carried in the trifling detail that

15. Leo Bersani, *A Future for Astyanax* (Boston: Little, Brown and Co., 1976). Bersani's stimulating case is made in chapter 2, entitled "Realism and the Fear of Desire."

is suddenly invested with immense significance. Based on an egregious disproportion between its assumed banality and the weight of revelation it comes to bear, the "significant trifle" is typically meant to surprise, even frighten. For in the same process where the detail is charged with meaning, it is invested with a power already capitalizing on that meaning. Power has taken hold where hold seemed least given: in the irrelevant. The process finds its most programmatic embodiment in detective fiction, where the detail literally incriminates. "I made a private inquiry last week," says Sergeant Cuff in *The Moonstone* (1868); "At one end of the inquiry there was a murder, and at the other end there was a spot of ink on a tablecloth that nobody could account for. In all my experience along the dirtiest ways of this dirty little world, I have never met with such a thing as a trifle yet."[16] The inquiries of Sherlock Holmes rely similarly upon trivia, as he repeatedly reminds us. "You know my method. It is based on the observation of trifles." "There is nothing so important as trifles." "My suspicions depend on small points, which might seem trivial to another."[17]

If the mainstream novel proves ultimately to be another instance of such detection, this is because, both in its story and in its method of rendering it, it dramatizes a power continually able to appropriate the most trivial detail. What makes Corentin a better agent than Peyrade in *Une ténébreuse affaire* is his ability to see such details and seize them as clues. While Peyrade, for instance, is fatuously "charmed" by Michu's wife Marthe, Corentin more acutely discerns "traces of anxiety" in her. "Ces deux natures se peignaient toutes entières dans cette petite chose si grande" (Their two characters were perfectly de-

16. Wilkie Collins, *The Moonstone* (Baltimore: Penguin, 1966), p. 136.

17. Arthur Conan Doyle, *The Complete Sherlock Holmes* (Garden City, N.Y.: Doubleday, 1930), pp. 214, 238, and 259. The quotations are respectively from "The Boscombe Valley Mystery," "The Man with the Twisted Lip," and "The Adventure of the Speckled Band."

picted in this so large little difference; 39). *Cette petite chose si grande*: if the incident that registers the contrast is thus *minor*, then the narration can cite Corentin's power only by sharing in it. We have already seen how Balzacian narration bases its interpretative mastery on minutiae (for example, Peyrade's breeches) that it elaborates into "telling" details. A semiological criticism might be tempted to take the conspicuous legibility of these details for a "readerly" assurance.[18] But its effects seem more disturbing than that, if only because such legibility is generally thematized as the achievement of a sinister power such as Corentin's. As in the detective story, meaningfulness may not always be comforting when what it appropriates are objects and events whose "natural" banality and irrelevance had been taken for granted. "Rien dans la vie n'exige plus d'attention que les choses qui paraissent naturelles" (Nothing in life requires more attention than the things that appear to be natural).[19] This remark from *La rabouilleuse* (1842) defines exactly the unsettling *parti pris* of Balzacian narration: what had seemed natural and commonplace comes all at once under a malicious inspection, and what could be taken for granted now requires an explanation, even an alibi. Balzac's fiction characteristically inspires a sense that the world is thoroughly traversed by techniques of power to which everything, anything gives hold. This world is not so much totally intelligible as it

18. Cf. Jonathan Culler, *Flaubert: The Uses of Uncertainty* (Ithaca, N.Y.: Cornell University Press, 1974), pp. 82–84 and 94–100; and Roland Barthes, *S/Z* (Paris: Seuil, 1970), pp. 79–80 ("La maîtrise du sens").

19. Honoré de Balzac, *La rabouilleuse* (Paris: Garnier, 1959), p. 15. The passage suggestively continues: "On se défie toujours assez de l'extraordinaire; aussi voyez-vous les hommes de l'expérience: les avoués, les juges, les médecins, les prêtres, attachant une énorme importance aux affaires simples; on les trouve méticuleux" (Everybody is sufficiently armed against what is out of the ordinary; but men of experience—lawyers, judges, doctors, priests—know to attach an enormous importance to the simplest matters as well—and people call them fussy!).

is totally suspicious. Even private life partakes of that extreme state of affairs in *Les chouans* (1829) once the war has begun: "Chaque champ était alors une forteresse, chaque arbre méditait un piège, chaque vieux tronc de saule creux gardait un stratagème. Le lieu du combat était partout. . . . Tout dans le pays devenait-il dangereux: le bruit comme le silence, la grâce comme la terreur, le foyer domestique comme le grand chemin" (Each field was now a fortress and each tree concealed an ambush; every old willow stump harbored a deadly contrivance in its hollow. The battleground had no boundaries. . . . Everything in the region had become dangerous: noise and silence alike, kindness as well as terror, the domestic hearth no less than the open road).[20]

What we spoke of as the "genetic" organization of narrative allows the significant trifle to be elaborated *temporally*: in minute networks of causality that inexorably connect one such trifle to another. One thinks most immediately of the spectacularly intricate plotting of sensation novelists like Collins and Braddon or *feuilletonistes* like Eugène Sue and Ponson du Terrail. But the "high" novel of the nineteenth century displays an analogous pride in the fineness of its causal connections. Maupassant argues in the preface to *Pierre et Jean* (1887) that, whereas an earlier generation of novelists relied on a single "ficelle" called the plot, the *romancier moderne* deploys a whole network of thin, secret, almost invisible "fils."[21] Inevitably, so threadlike a causal organization favors stories of entrapment, such as we are given in *Madame Bovary* (1857) or several times in *Middlemarch*. Lydgate unwittingly prophesies the disaster of his own career when he says that "it's uncommonly difficult to

---

20. Honoré de Balzac, *Les chouans* (Paris: Garnier, 1957), pp. 26–27.
21. Guy de Maupassant, "Préface à *Pierre et Jean*," collected in *Anthologie des préfaces de romans français du XIX⁰ siècle*, ed. Herbert S. Gershman and Kerman B. Whitworth, Jr. (Paris: Union Générale d'Editions, 1971), p. 369.

make the right thing work: there are so many strings pulling at once" (536); and Bulstrode is undone because "the train of causes in which he had locked himself went on" (665), to unforeseeable destinations. Much like Balzac's use of the significant trifle, George Eliot's insistence on causal ramification is meant to inspire wariness. "One fears to pull the wrong thread in the tangled scheme of things." Once a power of social control has been virtually raised to the status of an ontology, action becomes so intimidating that it is effectively discouraged.

Though power thus encompasses everything in the world of the novel, it is never embraced by the novel itself. On the contrary, the novel systematically gives power an unfavorable press. What more than power, for instance, serves to distinguish bad characters from good? Oliver Twist can represent "the principle of Good" (33, Dickens's preface) because he is uncontaminated by the aggression of his exploiters; and the supreme goodness of Lucy Morris in *The Eustace Diamonds* and Victorine Taillefer in *Père Goriot* depends similarly on their passivity vis-à-vis the power plays going on around them. Conversely, the characters who openly solicit power are regularly corrupted by it: the moral failings of a Rastignac or a Bulstrode are simply gradual, nuanced versions of the evil that arises more melodramatically in a Machiavellian like Corentin or a "poème infernal" like Vautrin. If they are to remain good, good characters may only assume power when—like Oliver's benefactors—they are seeking to neutralize the negative effects of a "prior" instance of it. The same "ideology of power" is implied by the form of the novel itself, which, as we have seen, fastidiously separates its "powerless" discourse from a fully empowered world.

Yet to the extent that power is not simply made over to the world, but made over *into* the world, literally "secularized" as its ontology, the novel inspires less a distaste for power than a fear of it. What ultimate effects the fear is calculated to produce may be suggested if we turn to a master of fear, who, though not a novelist and living in the seventeenth century, articulated the vision of power which the nineteenth-century novel would so effectively renovate.

Le moindre mouvement importe à toute la nature; la mer entière change pour une pierre. Ainsi, dans la grâce, la moindre action importe par ses suites à tout. Donc tout est important.

En chaque action, il faut regarder, outre l'action, notre état présent, passé, futur, et des autres à quoi elle importe, et voir les liaisons de toutes ces choses.

(The slightest physical movement bears on all of nature; the entire sea is altered by a single stone. Similarly, in the spiritual realm, the least action entails consequences for everything else; everything therefore is important.

In every action, our scrutiny must pass beyond the action itself to examine our present, past, and future states, the others it will affect, and how all these things are interconnected.)[22]

In his first paragraph, Pascal evokes the world of significant trifles related to one another in a minute causal network: the world to which the nineteenth-century novel gives solidity of specification. In his second, he points to what it entails to act wisely in this world: the nineteenth-century virtues of caution and prudence. And finally, in his last sentence, which I have not yet given because it will also be my own, he discloses the natural consequences of thus living in a world thus constructed: "Et lors on sera bien retenu." The novelistic Panopticon exists to remind us that we too inhabit it. "And then we shall indeed be put under restraint."

22. Blaise Pascal, *Pensées*, in *Oeuvres complètes* (Paris: Bibliothèque de la Pléiade, 1969), p. 1296 [no. 656].

TWO

From *roman policier* to *roman-police*: Wilkie Collins's *The Moonstone*

I

The classical detective story disposes of an interestingly paradoxical economy, at once prodigal and parsimonious. On one hand, the form is based on the hypothesis that *everything might count*: every character might be the culprit, and every action or speech might be belying its apparent banality or literalism by making surreptitious reference to an incriminating Truth. From the layout of the country house (frequently given in all the exactitude of a diagram) to the cigar ash found on the floor at the scene of the crime, no detail can be dismissed a priori. Yet on the other hand, even though the criterion of total relevance is continually invoked by the text, it turns out to have a highly restricted applicability in the end. At the moment of truth, the text winnows grain from chaff, separating the relevant signifiers from the much larger number of irrelevant ones, which are now revealed to be as trivial as we originally were encouraged to suspect they might *not* be. Sinister objects recover their banality, just as secret subjects resume their inconsequence. That quarrel overheard in the night, for example, between Mr. and Mrs. Greene proves to be an ordinary marital row. That cigar ash—unmistakably pointing, say, to Colonel Mustard's brand—is shown to have been deposited on the parquet *before* the crime took place. Of the elaborate house-plan, only this door or that window enters into the solution, and of

the exhaustive description of the scene of the crime only a few
items count while the rest relapse into insignificance. For the
detective's final summation offers not a maximal integration of
parts into whole, but a minimal one: what is totalized is just—
and no more than—what is needed to solve the crime. Everything and everybody else is returned to a bland, mute self-
evidence.

This observation is, of course, meant to shift the emphasis
from where it usually falls in discussions of the detective story:
away from a concern with the mystery that is finally solved toward a recognition of the hypothetical significances that are simultaneously dissolved. Though the detective story postulates
a world in which everything might have a meaningful bearing
on the solution of the crime, it concludes with an extensive repudiation of meanings that simply "drop out."[1] It is often argued that the detective story seeks to totalize its signifiers in a
complete and all-encompassing order. On the contrary, it is
concerned to restrict and localize the province of meaning: to
guarantee large areas of irrelevance. One easily sees, moreover,
what else is guaranteed in such a form. For as the fantasy of
total relevance yields to the reality of a more selective meaningfulness, the universality of suspicion gives way to a highly
specific guilt. Engaged in producing a social innocence, the detective story might well take for the motto of its enterprise,
"The truth shall make you free."

One may take a further step: the detective story is invariably
the story of a power play. The quasi-universal suspicion is only
another way of putting the quasi-total investigation. When the
sheer fact of meaningfulness incriminates and has a policing
force, the limits of the detective's knowledge become the limits
of his power as well: his astonishing explications double for a

1. As Sherlock Holmes tells his client in "The Naval Treaty," "The principal difficulty of your case lay in the fact of there being too much evidence. What was vital was overlaid and hidden by what was irrelevant."

control exercised in the interests of law and order. Detective fiction is thus always implicitly punning on the detective's brilliant *super-vision* and the police *supervision* that it embodies. His intervention marks an explicit bringing-under-surveillance of the entire world of the narrative. As such, it can be alarming. When Poe's Dupin reads his sidekick's mind in "The Murders in the Rue Morgue"; when, after a half-hour's sniffing about the scene of *L'affaire Lerouge*, Emile Gaboriau's Père Tabaret announces how and when the murder was committed as well as offers a physical description of the murderer; when Sherlock Holmes deduces a man's moral and economic history from his hat in "The Adventure of the Blue Carbuncle"—these prodigies are greeted as though they opened up the fearful prospect of an absolute surveillance under which everything would be known, incriminated, policed.

Typically, the detective's super-vision is dramatized by being exercised on what would seem to resist it most: the ordinary, "trivial" facts of everyday life. During the police investigation in *The Moonstone* (1868), for example, a smear is noticed on Rachel Verinder's newly varnished door. Superintendent Seegrave, an impressive-looking but incompetent local, dismisses the detail as a "trifle." Expert Sergeant Cuff, however, knows better: "In all my experience along the dirtiest ways of this dirty little world, I have never met with such a thing as a trifle yet."[2] He goes on to discover that the varnish dries after twelve hours; that it was applied at 3 P.M.; that it was still intact at midnight. Therefore, he concludes with classical acuity, the theft of the Moonstone was committed between midnight and 3 A.M. by someone whose dress—possibly a nightgown—is stained with varnish. The whole sequence makes a neat parable of the detective's work: to turn trifles into "telling" details, telling—what else?—a story of dirty linen.

2. Wilkie Collins, *The Moonstone* (Baltimore: Penguin, 1966), p. 136. Subsequent page references to this edition will be made in the text.

Yet, as we know, the investigation from which nothing seems safe is also subject to clear and strict limits, and so ultimately reassures the community that it initially frightens. In the first place, it restricts its scope to a socially approved enterprise: the identification and apprehension of a criminal who is by definition the "other"; and it lasts no longer than the criminal goes uncaught. In the second place, it is characterized as a dramatic instance of intervention and, as such, it is marked with a high degree of visibility. In this sense, the detective's extraordinary power of vision can be seen in turn by the community he appears to investigate. And just as the community invariably perceives the detective's personality as "eccentric," it views the sheer disruptiveness of his investigation (think of the hysterical housemaids in *The Moonstone*) as an anomaly, a dramatic exception to a routine social order in which police and surveillance play no part.

The final localization of culpability within a single individual might thus be thought of as a tactic in the more fundamental strategy of *localizing the investigation*: confining its aim (to the apprehension of a single criminal), limiting its agency (to a single eccentric detective), and highlighting its interventionary character (as an exception to the social norms usually in effect). In this respect, the social innocence established by the detective story would be far more substantial than a mere freedom from criminal guilt. For if the community is not finally the object of detection, neither is it the *subject* of detection: innocent of crime, it is—a fortiori—innocent of criminology too. Its most radical innocence, then, derives from its sheer ignorance of power, its incapacity to assume a machinery of surveillance, control, and punishment. The crime and the failure to solve it both testify to the community's naive state of vulnerability. Taken charge of by an eccentric outsider, the investigation preserves such naïveté while neutralizing the vulnerability that attends it. If one were to speak of an ideology borne in the form of the detective story, here would be one of its major sites: in the perception of everyday life as fundamentally "out-side" the network of policing power.

II

It is not difficult to recognize that *The Moonstone* begins by invoking and observing the norms of detective fiction. Rachel Verinder's Indian diamond is mysteriously stolen, and her mother, Lady Julia, has "no alternative but to send for the police" (116). The police investigation quickly proves to require "a cleverer head than Superintendent Seegrave's" (127), and the brilliant Sergeant Cuff—of whom "when it comes to unravel-ling a mystery, there isn't the equal in England" (132)—is called in to take charge. Cuff's powers of penetration are an-ticipated in the description of his gaze: "His eyes, of a steely light grey, had a very disconcerting trick, when they encoun-tered your eyes, of looking as if they expected something more from you than you were aware of yourself" (133). And such promise is soon made good in the impressive piece of reasoning about the varnish smear. In short order, the text organizes itself as a movement from mystery to solution supervised by an ex-traordinary police detective. It comes somewhat as a puzzle, then, when the text abandons the scenario it has so conscien-tiously set up. Cuff's investigation is broken off, suspended, and even its provisional conclusions are revealed to be erro-neous. The detective disappears from what remains a novel of detection, and although he reappears to clear up some inciden-tal matters at the end, the mystery is solved *without his doing*.

We can begin to elaborate what is at stake in this change of program by looking at what motivates it in the novel. For Cuff's failure and departure are precisely what the novelistic com-munity *has wished for*. In the First Period of the novel, his sheer presence is a disgrace, and he bears the burden of a general dis-like. Franklin Blake treats him "haughtily" (181); Lady Julia, who has an "unaccountable objection" to him, is always "eager" to be "out of [his] society" (146, 147); and even as Gabriel Betteredge serves him with the best of everything, he "shouldn't have been sorry if the best of everything had choked him" (174). Part of what these characters are responding to is the obvious affront of police intervention. Cuff is considered largely responsible for the fact that, as Betteredge's daughter puts it, "nothing is like what is used to be" (176). The natural order of the Verinder estate is brutally democratized, in the sense that all members of its hierarchy stand equal before Cuff's inquiry and suspicion. In his search for the stained garment, he intends "to examine the wardrobes of *everybody*—from her ladyship downwards" (145), and he is capable of advancing a hypothesis that links in guilt a maidservant who is a former convict and a young lady who is the mistress's daughter. His, indeed, is "an abominable justice that favoured nobody" (206).

Cuff's investigation threatens the community in even more radical ways as well. Systematically, his "roundabout" and "underground" practices (155, 177) violate the common decencies and genteel forebearances on which daily social life is based. He trails Rosanna Spearman "privately" on her walk (155); he eavesdrops on Betteredge and Blake on a couple of occasions; and he sets a spy on the rumble of Rachel's carriage. Ordinary actions and encounters are no longer protected either by the socially accepted conventions that prohibit scrutiny or by the socially given obviousness that precludes it. The community's sense of outrage, then, stems from a double infringement of the social contract ordinarily in force: not only does an outsider watch what is not supposed to be watched, but he also construes what he sees by other rules than the ones this community uses to regulate itself.

It is just this "heteronomous" reconstruction of its world that the community resists. Practically, resistance takes the form of a reluctance and even refusal to collaborate with Cuff. Rachel virtually declines to speak with him at all. Blake is determined to shield Rosanna Spearman from him ("I can't, and won't, help Sergeant Cuff to find the girl out" [183]). And even Betteredge, whose fascination and compliance with Cuff registers his scruples all the more effectively, tries to conceal information about Rosanna from him (152). In all cases, there stands behind such resistance a genteel code of honor and loyalty. A lady does not betray the gentleman she loves; a gentleman does not expose an unfortunate woman to suspicion; and a faithful retainer does not fail to imitate the code of his betters. It is already apparent that resistance is also offered ideologically, in the form of a sociomoral critique of Cuff's operations. When Blake infers that his conversation with Betteredge has been overheard, he says of Cuff: "He had done worse than listen. . . . He had remembered my telling him that the girl was in love with Mr. Franklin; and he had calculated on *that*, when he appealed to Mr Franklin's interest in Rosanna—in Rosanna's hearing" (183). Cuff's interventions always strike the community as being unfair, and it is easy to see why. The very "manners" whose traditional, taken-for-granted authority has maintained the self-identity of the community are now exploited to produce an alienated knowledge that rives it apart. Not the least of Cuff's sins in this perspective is that he is a liar, one who abuses the conventional stability of language and contexts of communication in order to mislead and deceive. Seeking information about Rosanna from her friends, the Yollands, Cuff tells Mrs. Yolland that his purpose is to clear Rosanna "from the unjust suspicions of her enemies in the house" (164), even though he has done more than anyone to accumulate evidence for such suspicions. Betteredge's indignation is qualified only by the comically literal terms in which it is cast: "It might be all in the way of the Sergeant's business to mystify an honest woman by wrapping her round in a network of lies; but it was my duty to have remembered, as a good Protestant, that the father of lies is the Devil—and that mischief and the Devil are never far apart" (164–65).

If Cuff's methods are troubling, their findings are untenable. Superintendent Seegrave has already implied a willingness to suspect Betteredge's own daughter, and Cuff proves even more perverse in suspecting Rachel Verinder herself. "I don't suspect," claims Cuff, moreover, "I know" (173). Unable rationally to extricate Rachel from Cuff's impressively taut weave of evidence, the community relies most simply on disavowal. Listening to Cuff's persuasive case, Betteredge rejoices that he is "constitutionally superior to reason" (208). Yet even Betteredge, whose comical intuitions nonetheless embody community norms, is capable of refuting Cuff's "knowledge" in less merely willful ways: "If Sergeant Cuff had been Solomon in all his glory, and had told me that my young lady had mixed herself up in a mean and guilty plot, I should have had but one answer for Solomon, wise as he was, 'You don't know her; and I do'" (174). With greater authority, Lady Julia makes the same point when Cuff confronts her with his "truth."

". . . I have to tell you, as Miss Verinder's mother, that she is *absolutely incapable* of doing what you suppose her to have done. Your knowledge of her character dates from a day or two since. My knowledge of her character dates from the beginning of her life. State your suspicion of her as strongly as you please—it is impossible that you can offend me by doing so. I am sure, beforehand, that (with all your experience) the circumstances have fatally misled you in this case. Mind! I am in possession of no private information. I am as absolutely shut out of my daughter's confidence as you are. My one reason for speaking positively, is the reason you have heard already. I know my child." (205)

The nature of her and Betteredge's quarrel with Cuff is thus explicitly epistemological: at one extreme, an "outside" knowledge constituted by an interventionary reconstruction of its object; at the other, an "inside" knowledge consubstantial with what it comes to know. Lady Julia's knowledge is analogous to the "old money" her estate represents: so gradually acquired that it becomes a "natural" possession that never had to be actively possessed. Conversely, just as Cuff's status as a detective would have announced his upward mobility to a mid-Victorian readership, his knowledge too bears the mark of the "nouveau," at once impressive and in bad taste, quickly assertive and asserting only monstrous propositions.

Now, before all else, Cuff's intervention is a sign that the community has failed to know itself. And if the results of his inquiry were verified, that failure of self-knowledge would become definitive. As it happens, however, Cuff is positively wrong. The diamond has been stolen not by Rachel or Rosanna (whose suspicious behavior is only intended to screen Franklin Blake, the man they love and think has stolen it), but by Godfrey Ablewhite, who needs ready cash to pay off his debts. By producing a solution that contradicts Cuff's conclusions but is consonant with the community's intuitions, the text blatantly endorses the latter. At a moment in Cuff's investigation, he scolds Betteredge for doing some detection on his own: "For the future, perhaps you will be so obliging as to do your detective business along with me" (157). In fact, in a striking reversal of the pattern of detective fiction, it is rather the blinded Cuff who ought to have done his "detective business" along with the community. And the main effect of Cuff's departure is to turn over the work of detection to prominent members of this community, like Matthew Bruff, its lawyer, and Franklin Blake, its *jeune premier*.

In a way, such a shift is bound to remind us of the typical displacements of detective fiction, where the function of detection passes either from a local to a national agent (from Seegrave to Cuff in the First Period of *The Moonstone*), from a police to a private detective (from Scotland Yard to Sherlock Holmes in "The Naval Treaty"), or from a professional to an amateur one (from Inspector G—— to Dupin in the Poe stories). Taken as a whole, *The Moonstone* obviously exemplifies the third type of displacement. Yet too many "amateurs" are involved here for the term to be wholly adequate. It is not just Betteredge who contracts "the detective fever." Nor is it merely the obvious detective figures (Blake, Bruff, Ezra Jennings) who together with their helpers (Murthwaite, Gooseberry) prosecute the case to a successful conclusion. Necessary information is provided by Rachel (who confesses that she saw Blake take the diamond), Mr. Candy (whose partially recovered memory helps bring his drugging of Blake to light), Limping Lucy (who delivers Rosanna's letter), and even Rosanna herself (whose letter puts Blake in possession of the missing nightgown). That none of these characters *intends* to assist the work of detection is irrelevant to the fact of their practical collaboration, without which the mystery would never be solved. In effect, the work of detection is carried forward by the novel's entire cast of characters, shifted not just from professional to amateur, but from an outsider to a whole community. Thus, the move to discard the *role of the detective* is at the same time a move to disperse the *function of detection*.

It might of course be thought that the community simply represents an alternative agency of detection, just as unified and localizable as that embodied in Sergeant Cuff. At its most radical, however, the dissemination of the detective function precludes the very possibility of identifying the agency in charge of it. For not only does the work of detection fail to correspond to any one character's design, it never even corresponds to an implicitly "collective" intentionality. What integrates and consolidates the efforts of characters is a master plan that no one governs or even anticipates. The community serves such a master plan but is not its master. Significantly, the work of detection is prosecuted in large degree as a result of chance and coincidence. It would have been impossible to calculate on Mr. Candy's recovery from amnesia, or on an Ezra Jennings turning up in the right place at the right time. Such happy chances, moreover, are produced only in the course of time, which is also invested with the detective function. One recalls the following exchange from Dickens's *The Mystery of Edwin Drood* (1870):

"It seems a little hard to be so tied to a stake, and innocent; but I don't complain."

"And you must expect no miracle to help you, Neville," said Mr. Crisparkle, compassionately.

"No, sir, I know that. The ordinary fulness of time and circumstance is all I have to trust to."

"It will right you at last, Neville."

"So I believe, and I hope I may live to know it."[3]

Though Dickens's novel is unfinished, it seem obvious that it writes here a promissory note that any possible ending would have met. *The Moonstone* promotes a similar reliance on the "ordinary fulness of time and circumstance," which, while it accommodates characters' efforts to speed its ripening process along, is not fully or finally identified with them. "Let us trust to time," says Mr. Bruff, "time would show" (452), and the text bears him out. In the course of time, Franklin Blake returns from abroad, Limping Lucy delivers Rosanna's letter, Rachel reveals what she has been hiding, Mr. Candy makes a recovery, and Luker's term of deposit on the diamond expires. What needs to come out somehow does, and the work of detection advances, an intentionality without a subject, a design that no one is allowed to assume responsibility for forming.

Confronted with this phenomenon, critics like Ian Ousby have been tempted to invoke the familiar notion of Providence, which would enable us to ascribe the work of detection to an agency in control of it. Yet one should beware of using the notion of Providence to neutralize the ways in which the "providential" is characterized in the novel. Contrary to Collins's practice in, say, *Armadale* (1866), the "providential" here is di-

3. Charles Dickens, *The Mystery of Edwin Drood* (Oxford: Oxford University Press, 1956), p. 197.

vested of any explicit religious dimension. We are meant to respond with a very worldly smile when Betteredge speaks, like a good Protestant, of the Devil, and only in hypocrites like Miss Clack or Ablewhite do we find the traditional pious belief in divine will. Moreover, if such a will is at work in the novel, it functions only through the established logic of a thoroughly ordinary world. The providential effect of detection in *The Moonstone* does not depend on its proximate causes. These are individual psychologies, social institutions and scenarios, even ontological laws that operate in overwhelmingly conventional ways. Rather, it depends on the fact that detection, working exclusively through its agents' intentions, uncannily but benignly transcends them. Discreet and, in the last analysis, agentless, the detective function is able to organize the text without raising the moral problems posed by Cuff's interventionary police inquiry.

In order to elicit this latent detection, blandly and automatically attaching to the way things are, we might begin by noticing that Cuff's morally unacceptable investigation has its precondition in a prior investigation. In his clever deduction regarding the door smear, all Cuff really does is assemble and coordinate the information gathered and given to him by members of the community. Blake knows the drying time of the varnish and when it was applied; Penelope has noticed that it was still intact at midnight. The door was under a patchy and unconscious surveillance well in advance of Cuff's arrival. What may seem a gratuitous observation becomes more significant when Cuff proceeds to find the stained article of dress: "Before we begin, I should like, if convenient, to have the washing-book. The stained article of dress may be an article of linen. If the search leads to nothing, I want to be able to account next for all the linen in the house, and for all the linen sent to the wash. If there is an article missing, there will be at least a presumption that it has got the paint-stain on it, and that it has been purposely made away with, yesterday or today, by the person owning it" (146–47). Suggestively, the washing-book belongs to a preestablished system for accounting for the linen. Cuff's hypothesis, in other words, would verify itself by a means that already exists *as a means of verification*. And later, when he has traced Rosanna to a linen-draper where she purchased "enough [cloth] to make a nightgown" (188), he explains: "her nightgown must have brushed the wet paint on the door. . . . She couldn't safely destroy the nightgown without first providing another like it, to make the inventory of her linen complete" (189).

"To make the inventory of her linen complete": even as it tells us what Rosanna would have had to circumvent, the phrase glances at the extent to which the servants' lives are already administered and controlled. A preventive detection inheres in the very management of the estate. One might also recall how Rosanna's secret signs of interest in Franklin Blake are "surprised" and "surprised again" by Penelope (79); or how, again by Penelope, the private meeting between Rachel and Godfrey Ablewhite is watched and overheard from "behind the holly" (98). In both cases, Penelope hastens to report to her father, who happens also to be head servant. Natural curiosity and common gossip double for an informal system of surveillance observed on the estate long before the Moonstone is stolen.

In a more diffuse way, the system is implied in the very "knowledge" characters have of one another. Everyone's behavior in this world is being continuously encoded according to shared norms of psychological and moral verisimilitude. Invariably, the points at which behavior seems insufficiently motivated by these norms are points of *suspicion*. As early as the First Period, one could make an accurate guess at the thief simply by ranking the main suspects (Rachel, Rosanna, Blake, and Ablewhite) in the distance to which each stands outside the collective cognition whose spokesman is Betteredge. He too has known Rachel from birth. He intuits the goodwill of Rosanna, who in any case has been thoroughly watched both at the reformatory and at the Verinder estate. He knew Blake as a boy, and though he is somewhat baffled by the man, he notes that the passing years have left "the bright, straightforward look in his eyes" (60). Blake's eccentricities (his moodiness, his frivolousness, his foreign "sides") are soon accommodated as idiosyncrasies, not deviations. Only in the case of Ablewhite does Betteredge claim no more than an extrinsic knowledge, gathered from hearsay and as a spectator:

I do suppose this was the most accomplished philanthropist (on a small independence) that England ever produced. As a speaker at charitable meetings the like of him for drawing your tears and your money was not easy to find. He was quite a public character. The last time I was in London, my mistress gave me two treats. She sent me to the theatre to see a dancing woman who was all the rage; and she sent me to Exeter Hall to hear Mr Godfrey. The lady did it, with a band of music. The gentleman did it, with a handkerchief and a glass of water. Crowds at the performance with the legs. Ditto at the performance with the tongue. (89)

It ought to come as no surprise that Godfrey is leading a double life when, even in Betteredge's apparent commendation, one can read a hollowness—an absence of the "real" Godfrey. Significantly, Betteredge praises his *rhetoric*, traditionally the sign of an outward appearance whose correspondence with inward being is not to be taken for granted. By the time Godfrey is associated with Miss Clack, and it is known that he has asked to see Lady Julia's will, there is little to learn except the logistics of the theft and the details of the secret life motivating it. Indeed, one might say that the remaining actions in the novel—the discovery that Franklin Blake stole the diamond, its confirmation and disconfirmation—merely distract characters from the obvious epistemological gaps that identify Godfrey as the thief. In this sense, the revelation at the end is a fact that the community knew all along, but simply didn't know that it knew.

In effect, then, a policing power is inscribed in the ordinary practices and institutions of the world from the start. The full extent of this inscription can already be measured in the prologue, where a cousin writing to relatives in England accuses Colonel John Herncastle of stealing the Moonstone from its Indian shrine. "I declare, on my word of honour, that what I am now about to write is, strictly and literally, the truth" (33). Beginning like a legal deposition, the cousin's manuscript proceeds to marshal the "moral evidence" for his accusation, and concludes by submitting the case to the family's judgment. And the family network that detects and judges crime is also empowered to enforce its own sentence: "[Herncastle] came back with a character that closed the doors of all his family against him. . . . The mystery of the Colonel's life got in the Colonel's way, and outlawed him, as you may say, among his own people. The men wouldn't let him into their clubs; the women—more than one—whom he wanted to marry, refused him; friends and relations got too near-sighted to see him in the street" (63–64). The quasi-legal status of the prologue extends to the entire novel, as a "record in writing" (39) containing "the attestations of witnesses who can speak to the facts" (236). Each deposition is under the juridical restraint not to overstep the boundaries of the "personal experience" (40) of the deposer. Betteredge is only the first to remind us that he is forbidden to tell more in his narrative than he knew himself at the time: "In this matter of the Moonstone the plan is, not to present reports, but to produce witnesses" (233). According to the same plan, the narratives are being collected to provide "a record of the facts to which those who come after [the protagonists] can appeal" (39). Betteredge imagines "a member of the family" reading his narrative fifty years later: "Lord! what a compliment he will feel it, to be asked to take nothing on hearsay, and to be treated in all respects like a Judge on the bench" (233). In the most active sense of the term, the community is concerned to "justify" itself—*to make its own justice*. If this com-

munity can afford to dispense with the legal systems of surveillance, trial, and punishment, this is because its own organization anticipates and contains them.

With one crucial difference: the community's policing apparatus is inscribed not just "in" but "as" the ordinary practices
of the world. Everyday roles, motivations, scenarios naturalize
this apparatus effortlessly. Herncastle's cousin swears not in the
name of God, as he would in a court of law, but on his honor,
as he would in ordinary intercourse among ladies and gentlemen. The institution of justice to which he appeals is also, on
its most visible face, the institution of the family. Herncastle
is not so much punished as he is snubbed—the natural response
of gentility to someone with a bad character. Penelope's spying
is perceived as "the natural curiosity of women" (79), a young
girl's innocent interest in the love relationships of her mistress
and her fellow servants. She doesn't, moreover, go tattle to the
head servant; she quite properly confides in her father. As for
the washing-book, its function is presumably to make sure that
nothing is lost. Even many of the depositionlike narratives that
record the story are no more than everyday forms of writing
(letters, journals, diaries), or are at least derived from them.

In a similar pattern, detective figures such as Blake, Bruff,
and Jennings have no intrinsic interest in detection at all. Blake
needs to clear up the mystery in order to gain Rachel's hand.
A close family friend, Bruff is naturally concerned to protect
the fatherless and soon altogether orphaned Rachel from ad-
venturers, as well as to promote the course of true love between
her and Blake. And Jennings gets involved because he feels
sorry for Blake, whom he sees as a double of himself. Typically,
characters become detectives in the exact degree that they remain what they already are. As an eminent lawyer, Bruff can
easily find out who has asked to see his client's will; as a psy-
chologist, Jennings is able to decipher Mr. Candy's fragmentary
utterances and to create the opium experiment that exculpates
Blake once for all. At the most basic level, what assists the work

of detection can be as "natural" as one's physical constitution. Candy helps simply by recovering from his amnesia, and Blake merely by having the same somatic responses to his second dose of opium as to his first. In the end, moreover, even the most voluntaristic efforts of detection are sublated in a self-regulating moral ontology. For the thief of the Moonstone is identified and discovered only after he is dead—murdered by Indians who have recovered the jewel for their Hindu shrine. The text's suggestion is obvious: the nature of things is so arranged that Godfrey's crime inevitably designates and punishes itself. "Questo è il fin di chi fa mal."

In general, the effects of a police apparatus are secured as side effects of their motivation *in another register*. They surface as incidental consequences of actions and institutions that have other, more obvious and "natural" explanations for their being. Thus, without having to serve police functions in an ex officio way, gossip and domestic familiarity produce the effect of surveillance; letters and diaries, the effect of dossiers; closed clubs and homes, the effect of punishment. The intention to detect is visible only at a microscopic level, casually implied in self-evident moral imperatives (to love, to take care of, to feel sorry for), or at a macroscopic level, inscribed in the fullness of time and in the moral-ontological law that compels guilt to confess itself. In either case, a direct assumption of policing power by the community is avoided. In a way, then, *The Moonstone* displaces the structures of detective fiction only to restage its ideology of everyday life in more ambitious ways. The detective story, I claimed, put policing power at the margins of everyday life, from which it made an occasional, anomalous incursion. More radically, *The Moonstone* dismisses the police altogether, and the mysterious crime is worked to a solution by a power that no one has charge of. The equivocal role of the "providential"—immanent in the social world yet distinct from its intentionalities—is thus part of a strategy whose ideological implications should be plain. The exercise of policing power inheres in the logic of the world, but only as a discreet "accident" of normative social practices and models of conduct. The community does not mobilize in a concerted scheme of police action, and yet things turn out as though it did. *The Moonstone* satisfies a double exigency: how to keep the everyday world entirely outside a network of police power and at the same time to preserve the effects of such power within it. Indeed, the novel *increases* this power in the very act of arranging for it to "disappear," absorbed into (as) the sheer positivity of being in the world. It cannot be decried as an intervention because it is already everywhere. It cannot be resisted for long since it exerts the permanent pressure of "reality" itself. Finally, it cannot even be seen, for it is a power that never passes as such: therein lies its power.

III

Students of detective fiction commonly grow wistful when discussing its ancestors in the nineteenth-century novel. Such novels, it is usually lamented, approach the so-called classical detective story, but stop disappointingly short of realizing its program fully and point by point.[4] Yet if these novels are not detective stories, it is, as we say, because they do not wish to be. In the case of *The Moonstone*, this is a highly active truth.

4. Régis Messac's standard history—*Le detective novel et l'influence de la pensée scientifique* (Paris, 1929)—sets the standard here as well. *Primo tempo*: "Collins était probablement celui qui eût été le mieux doué pour reprendre et continuer l'oeuvre de Poe. . . . Collins, comme les autres, a entrevu ce que pouvait être le genre"; *secondo tempo*: "Mais il n'a jamais réalisé pleinement et de point en point le programme qu'il esquissait" (Collins was probably the one who was best qualified to resume and continue the work of Poe. . . . Collins, like the others, glimpsed what the genre might be, but he never realized, fully and point by point, the program that he sketched out. Pp. 550–51).

The text, we have seen, invokes the norms of detective fiction precisely to rework and pass beyond them. It moves from a story of police action to a story of human relationships in less "specialized" contexts. The move seems a shift in genre as well: from the detective novel to what can only be called the Novel *tout court*. The text might thus be taken to imply a certain genealogy of the Novel, as the form that results when the detective story is exploded and diffused. The genealogy, of course, is not a genesis. Historically, it would be absurd to derive the novel from the detective story, whose "classical" period of development neither precedes nor even (excepting three stories by Poe) coincides with the novel's own. More accurately, the detective story first emerges as an aborted function *within* the novel, as part of the novel's characteristic double pattern of circumscribing the professional offices of detection the better and more broadly to reinscribe them in everyday life. This is one reason why the criticism of the traditional novel inevitably brings up the model of detective fiction and inevitably finds it wanting. This is also why, at once incited and inhibited by the novel that forestalls it, the detective story can only "arrive" on the demise of that novel, at the end of the nineteenth century and after, with Doyle, Christie, Leroux, and others.

Yet the turn in *The Moonstone* from a professional detective to lay detection acquires its widest resonance as a parable of the modern policing power that comes to rely less on spectacular displays of repressive force than on intangible networks of productive discipline. As our analysis has already suggested, even the functions of the Panopticon are finally, in Poe's phrase, "a little *too* self-evident" to be fully exemplary of this discipline, whose subtlety, mobility, and sheer off-handedness also resist identifying it with any of the other, "nonpenal" institutions that it may traverse. Furthermore, although I have argued that *The Moonstone* rehearses the story of modern power, it would ultimately be more pertinent to show how this story recurs in the novel's own telling of it. For if discipline is a general phenomenon in the nineteenth-century Occident, then the texts we call nineteenth-century novels would not merely register it (as a feature of a referent in the world), but relay it as well (within the literary institution of the Novel). *The Moonstone*, for instance, would do more than dramatize a certain ideology of power; it would produce this ideology as an effect—and in the mode—of its being read as a novel. Accordingly, our attention needs to turn from the discipline narrated in the novel to the discipline inherent in the novel's technique of narration.

Unlike the majority of Victorian novels, *The Moonstone* is not related by an "omniscient narrator," whose unimpeachable authority imposes itself on the reader. Instead, the story is told in a succession of narratives written by some of the characters and organized through their limited points of view. The "modernity" of such a procedure is seductively apparent, as are the implications that a post-Jamesian criticism might wish to draw from it. Thus, *The Moonstone* is currently thought to offer "a narrative structure that is thoroughly subjective and unreliable" (A. D. Hutter) and "to provide a continually shifting viewpoint on the action, offering not merely different but sometimes contradictory views of the same event or character" (Ian Ousby).[5] The text, it is implied in such claims, opens up the notion of truth to radically relativistic challenge—in the manner, say, of *Rashomon*. In Kurosawa's film (1950), one remembers, a crime is recounted four times, each time by a different protagonist. Not only are the accounts incompatible, but there is no compelling standard of plausibility by which the contradictions might be adjudicated. The "truth" is dissolved into four conflicting interpretations. Contrary to the example of *Rashomon*, however, the "unreliable" and "contradictory" narrative structure of *The Moonstone* works only as a ruse. To be

5. A. D. Hutter, "Dreams, Transformations, and Literature: The Implications of Detective Fiction," *Victorian Studies* 19 (December 1975): 191; and Ian Ousby, *Bloodhounds of Heaven* (Cambridge, Mass.: Harvard University Press, 1976), p. 117.

sure, the text *claims* for itself all that Hutter and Ousby are ready to grant it. A reader is supposed to listen to the various witnesses, and to make up his mind about the validity of their reports as he will, "like a Judge on the bench." To all formal appearances, his reading is deprived of any grounding in an authoritative version. Yet the possibility of an authentic "dialogism" in the text disappears once we recognize that, in every crucial case, all readers (including Hutter and Ousby) pass *the same judgment*. The different points of view, degrees of information, tendencies of suspicion are never allowed to tamper with more basic interpretative securities about character and language. Characters may be *known* because they are always equipped with stable, centered identities; and they may be known *in language* because it is incapable of ever escaping from its own truthfulness.

For all its apparent "subjectivity," for example, Betteredge's narrative can be counted on to give us a valid cognition of its "subject": the faithful retainer himself, whose very naïveté is a guarantor of the plain dealing of his self-presentation. Moreover, to the degree that Betteredge's language unproblematically "names" him, we know exactly what weight to give to its cognitive claims about other matters in the novel. To suspect this language, as a reader of *The Murder of Roger Ackroyd* might well try to do, is to play a more strenuous interpretative game against the text than it is ever willing to reward: Betteredge's normative-seeming perceptions are normative in fact, fully borne out in the rest of the novel. For all practical purposes of reading, the head servant's subjectivity shrinks down to a few idiosyncrasies that differentiate him as a "character" and that we know enough to discount. Though he treats *Robinson Crusoe* like an oracle, we don't seriously expect that book to figure in the solution to the mystery. Nor do we ever feel that the misogyny he professes interferes with the good sense of his intuitions about Rachel (high-tempered, but honorable) or Rosanna (fatally weak, perhaps, but no criminal). His narrative may not tell us "the whole truth," but it can be relied on to tell us "nothing but the truth." The local uncertainties in his report never impair the possibility of his or our cognition, which is always able to designate them as such, and so to initiate a process of mastering them. Whatever Betteredge doesn't know, he knows he doesn't know, and so do we. In this sense, the actual cognitive problems posed by his language are infrequent and strictly minor. Thus, when he introduces Godfrey Ablewhite in the passage we cited earlier, it is unclear whether he means his language to be "straight" or sarcastic. The undecidability of what Betteredge means, however, never carries over into what his language actually says. The reader inevitably recognizes that, with or without Betteredge's knowledge, his text refuses to endorse Godfrey in any full way. That Betteredge's language is ambiguously motivated is irrelevant to a more fundamental readerly certainty about Godfrey's unique and suspicious hollowness.

The Moonstone, I am arguing, is more fundamentally about the securities of perception and language than about the problems they pose. To use Mikhail Bakhtin's term, the novel is thoroughly *monological*—always speaking a master-voice that corrects, overrides, subordinates, or sublates all other voices it allows to speak. This basic monologism shows up best, in fact, where it seems threatened most: in the narrative of Miss Clack. In obvious ways, Clack's perception differs radically from that of the rest of the community: she suspects Rachel, dislikes Franklin Blake, and adores Godfrey Ablewhite. Yet at least when it comes to representing the self-deceived spinster herself, Clack's language is incontestably truthful. At the start of her narrative, Blake appends a footnote telling us that " 'the person chiefly concerned' in Miss Clack's narrative, is happy enough at the present moment, not only to brave the smartest exercise of Miss Clack's pen, but even to recognize its unquestionable value as an instrument for the exhibition of Miss Clack's character" (236). In addition to exculpating Rachel (who is, of course, "the person chiefly concerned"), the note invites us to read Clack's narrative against its grain—to locate its truth in the blinds of its narrator's *inconscience*. Even without the invitation, Clack's perceptions are so blatantly self-betraying that a reader inevitably revises them to mean something very different from what Clack imagines. When she insists, for instance, that Rachel's haughtiness didn't anger her ("I only made a private memorandum to pray for her"), the piety is effectively "desublimated" only a paragraph later: "For my own part, knowing Rachel's spirit to have been essentially unregenerate from her childhood upwards, I was prepared for whatever my aunt could tell me on the subject of her daughter. It might have gone on from bad to worse till it ended in Murder; and I should still have said to myself, The natural result! oh, dear, dear, the natural result!" (244). The ardent concern for Rachel's imperiled soul merely aggrandizes the ressentiment of a poor relation, just as the hero-worship of Godfrey Ablewhite merely returns the sexual repression of a frustrated old maid. In the context of these transparent psychological aberrations, Clack's mistaken views of Rachel and Godfrey point to themselves as such, and thus they are neutralized even as they are presented. More than neutralized: they reinforce the dominant perceptions that a reader has already derived from Betteredge's narrative and will find confirmed in the narratives of Bruff and Blake. Although *The Moonstone* formally lacks a monological *narrator* who could refute Clack's words by direct comment ("Clack was lying to herself") or indirect insinuation ("Clack persuaded herself that Rachel's insolence roused no anger in her"), the text remains an essentially monological narration. Despite the intentions of its "author," Clack's narrative is reduced to no more than a loyal opposition within a single and coherent movement of disclosure.

There is a further point to be made. Not only is *The Moonstone* a monological text, but also its monologism quite literally *goes without saying*. Formally and linguistically, the master-discourse that organizes the text is unwritten: carried only through the subjective narratives that are unwittingly but regularly obliged to postulate it. Collins's technique is a way to inscribe the *effects* of monologism in the text without ascribing them to the *agency* of an actual monologist. As a result, monologism doesn't strictly seem *in* the text (like the shifters and first-person pronouns that identify the narrator in George Eliot or Trollope); nor does it seem fully *outside* the text (like an interpretative choice that one may, or may not, impose on it). Rather, it is staged like an "invisible hand," programming the text without needing to be programmed into it. As such, of course, the monologism of the narration is exactly analogous to the work of detection in the representation. Just as a common detection transcends the single efforts of various detective figures, a common narration subsumes the individual reports of various narrators. The world resolves its difficulties, and language finds its truth, according to the same principle of quasi-automatic self-regulation.

At both levels, *The Moonstone* promotes a single perception of power. In a consistent pattern, power in the novel is never gathered into an identifiable (and hence attackable) center. Neither is it radically "disseminated" so that the totality it claims to organize breaks down into discontinuities and incoherencies. Its paradoxical efficiency lies in the fact that an apparent lack of center at the level of *agency* secures a total mastery at the level of *effect*. What finally justifies us in calling the novel's perception of power "ideological" is that *The Moonstone* never really perceives power as such at all. The novel is itself blinded by the mystificatory strategy of power in the very act of tracing it. In practical terms, this means the novel must always "say" power as though it were saying *something else*. As I've tried to suggest, the "something else" is no less than the irresistible positivity of words and things "as they are." Just as detection surfaces only in the ordinary activities of amateurs, and monological narration only in subjective narratives, so too the discourse on power only comes to light in (as) a discourse on "the way things are." "Revealing" the character of modern power only insofar as it "masks" it as an ontology, *The Moonstone* is thus perfectly obedient to the imperatives of such power. Accordingly, the novel's discourse on power must finally be taken as a discourse *of* power—a discourse *spoken through* by a power that is simply extending its blinding strategy of displacement.

An argument might even be made that monologism forwards (is forwarded by) this "discourse of power" in novels that make use of an omniscient narrator as well. For the omniscient narrator (say, as he appears in George Eliot or Trollope) is typically presented as one who merely *tells* a story that is assumed to have happened already. The staging of the text as the narration of an autonomous story thus advances both the reality effect of the story and the reality effect of its self-regulation. Power, on this showing, is not felt to lie in the hands of the teller (who in general appears to regret the adventures he recounts). Instead, power is seen to coincide with the "reality" that is merely being re-presented: a reality whose authority may be lamented, but is never finally arguable. The case of *The Moonstone* would thus implicate the canonical or serious novel tradition to which, not altogether unsuitably, it has been considered to stand in a "trivial" relation.

THREE

Discipline in Different Voices: Bureaucracy, Police, Family, and *Bleak House*

I

The Court of Chancery in *Bleak House* (1852–53) makes a certain difference in Dickens's representation of social discipline. This representation had hitherto been restricted to places of confinement that, as much as they referred to a disciplinary society committed to the manufacture and diffusion of such enclosures, carried an even more emphatic allusion to the space between them: a space of freedom or domestic tranquillity that was their "other." The often ferocious architecture that immured the inmates of a carceral institution seemed to immure the operations practiced on them there as well, and the thick, spiked walls, the multiple gateways, the attendants and the administrators that assured the confinement of those within seemed equally to provide for the protectedness of those without, including most pertinently the novelist and his readers. Embodied in the prison, the workhouse, the factory, the school, discipline became, quite precisely, a *topic* of Dickensian representation: a site whose redoubtable but all the more easily identified boundaries allowed it to be the target of criticism to the same extent that they isolated it from other, better sites. The topic of the carceral in Dickens—better, the carceral as topic—thus worked to secure the effect of difference between, on the one hand, a confined, institutional space in which power is violently exercised on collectivized subjects, and on the other, a space of "liberal society," generally determined as a free, private, and individual domain and practically specified as the family. Yet clear though the lines of demarcation were, it was alarmingly easy to cross them. After all, what brought carceral institutions into being in the first place were lapses in the proper management of the family: in its failure to constitute itself (the problem of illegitimate or orphaned children and the institutional solution of foundling hospitals and baby farms) or in its failure to sustain itself by means of a self-sufficient domestic economy (the problem of poverty and debt and the institutional responses of workhouses and debtor's prisons). And in the portrayal of its hero in the workhouse, *Oliver Twist* (1838) dramatized the shameful facility with which such institutions might mistakenly seize upon what were middle-class subjects to begin with. Still, if to witness the horror of the carceral was always to incur a debt of gratitude for the immunities of middle-class life, then to sense the danger from the carceral was already to learn how this debt had to be acquitted. When Oliver Twist, enchanted by the difference between his previous experience and his life at Mr. Brownlow's, begged the latter not to send him back to "the wretched place I came from," Brownlow declared: "You need not be afraid of my deserting you, unless you give me cause." Earlier he had promised Oliver access to the culture represented by the books in his library on similar conditions: "You shall read them, if you behave well."[1] The price of Oliver's deliverance from the carceral (either as the workhouse or as Fagin's gang) would be his absolute submission to the norms, protocols, and regulations of the middle-class family, in which he received tuition not just from Brownlow but from the Maylies as well. Liberal society and the family were kept free from the carceral institutions that were set up to

1. Charles Dickens, *Oliver Twist* (Oxford: Oxford University Press, 1949), pp. 95 and 94.

remedy their failures only by assuming the burden of an immense internal regulation. If discipline was confined to the carceral, then, this was so in order that it might ultimately be extended—in the mode of what was experientially its opposite—to the space outside it.

The Court of Chancery in *Bleak House* forces upon this representation the necessity of a certain readjustment. In the first place, an essential characteristic of the court is that its operations far exceed the architecture in which it is apparently circumscribed. The distinctive gesture of the carceral—that of locking up—makes little sense here when, at the end of the day, what is locked up is only "the empty court" and not "all the misery it has caused."[2] Though the court is affirmed to be situated "at the very heart of the fog" (2), this literally nebulous information only restates the difficulty of locating it substantially, since there is "fog everywhere" (1). The ultimate unlocalizability of its operations permits them to be in all places at once. "How many people out of the suit, Jarndyce and Jarndyce has stretched forth its unwholesome hand to spoil and corrupt, would be a very wide question" (5), but it would perhaps also be a moot one, since nearly all the characters we meet in the novel are in the cause, either as parties to it or administrators of it, even those such as Esther who seem to have nothing to do with it. And the suit is as long as it is wide, the spatial extension of its filiations being matched by the temporal duration that unfolds under its "eternal heading" (5). Dickens's satire on the inefficiency of the court begins to seem a feeble, even desperate act of whistling in the dark, for the power organized under the name of Chancery is repeatedly demonstrated to be all too effective. Like the fog and dirt that are its first symbols, this power insinuates itself by virtue of its quasi-

2. Charles Dickens, *Bleak House* (Oxford: Oxford University Press, 1948), p. 7. For all future citations from the novel, page references to this edition will be given parenthetically in the text.

alchemical subtlety. To violent acts of penetration it prefers the milder modes of permeation, and instead of being densely consolidated into a force prepared to encounter a certain resistance, it is so finely vaporized—sublimated, we should say, thinking of alchemy and psychoanalysis together—that every surface it needs to attack is already porously welcoming it. Unlike, say, the power that keeps order in Dotheboys Hall in *Nicholas Nickleby* (1839), this power does not impose itself by physical coercion (though, as the case of Gridley reminds us, it does dispose of carceral sanctions for those who hold it in contempt). Rather, it relies on being voluntarily assumed by its subjects, who, seduced by it, addicted to it, internalize the requirements for maintaining its hold. "Fog everywhere." What Chancery produces, or threatens to produce, is an organization of power that, ceasing entirely to be a *topic*, has become topography itself: a system of control that can be all-encompassing because it cannot be compassed in turn. Writing in the nineteenth century, John Forster would not be the last critic of *Bleak House* to notice how "the great Chancery suit, on which the plot hinges, on incidents connected with which, important or trivial, all the passion and suffering turns, is worked into every part of the book."[5] Yet though we see nothing but the effects of Jarndyce and Jarndyce, everywhere present, affecting everyone, everything, we never come close to seeing what the suit is all about, as though this were merely the pretext that allowed for the disposition and deployment of the elaborate channels, targets, and techniques of a state bureaucracy. The interminable process of interpretation to which the original will gives rise, literally maddening to those who bring to it the demand that it issue in final truths and last judgments, is abandoned rather than adjudicated. If Chancery thus names an organization of power

---

5. John Forster, in an unsigned review for the *Examiner* (October 8, 1853): 643–45; reprinted in Philip Collins, ed., *Dickens: The Critical Heritage* (New York: Barnes and Noble, 1971), p. 291.

that is total but not totalizable, total *because* it is not totalizable, then what is most radically the matter with being "in Chancery" is not that there may be no way out of it (a dilemma belonging to the problematic of the carceral), but, more seriously, that the binarisms of inside/outside, here/elsewhere become meaningless and the ideological effects they ground impossible.

Furthermore, the nature of Chancery necessarily affects the nature of the resistance to it. Whereas the topic of the carceral, localizing disciplinary practices that thereby seemed to require only local remedies, always implied a feasible politics of reformism, the total social reticulation of Chancery finds its corresponding oppositional practice in the equally total social negation of anarchism. Repeatedly, the court induces in the narration a wish for its wholesale destruction by fire: "If all the injustice it has committed, and all the misery it has caused, could only be locked up with it, and the whole burnt away in a great funeral pyre—why, so much the better for other parties than the parties in Jarndyce and Jarndyce!" (7). Even the elision of agency managed by the passive voice (who, exactly, would burn the court?), stopping short of any subjective assumption of the action, mirrors perfectly the court whose operations are in no one's control. The wish, moreover, may be considered fulfilled (albeit also displaced) when Mr. Krook, who has personified the Chancellor and Chancery from the first, dies of spontaneous combustion. It is as though apocalyptic suddenness were the only conceivable way to put an end to Chancery's meanderings, violent spontaneity the only means to abridge its elaborate procedures, and mere combustion the only response to its accumulation of paperwork. One of the least welcome implications of an all-inclusive system, such as Chancery appears to be, is that even opposition to it, limited to the specular forms of reflection and inversion, merely intensifies our attachment to the perceptual grid constructed by its practices.

To say so much, of course, is to treat Chancery, if not more radically, then certainly more single-mindedly, than Dickens is ever willing to do. For while a major effort of *Bleak House* is to establish Chancery as an all-pervasive system of domination, another is to refute the fact of this system and recontain the court within a larger spatial organization that would once again permit an elsewhere along with all the ideological effects attaching to it. If Krook's death, for instance, illustrates the apocalyptically antisocial kinds of retribution that are the only adequate responses to Chancery remaining, it can also be seen to reinstate precisely those social and political possibilities that Chancery, as a total order, ought to have made impossible. For insofar as Krook dies, as in certain modern etiologies of cancer, of his own internal repressions, then Chancery can be safely trusted to collapse from its own refusal to release what is unhealthily accumulating in its system. Alternatively, insofar as Krook's violent end is meant to foreshadow what is in store for the institution he figures, then his death carries a warning to the court to amend its ways or else. In either case, we are reinstalled within the reformist perspectives that Chancery had, we thought, in principle annulled.

Even the omnipresence of the Chancery suit that Forster rightly noted is frequently neutralized by a certain inconsequentiality. John Jarndyce, Ada Clare, and Esther Summerson are all in the suit without being spoiled or corrupted by it—indeed, they constitute the domestic retreat to which the institutional, social space of the court can then be contrasted. Richard Carstone, whose aimlessness internalizes the procedural protractions of the court, makes a better example of Chancery's power to spoil and corrupt. Yet it is also possible to argue, as did an early critic of the novel, under the impression that he was exposing its deficiency, that Richard "is not made reckless and unsteady by his interest in the great suit, but simply expends his recklessness and unsteadiness on it, as he would on something else if it were non-existent."[4] It is, of course, Dickens's own text that opens up the possibility of this moral

4. George Brimley, in an unsigned review, *Spectator* 36 (September 24, 1853): 923–25; reprinted in Collins, p. 283.

explanation in its reluctance to commit itself to social determination:

> "How much of this indecision of character," Mr. Jarndyce said to me, "is chargeable on that incomprehensible heap of uncertainty and procrastination on which he has been thrown from his birth, I don't pretend to say; but that Chancery, among its other sins, is responsible for some of it, I can plainly see. It has engendered or confirmed in him a habit of putting off—and trusting to this, that, and the other chance, without knowing what chance—and dismissing everything as unsettled, uncertain, and confused. The character of much older and steadier people may be even changed by the circumstances surrounding them. It would be too much to expect that a boy's, in its formation, should be the subject of such influences, and escape them." (167)

Jarndyce kindheartedly proposes the sociological key to Richard's character in the same breath as he admits its insufficiency. And what is at stake in his hesitation between "engendered" and "confirmed," between the court as cause and the court as occasion, goes beyond the double view of Richard. Ultimately, the text oscillates between two seemingly incompatible sets of assumptions about the nature of Chancery's power—one deriving from the perception of total domination, the other still attached to the topic of the carceral. Thus, just as the satire on the inefficiency of the court contradicts the demonstrated power of such inefficiency, so too the anachronism of Chancery, upheld as "a slow, expensive, British, constitutional sort of thing" (13) by such fossils as Sir Leicester, counters the newness of the phenomenon that Dickens is describing under that name: the expanded development of the Victorian state bureaucracy that is at least as current as the novel's official exhibit of modernity in the Detective Police.[5]

5. A euphoric account of the destiny of Victorian bureaucracy may be found in David Roberts, *The Victorian Origins of the Welfare State* (New Haven: Yale University Press, 1961). For a detailed treatment of Dick-

All the evidence of Chancery's totalizing effects—of its productivity as an all-engloving system of power—is equivocal in such ways, as the text at once claims that this system is and isn't efficient, is and isn't everywhere, can and can't be reformed. In the literal sense of giving utterance to a double discourse, *Bleak House* is a contradictory text. Yet as we continue to consider the operation of such "contradiction" in the text, we should be wary of prejudging it, in a certain Marxist manner, as the "symptom" of an ideological bind, obligingly betrayed to our notice in the text's taken-for-granted "distanciation" from its own program.[6] We need rather to be prepared to

---

ens's attitude toward the Detective Police, see the pertinent chapter in Philip Collins's invaluable study, *Dickens and Crime*, 2d ed. (London: Macmillan, 1964).

6. I have in mind the tradition founded in Louis Althusser, "A Letter on Art," in his *Lenin and Philosophy*, trans. Ben Brewster (New York and London: Monthly Review Press, 1971), pp. 221–27, and elaborated in Pierre Macherey, *A Theory of Literary Production*, trans. Geoffrey Wall (London: Routledge and Kegan Paul, 1978). Althusser's claim that art performs an "internal distanciation" on ideology in the course of representing it ("Letter," p. 222) receives its working-through in the theory and practical criticism of Macherey, for whom "the finished literary work . . . *reveals* the gaps in ideology" by "specifically literary means" (*Literary Production*, pp. 60, 238). The best example of this tradition in English (and also the most relevant to the work in progress here) is Terry Eagleton, *Criticism and Ideology* (London: New Left Books, 1976). In the chapter called "Ideology and Literary Form," which includes a discussion of Dickens and other nineteenth-century English novelists, "ideology" (qua "organicism") once again provides the principle of coherence that "literary form" once again brings into disarray: "In English literary culture of the past century, the ideological basis of organic form is peculiarly visible, as a progressively impoverished bourgeois liberalism attempts to integrate more ambitious and affective ideological modes. In doing so, that ideology enters into grievous conflicts which its aesthetic forms betray in the very act of attempted resolution" (p. 161). In all cases, the category of artistic form remains where bourgeois aesthetics used to situate it: beyond social tensions or, what comes to the same, invariably on the right side of the struggle.

find in the source of "incoherence," the very resource on which the text draws for its consistency; in the ideological "conflict," a precise means of addressing and solving it; in the "failure" of intention on the part of the text, a positively advantageous *strategy*.

II

Of all the mysteries that will crop up in *Bleak House*, not the least instructive concerns the curious formal torsion whereby a novel dealing with a civil suit becomes a murder mystery, and whereby the themes of power and social control are passed accordingly from the abyssal filiations of the law into the capable hands of the detective police. By what kinds of logic or necessity is the law thus turned over to the police, and the civil suit turned into the criminal case? For if Jarndyce and Jarndyce provides the ground from which mysteries and the consequent detections originate, it is certainly not because the suit is itself a mystery. In one way, it is so illegible that we don't even have a sense, as we should with a mystery, of what needs to be explained or, more important, of what might constitute either the clues or the cruxes of such an explanation. In another, the suit may be read fully and at leisure: in the reams of dusty warrants, in the tens of thousands of Chancery-folio pages, in the battery of blue bags with their heavy charges of paper—in all the archival litter that has accumulated over the dead letter of the original will. Dickens's presentation offers either too little or else too much to amount to mystery. Besides, nothing about the suit is secret or hidden, unless we count the second will found late in the novel, and this hardly brings us closer to a judgment. All that is ever unavailable is the dead legator's intentions.

It would be seriously misleading, however, on the basis of this exception, to deconstruct the suit into an allegory of inter-

pretation as that which, confronting the absence of an immediate meaning effected by the very nature of the sign or text,
must unfold as an interminable proliferation of readings.[7] For
one thing, if the suit can be thought to give expression to such
difficulties of interpretation, this is because, more than merely
finding them acceptable, it goes out of its way to manufacture
them; and no response would serve Chancery or the logic of its
law better than to see this manufacture as inhering in the nature
of "textuality" rather than belonging to an institutional practice that seeks to implant and sanction its own technical procedures. For another, it seems willful to see the work of interpretation occurring in what is far more obviously and actually
the profitable business of deferring it indefinitely. With its
endless referrals, relays, remands, its ecologically terrifying
production of papers, minutes, memoranda, Dickens's bureaucracy works positively to elude the project of interpretation
that nominally guides it. (And by the time that the Circum-
locution Office in *Little Dorrit* [1857] avows the principle
"HOW NOT TO DO IT," even the nominal commitment seems
abandoned.)[8] Esther properly recognizes how "ridiculous" it is
to speak of a Chancery suit as "in progress," since the term implies a linear directedness that, while fully suitable to the project that subtends Esther's own narration (indicatively begun
under the title of "A Progress"), must be wholly absent from a
case that, typically, "seemed to die out of its own vapidity,
without coming, or being by anybody expected to come, to any
result" (345). Moreover, to see that, in Chancery, the process
of decision and interpretation is diverted is also to see that it is
diverted *into* Chancery, as an apparatus. It is diverted, in other
words, into the work of establishing the very channels for its

---

7. A first, but decisive expression of this view is given in J. Hillis Miller's
   introduction to *Bleak House*, by Charles Dickens (Baltimore: Penguin,
   1971), pp. 11–34.
8. Charles Dickens, *Little Dorrit* (Oxford: Oxford University Press, 1953),
   p. 104.

diversion: channels by means of which a legal establishment is ramified, its points of contact multiplied, and routes of circulation organized for the subjects who are thus recruited under its power.[9]

Yet Chancery can never dispense with the judgments that it also never dispenses. Though the project of interpretation is virtually annulled in the workings of its formalism ("the lantern that has no light in it"), the *promise* of interpretation, as that which initiates and facilitates this formalism, remains absolutely necessary. At the theoretical level of ideology, the promise functions to confer legitimacy on Chancery proceedings: as even poor crazed Miss Flyte, in her confusion of the Last Judgment with the long-delayed judgment in her own case, is capable of revealing, the legal system must appeal for its legitimacy to transcendent concepts of truth, justice, meaning, and ending, even when its actual work will be to hold these concepts in profitable abeyance or to redefine and contain them as functions of its own operations. And at the practical and technical level of such operations, the promise of judgment becomes the lure of advertising, extended by venalities such as Vholes to promote the purchase and exercise of their services.

Perhaps the most interesting effect of all produced by the promise, however, considerably exceeds these theoretical and practical functions. If Chancery exploits the logic of a promise

9. Trollope, the only other major Victorian novelist to take up the subject of bureaucracy, offers us a similar perception in *The Three Clerks* (1858), where the new system of competitive examinations introduced by the Civil Service Reform inspires one of the examiners with the definitive dream of bureaucracy: to turn the end it serves into the means of its own expansion. "Every man should, he thought, be made to pass through some 'go.' The greengrocer's boy should not carry out cabbages unless his fitness for cabbage-carrying had been ascertained, and till it had also been ascertained that no other boy, ambitious of the preferment, would carry them better" (Anthony Trollope, *The Three Clerks* [Oxford: Oxford University Press, 1943], p. 128).

by perpetually maintaining it as *no more than such*, then the suit must obviously produce as much frustration as hopefulness. Accordingly, one consequence of a system that, as it engenders an interpretative project, deprives it of all the requirements for its accomplishment is the desire for an interpretative project that would *not* be so balked. This desire is called into being from within the ground of a system that, it bears repeating, resists interpretation on two counts: because it cannot be localized as an object of interpretation, and because it is never willing to become the agency or subject of interpretation. What such a desire effectively seeks, therefore, is a reduced model of the un-totalizable system and a legible version of the undecidable suit. What such a desire calls for, in short, both as a concept and as a fact, is the detective story.

The detective story gives obscurity a name and a local habitation: in that highly specific "mystery" whose ultimate uncovering motivates an equally specific program of detection. If the Chancery system includes everything but settles nothing, then one way in which it differs from the detective story is that the latter is, precisely, a *story*: sufficiently selective to allow for the emergence of a narrative and properly committed, once one has emerged, to bringing it to completion. In relation to an organization so complex that it often tempts its subjects to misunderstand it as chaos, the detective story realizes the possibility of an easily comprehensible version of order. And in the face—or facelessness—of a system where it is generally impossible to assign responsibility for its workings to any single person or group of persons, where even the process of victimization seems capricious, the detective story performs a drastic simplification of power as well. For unlike Chancery, the detective story is fully prepared to affirm the efficacy and priority of personal agency, be it that of the criminal figures who do the work of concealment or that of the detective figures who undo it. It is not at all surprising, therefore, that the desire for the detective story first emerges from within the legal community itself, in Tulkinghorn and Guppy, since lawyers, having charge of the system, are most likely to be aware of the extent to which they merely convey a power which is theirs only to hold and not to have. It is entirely suitable that those who continually *exercise* this power—in the root sense, that is, of driving it on—should be the first to dream of *possessing* it, so that the calling of Mr. Tulkinghorn, for instance, "eke solicitor of the High Court of Chancery" (11), becomes "the acquisition of secrets and the holding possession of such power as they give him, with no sharer or opponent in it" (511). At the other end of the legal hierarchy (though not, one may be sure, for long), Mr. Guppy prepares for a similar vocation: "Mr. Guppy suspects everybody who enters on the occupation of a stool in Kenge and Carboy's office, of entertaining, as a matter of course, sinister designs upon him. He is clear that every such person wants to depose him. If he be ever asked how, why, when, or wherefore, he shuts up one eye and shakes his head. On the strength of these profound views, he in the most ingenious manner takes infinite pains to counter-plot, when there is no plot; and plays the deepest games of chess without any adversary" (272). Guppy's counter-plotting "when there is no plot" may be seen as the usefully paranoid attempt of an ambitious clerk to grasp the power of the legal system over him by turning everybody in it into his personal enemy. It may also be seen as the desperately fanciful effort of an otherwise bored office worker to overwrite the impersonal and inconsequential tedium of his tasks with lively dramas centered on himself. In either case, it suggests precisely the sense in which the nonnarrative system of Chancery generates narratives both to grasp its evasiveness and to evade its grasp.

Yet within this perspective, one must register the general failure of the amateur detectives in *Bleak House* to impose a will to truth and power. Anecdotally, their stories all reach a final point of checkmate. Guppy's chance to lay his hands on the decisive evidence goes up in smoke with Krook; Tulkinghorn is murdered before he has quite decided how to make use of his discovery; and even Mrs. Snagsby is still "on the great high road that is to terminate in Mr. Snagsby's full exposure" (734) when Mr. Bucket is obliged to set her straight. These abortive endings, which effectively place the stories under the paradigm of the interminable Chancery suit, also carry "political" rebukes, as the detectives are denied the power to which their knowledge seemed to entitle them. Tulkinghorn's violent death at the hands of a woman over whom he had flaunted his control is the most dramatic example of such chastisement; but another is Guppy's rejection by Esther, the woman who initially inspired his detective work and who he hoped might reward it with her hand; and still another is the gentle but public reprimand that Mrs. Snagsby receives from Mr. Bucket. The profound reason for the anecdotal failure of these stories is that they are undertaken as individual projects. That individuality not only must debilitate the power of the will-to-power, but also qualifies the general validity of the production of truth. Even when the stories have more to go on than does Mrs. Snagsby's—exemplary in its forced, false, but flawless coherence—they are marred by an egocentricity that confers on them the epistemologically suspect tautology of wish-fulfillments. Just as Guppy's detection is part and parcel of his *arrivisme*, an ambitious attempt to ennoble the woman of his choice and to win her gratitude for doing so, similarly, Tulkinghorn, who holds that women "are at the bottom of all that goes wrong in [the world]" (222), finds his sexual resentment justified in a story of female error and deceit. Even Mrs. Snagsby's fantasy that Jo has been illegitimately sired by her husband likewise satisfies her need to see herself as wronged, and so consolidates the basis of her domestic tyranny. It is not enough to say that, if the detective story is meant to be an individual rendition of an order and a power that are social and institutional in nature, then a great deal must be lost in the translation. For that loss to be registered as *its* loss, in its formal incompletion, its cognitive inadequacy, and its political failure, what must also be asserted is the priority assumed by social and institutional categories over the individual projects that they will ultimately reabsorb.

Even as a failure, however, the project of detection enjoys a certain dangerous efficacy. For it fails in every respect except that of catching on. Its weakness as an individual enterprise becomes a demonstrable strength as the number of individuals undertaking it increases and it thereby acquires a certain social distribution and consistency. As a *common* individual project, detection poses a threat to the social and institutional orders that continue to doom it to failure as a single undertaking. From beginning to end, the project sanctions the deviate erotic desire that inspires it and that it releases into action. The unsavory sexual secrets that ultimately gratify this desire are themselves subversive of socially given arrangements. Regularly involving a double transgression, of class as well as conjugal boundaries, they give scandal to the twin unities that Dickens puts at the basis of a decent social order, family and station. To disclose these secrets, moreover, exacerbates their scandalous effects, as when what Mrs. Snagsby thinks she knows leads her to seek a marital separation, and what Tulkinghorn tells Lady Dedlock prompts her public flight. In a context where home and family are the chief bulwarks against drifting into the interminable circulations of Chancery, the kind of individuality implied and exfoliating in the project of detection must seem ultimately anarchic. Born, as Tulkinghorn's case makes particularly clear, when the law is taken into one's own hands, it gives birth to the familiar rivalrous, self-seeking world of which the tension between Tulkinghorn and Guppy is an early symptom, and in which the murderous personal arrogations of Mademoiselle Hortense are, though shocking, perfectly proper.

We begin to see why the detective narratives require to come under the management of a master-agency charged with the task both of suppressing their successes (in fostering extreme threats to social order) and of supplying their failures (to provide a widely available, consoling simplification of this order). We begin to understand, in other words, the profound necessity of the police in *Bleak House*. Though the Court of Chancery, to make itself tolerable, produces a desire for the detective story, as for that which will confer on it the legibility of a traditionally patterned meaning, this desire, far from issuing in an order that can be comfortingly proffered and consumed as the essence of the chaos that is Chancery's appearance, threatens to reduplicate such chaos in the yet more explicit form of social disaggregation. What keeps the production of this desire from being dangerously excessive—what in fact turns the dangerous excess back into profit—is that the detective story, following the same logic whereby it was produced among the effects of Chancery, produces among *its* effects the desire for its own authoritative version and regulatory agency. Out of control to the point that, at Tulkinghorn's murder, the very principle of sense-making appears to have gone "stark mad" (665), the detective story eventually asks to be arrested by the Detective Police.

Such regulation should not be seen purely as a repressive practice, involving, for instance, the capture of a murderer like Mademoiselle Hortense or a runaway like Lady Dedlock. The police not only repress but also, profoundly, satisfy the desire to which Chancery gives rise. For in addition to doing the negative work of correcting for the socially undesirable consequences of amateur projects of detection, they perform the positive work of discharging for society as a whole the function that these amateur projects had assumed unsuccessfully: that of providing, within the elusive organization of Chancery, a simplified representation of order and power. The novel's shift in focus from the Court of Chancery to the Detective Police en-

compasses a number of concomitant shifts, which all operate
in the direction of this simplification: from civil law and questions of liability to criminal law and less merely legal questions
of guilt; from trivial legal hairsplitting to the urgency of the
fact, beyond such disputing, of murder; from a cause with
countless parties represented by countless attorneys in an anonymous system, to a case essentially reduced to two personal
duels, between the criminal and his victim and between the
criminal and the detective; from long, slow, to all appearances
utterly inefficient procedures to swift and productive ones; and
finally, from an institution that cannot justify its power to one
that, for all the above reasons, quite persuasively can. It is as
though every complaint that could be made about the one institution had been redressed in the organization of the other,
so that one might even argue, on the basis of Dickens's notorious willingness to serve as a propagandist for the New Police,
that the excruciating *longueurs* of Chancery existed mainly to
create the market for Mr. Bucket's expeditious *coups*.[10] Along
these lines, one might even want to read, in the police activity

10. Frequently drawn from the end of the eighteenth century to our own
day, the contrast between the law's delay and the dispatch of the police
typically emerges (as here in Dickens) on the side of the police. A locus
classicus: "Entourée de formes qu'elle ne trouve jamais assez multipliées,
la justice n'a jamais pardonné à la police sa rapidité. La police, affranchie
de presque toutes les entraves, n'a jamais excusé dans la justice, ses len-
teurs; les reproches qu'elles se font mutuellement, la Société les fait sou-
vent à l'une ou à l'autre. On reproche à la police d'inquiéter l'innocence,
à la justice de ne savoir ni prévenir, ni saisir le crime" (Surrounded by
forms that it never finds elaborate enough, the judicial system has never
pardoned the police its speed. The police, freed from nearly all such
shackles, has never forgiven the judicial system its sluggishness. The re-
proaches that each makes to the other are made to both by Society, which
upbraids the police for disturbing the innocent and the judicial system
for being unable to deter or apprehend the criminal. Joseph Fouché,
Minister of Police, in a circular addressed to the prefects of France, 30
Brumaire, Year VIII; quoted in Henry Buisson, *La police, son histoire* [Vi-
chy: Imprimerie Wallon, 1949], p. 167).

that develops over the dead body of the law ("or Mr. Tulking-horn, one of its trustiest representatives" [305]), Dickens's exhilarated announcement of the agencies and practices of social discipline that, claiming to be merely supplementing the law, will come in large part to supplant it.[11] Yet to the extent that we stress, in the evident archaism of Chancery, the emergence of a new kind of bureaucratic organization, and in the blatantly modern Detective Police (instituted only ten years before the novel began to appear), a harkening back to a traditional and familiar model of power, then we need to retain the possibility that Dickens's New Police still polices, substantively as well as nominally, *for* the law, for the Chancery system, and that, as a representation, it serves a particular ideological function within this system, and not against it. Made so desirable as a sort of institutional "alternative" to Chancery, the police derive their ideological efficacy from providing, within a total system of power, *a representation of the containment of power*. The shift from Chancery to the police dramatically localizes the field, exercise, and agents of power, as well as, of course, justifies such power, which, confined to a case of murder and contained in a Mr. Bucket, occupies what we can now think of as the right side. And when the novel passes from adulatory wonder at the efficiency of the police to sad, resigned acknowledgment of their limits (such as emerges in Hortense's last exchange with Bucket), the circumscription of power, reaching the end to which it always tended, has merely come full circle.

III

The police thus allow for the existence of a field outside the dynamic of power and free from its effects. Once installed in

11. See Michel Foucault, *Discipline and Punish*, trans. Alan Sheridan (New York: Pantheon, 1977), esp. pp. 222–23.

this realmless realm, one could cease to internalize—as the desperate, hopeful psychology of compulsion—the lures of the Chancery system; from within it, one could bear witness to the possibility of a criticism of that system that would no longer be merely the sign of the impossibility of withdrawing from it. Shifting focus from the Court of Chancery to the Detective Police, the novel works toward the recovery of this place elsewhere, in a two-pronged strategy whose other line of attack lies in Esther's absolute refusal to be touched by the suit and in the constitution of Bleak House that her refusal enables. For in point of fact the "outside" of power is specified as a domestic space, occupied by an ideal of the family. Not the least evil of the Chancery system in this respect was that, in it, police and family blurred into one another. As an apparatus of power concerned to impose, protect, and extend itself, Chancery naturally included a policing function, but it had the aspect of a family as well, not only because the suits that came before it arose from family disputes, but also because (as when it put its wards Ada and Richard under the guardianship of John Jarndyce) it sanctioned families of its own. In effect, the emergence of Bleak House on the one hand and of Mr. Bucket (who, though Mrs. Bucket is as fond of children as himself, has none) on the other achieves the extrication of the family from the police, a disarticulation into separate domains of what it was a trick of Chancery's domination to have knitted seamlessly together.

We mustn't be surprised, however, if there is a trick to this new arrangement too—and perhaps a far better one. When Mr. Bucket escorts Mr. Snagsby through Tom-all-Alone's (much as Inspector Field took Dickens with him on his tours of duty), the detective's thoroughgoing knowledge of the place as well as the extreme deference shown to him by its inhabitants (who call him "master") indicate the degree to which the police have saturated the delinquent milieu. If the saturation doesn't appear to have much curtailed delinquency, or even, strangely, to

have prevented Tom-all-Alone's from continuing to serve as a
refuge for those wanted by the police, these perhaps were never
the ends of police penetration. What such penetration apparently does secure is a containment of crime and power together,
which both become visible mainly in a peripheral place,
"avoided by all decent people" (220).[12] The raison d'être of
Tom-all-Alone's is that it *be* all alone, as the text is prepared to
admit when it speculates "whether the traditional title is a
comprehensive name for a retreat cut off from honest company"
(220). Yet the marginal localization of the police thus achieved
is subjected to a dramatic ambiguity as soon as, beyond ensur-
ing the circulation of vagrants like Jo or the apprehension of
murderers who, doubly exotic, come both from foreign parts
and from the servant class, the police pass into the fashionable
upper-class world of Chesney Wold or even the just barely re-
spectable shooting gallery of Mr. George. Though disturbed
by Bucket's nighttime visit, heralded only by the glare of his
bull's-eye, the denizens of Tom-all-Alone's are neither surprised nor shamed by what is evidently a very familiar occur-
rence. Compare their dull acceptance to Sir Leicester's appalled
imagination: "Heaven knows what he sees. The green, green

12. In installing criminals and police in the same seat—the conspicuous and
closed world of delinquency—Dickens follows what was routine practice
throughout the popular literature of the nineteenth century. To quote
from a single, but highly influential example: "Le quartier du Palais de
Justice, très circonscrit, très surveillé, sert pourtant d'asile ou de rendezvous aux malfaiteurs de Paris. N'est-il pas étrange, ou plutôt fatal,
qu'une irrésistible attraction fasse toujours graviter ces criminels autour
du formidable tribunal qui les condamne à la prison, au bagne, à l'é-
chafaud!" (The neighborhood of the Palace of Justice, though very circumscribed and under close surveillance, serves nonetheless as a refuge
or a rendezvous for the wrong-doers of Paris. Is it not strange, or rather
fated, that an irresistible attraction always draws criminals to the vicinity
of the fearful tribunal that condemns them to prison, the hulks, the scaf-
fold! Eugène Sue, *Les Mystères de Paris* [1843], 4 vols. [Paris: Editions
Hallier, 1977], 1:15).

woods of Chesney Wold, the noble house, the pictures of his forefathers, strangers defacing them, officers of police coarsely handling his most precious heirlooms, thousands of fingers pointing at him, thousands of faces sneering at him" (743–44). Compare it even to Mr. George's sharp mortification: "You see . . . I have been handcuffed and taken into custody, and brought here. I am a marked and disgraced man, and here I am. My shooting-gallery is rummaged, high and low, by Bucket; such property as I have—'tis small—is turned this way and that, till it don't know itself" (705). The sense of scandal that informs both passages, even as it acknowledges that the police can break out of their limits to become a total, all-pervasive institution like Chancery, reinforces our perception of the boundaries that ordinarily keep them in their place. It qualifies the police intervention in either case as an exceptional state of affairs, warranted only by the exceptional circumstances that call it into being.

The representation of the police, then, is not just organized by a comforting principle of localization; it is also organized within the fear-inspiring prospect of *the possible suspension of this principle*. One may read the resulting ambiguity in the very character of Mr. Bucket. The fact that the representation of the police is virtually entirely confined to the portrayal of this one character is of course revealing of the strategy of containment taken toward the police. The Court of Chancery required dozens of lawyers in the attempt to represent it, and even then the attempt had always to remain unequal to a system whose essential anonymity resisted its being seized as character. The police, however, can be adequately rendered in the character of a single one of their agents, and this fact, among others, makes them a superior institution. Whereas the law is impersonal and anonymous, the law enforcement is capable of showing a human face—if that is the word for the mechanically recurring tics and character traits that caused Inspector Bucket to be received at the time of the novel's publication as one of Dickens's most "delightful" creations.[13] Yet if police power is contained in Bucket, Bucket himself is *not* contained in the way that characters ordinarily are. A master of disguise, who makes himself appear in as "ghostly" a manner as, with a touch of his stick, he makes others "instantly evaporate" (308, 310), Bucket seems superhuman and his powers magical. To Mr. Snagsby, confused and impressed, he appears "to possess an unlimited number of eyes" (315); and Jo, in his ignorance and delirium, believes him "to be everywhere, and cognizant of everything" (639). With ironic reservations that only refine the ambiguity, the narration even offers its own language in support of these baffled perceptions: "Time and place cannot bind Mr. Bucket" (712), it tells us, and "Nothing escapes him" (713).

Another way to bring out the ambiguity that invests the established limits of the police is to ask: on behalf of whom or what does the Detective Police do its policing? Answers in the text, accurately reflecting a historical ambiguity, are various. Bucket works now in the capacity of a private detective employed by individuals such as Tulkinghorn; now as the public official of a state apparatus that enjoins him, for instance, to secure Gridley for contempt of court; and now in some obscure combination of the two functions, as when, at the end, he seems to police simultaneously on behalf of society at large and at the behest of Sir Leicester Dedlock. In a sense, the progress toward the legitimacy of power that we read in the focal shift from Chancery to the Detective Police occurs within the representation of the police itself, which, at the beginning, acting as the agent of an arbitrary system or an equally arbitrary individual will, acquires in the end—via murder and a missing person—the means of legitimizing the exercise of its power, even though this is still nominally in the hire of Sir Leicester. Yet this effort of the narrative sequence to legitimize the power

13. See the editor's summary of the Victorian reception of *Bleak House* in Collins, *Dickens: The Critical Heritage*, p. 273.

of the police leaves looking all the more unresolved the question of their whereabouts, which are established in so many places, as so many indistinct, overlapping, competing jurisdictions, that they cease to seem established at all.

All the ambiguities about the police serve to establish a radical uncertainty about the nature of private, familial space. "As [Mr. Bucket] says himself, what is public life without private ties? He is in his humble way a public man, but it is not in that sphere that he finds happiness. No, it must be sought within the confines of domestic bliss" (675–76). But as we know, Bucket here maintains the difference between public (institutional) and private (domestic) spheres as part of a successful attempt to neutralize it. The difference on which he affably insists allows him to be welcomed into the Bagnet household, where at the proper moment—no longer as a new friend of the family, but now a public official—he can arrest their friend and guest Mr. George. Is the private sphere autonomous or not? The representation of the police in *Bleak House* permits us to answer the question either way: to insist, when this is necessary, on the elsewhere opened up by the localization of the police (who considerately police, among other things, their own limits); or to suggest, when this is desirable, the extent to which this elsewhere is constantly liable to being transgressed by the police. The police simultaneously produce and permeate (produce as permeable) the space they leave to be "free."

If, therefore, we need to say that, in its representation of bureaucracy and the police, *Bleak House* regularly produces a difference between these institutions and the domestic space outside them, we must also recognize that it no less regularly produces this difference *as a question*, in the mode of the "problematic." The bar of separation and even opposition that it draws between the public and private spheres is now buttressed, now breached, firm and fragile by turns. On one hand, Chancery is a total system of domination, engendering resistances whose mere inversions or duplications of its injunctions only entrench its power more deeply. On the other hand, Chancery's domination seems to cease precisely at the points where one elects to erect bulwarks against it such as Esther's Bleak House. Or again: if the police represent a reduction of the domination of Chancery, and thus permit a domestic autonomy, it is also suggested that the police, as all-encompassing as Chancery, can at any moment abolish that autonomy. Or still again: the police are other, better than Chancery, but they are also the organ that polices on its behalf and thus works to preserve it. We cannot too strongly insist that these "paradoxes" are not merely confusions or historical contradictions that tug and pull at a text helpless to regulate them, but rather productive ambiguities that facilitate the disposition, functioning, and promotion of certain ideological effects, some of which we have already suggested. Neither, however, should *"Bleak House,* by Charles Dickens" be denounced—or congratulated—as the ultimate strategist of these effects, as though one could allow such effects their broad cultural resonance without also recognizing their broad cultural production and distribution. Yet if the novel no more "manipulates" the equivocations we have traced than "succumbs" to them, perhaps the most pertinent reason is that it lacks the distance from them required to do either. We shall see how, in the first place, these equivocations *are its own*, always already borne in the novel as a form; and also how, in the last instance, these equivocations *come to be its own*, as the novel reproduces in the relationship between form and content the dialectic that occurs within each of its terms.

IV

It would certainly appear as though the existence of that sheltered space which the novelistic representation labors to produce—but with, we have seen, such dubious results—is unconditionally taken for granted in the novel form, whose unfolding or consumption has not ceased to occur in such a space all along. Since the novel counts among the conditions for this consumption the consumer's leisured withdrawal to the private, domestic sphere, then every novel-reading subject is constituted—willy-nilly and almost before he has read a word—within the categories of the individual, the inward, the domestic. There is no doubt that the shift in the dominant literary form from the drama to the novel at the end of the seventeenth century had to do with the latter's superior efficacy in producing and providing for privatized subjects. The only significant attempt to transcend the individualism projected by the novel took place precisely in Victorian England as the practice of the *family reading*, which may be understood as an effort to mitigate the possible excesses of the novel written for individuals by changing the locus of reading from the study—or worse, the boudoir—to the hearth, enlivened but also consolidated as a *foyer d'intrigue*. A Victorian novel such as *Bleak House* speaks not merely for the hearth, in its prudent care to avoid materials or levels of explicitness about them unsuitable for family entertainment, but from the hearth as well, implicitly grounding its critical perspective on the world within a domesticity that is more or less protected against mundane contamination.

Yet if only by virtue of the characteristic length that prevents it from being read in a single sitting, the novel inevitably enjoins not one, but several withdrawals to the private sphere. Poe, who first raised the issue of the effects of this length, considered the discontinuousness of novel reading to be one of the liabilities of the form, which thereby had to forego "the immense benefit of *totality*." In the novel state, Poe thought, the autonomy of "literary concerns" was always being frustrated by the foreign intervention of "worldly interests."[14] If, however,

14. Edgar Allan Poe, "Tale-Writing—Nathaniel Hawthorne," in *The Complete Works of Edgar Allan Poe*, ed. James A. Harrison, 17 vols. (New York: George D. Sproul, 1902), 13:153.

novel reading presupposes so many disparate withdrawals to the private sphere, by the same token it equally presupposes so many matching returns to the public, institutional one. An important dimension of what reading a novel entails, then, would lie—outside the moment and situation of actual perusal—in the times and places that interrupt this perusal and render it in the plural, as a series. Just as we read the novel in the awareness that we must put it down before finishing it, so even when we are not reading it, we continue to "live" the form in the mode of *having to get back to it*. Phenomenologically, the novel form includes the interruptions that fracture the process of reading it. And the technical equivalent of this phenomenological interpenetration of literary and worldly interests would be the practice of various realisms, which, despite their manifold differences, all ensure that the novel is always centrally about the world one has left behind to read it and that the world to which one will be recalled has been reduced to attesting the truth (or falsehood) of the novel. It is not quite true, therefore, that the novel is simply concerned to attach us to individuality and domesticity, to privacy and leisure. What the form really secures is a close *imbrication* of individual and social, domestic and institutional, private and public, leisure and work. A drill in the rhythms of bourgeois industrial culture, the novel generates a nostalgic desire to get home (where the novel can be resumed) in the same degree as it inures its readers to the necessity of periodically renouncing home (for the world where the novel finds its justification and its truth). In reading the novel, one is made to rehearse how to live a problematic—always surrendered, but then again always recovered—privacy.

V

The same opposition—or at least the question of one—between private-domestic and social-institutional domains that is

produced in the representation and consumed as the form occurs again in the relationship between the representation and
the form. For though the form projects itself as a kind of home,
what is housed in this home, as its contents, is not merely or
even mainly comfortable domestic quarters, but also the social-
institutional world at large. If the novel is substantially to al-
lege its otherness in relation to this world, and thus to vouch
for its competence to survey, judge, and understand it, then far
from seeking to be adequate or isomorphic to its contents (when
these are carceral, disciplinary, institutional), it is instead
obliged to defend itself against them by differentiating the
practices of the world from the practices of representing it. The
current critical fondness for assimilating form and content (via
homologies, thematizations, *mises-en-abîme*) becomes no more
than a facile sleight-of-hand if it does not face the complication
it in fact encounters in the question of the difference between
the two that the novel regularly raises.[15] Specifically, as I hope

15. Even critics who propose an immediate identification of form and content in *Bleak House* are in practice compelled to acknowledge that the
novel resists their enterprise. J. Hillis Miller's claim that "*Bleak House*
has exactly the same structure as the society it exposes" has frequent recourse to concessive clauses that make allowance for "Dickens's generous
rage against injustice, selfishness and procrastination" or his "sympathy
for Gridley's indignant outrage" against the Chancery system (Introduction, pp. 29, 27). And Terry Eagleton, for whom the novel is
"obliged to use as aesthetically unifying images the very social contradictions . . . which are the object of [Dickens's] criticism," is quite
happy to register the "contradictory" nature of the unity thus established
(*Criticism and Ideology*, p. 129). Yet since both critics only recognize the
difference between the novel and its world in the process of annulling it,
they never permit themselves to consider seriously the *question* of the
difference, and each is finally willing to pass off as a weakness of the text
what is only a weakness in his account of it. In Miller's argument, in the
absence of further treatment, evidence of the difference goes only to show
that Dickens was curiously inconsistent. And in Eagleton's, such evidence would merely point to a text that is, to use his own expressive
phrase about *Dombey and Son* (1846–48), "self-divided and twisted by

to show in a moment, *Bleak House* is involved in an effort to distinguish its own enormous length from the protractedness of the Chancery suit, and also its own closure from the closed case of the Detective Police. But even remaining at a general and fundamental level, we can see the difference in the fact that, for instance, while the world of *Bleak House* is dreary enough, yet were the novel itself ever to become as dreary, were it ever to cease *making itself desirable*, it would also by the same token cease to be read. Pleasurably, at our leisure and in our homes, we read the novel of suffering, the serious business of life, and the world out-of-doors. Moreover, the critical and often indignant attitude that *Bleak House*, by no means untypically, takes toward its social world reinforces this "erotic" difference with a cognitive one: the novel views the world in better, more clear-sighted and disinterested ways than the world views itself.

The suit in *Bleak House* has only to be mentioned for its monstrous length to be observed and censured. "Jarndyce and Jarndyce still drags its dreary length before the Court, perenially hopeless" (4). The suit is not merely long, but—here lies the affront—excessively so, longer than it is felt it ought to be. Yet what Dickens calls the "protracted misery" of the suit (54)— by which he means the misery of its protractedness as well as vice versa—cannot be explained merely as the consequence of gratuitous *additions* to a necessary and proper length, left intact, which they simply inordinately "pad." One of the ill effects of the length of the suit has been precisely to render unavailable the reality of a proper measure, of which the suit could be seen as an unwarranted expansion and to which it

the very contradictions it vulnerably reproduces" (*Criticism and Ideology*, p. 127). Yet when, as it begins to appear, the difference between novel and world belongs to a series of analogous differences operating in the novel at several levels, then in dismissing the difference as an inconsequence or laying it to rest as a contradiction, we neglect a crucial aspect of the novel's own program, a central feature of its self-definition.

would be theoretically possible to restore it by some judicious abridgment. The further the length of the suit is elaborated, the more it abandons any responsibility to the telos or finality that originally called it forth, nominally continues to guide it even now, and would ultimately reabsorb it as the pathway leading to its own achievement. And along with the *formality* of an ending—the juridical act of decision—what would constitute the *substance* of one is put in jeopardy: namely, the establishment of the meaning of the original will. So nearly intertwined are ending and meaning that to adjourn the one seems to be to abjure the other: "This scarecrow of a suit has, in course of time, become so complicated that no man alive knows what it means" (4).

The suit's effective suspension of teleology is, of course, scandalously exemplary of a whole social sphere that seems to run on the principle of a purposiveness without purpose. The principle is enunciated and enforced not only by the bureaucratic officials who, when Jo is sick, "must have been appointed for their skill in evading their duties, instead of performing them" (432), but even by the various policemen in the novel who enjoin Jo to "move on" in his perpetually maintained, displaced itinerary to nowhere. Internalized, this lack of purpose emerges as character defects: the long-windedness of Chadband, the aestheticism of Skimpole (who begins sketches "he never finished"), the flightiness of Richard. Such instances, however, in which the sense of an ending seems entirely given up, are no more symptomatic of the general social suspension of finality than the abstract impatience and hopeful voluntarism with which the sense of an ending is merely imposed on a state of affairs that must thereby be misunderstood. Miss Flyte is mad to expect a judgment "shortly," and Richard is certainly on the way to madness when, choplogically, he argues that "the longer [the suit] goes on, . . . the nearer it must be to a settlement one way or other" (182). In the progress of Hegelian Spirit, "the length of this path has to be endured because, for one thing, each moment is necessary" to the emergence of the result;[16] whereas, the mere ongoingness of the un-Hegelian suit brings madness to any attempt to make sense of this length as a necessity, or in terms of the end-orientation that it formally retains but from which it has substantially removed itself. Finally, however, the length of the suit is devoid of necessity only in terms of an eventual judgment. Just as the inefficiency of power in Chancery showed up from another standpoint as the power of inefficiency, so too what are in one perspective the superfluous, self-subversive elongations of procedure become in another the necessary developments of a power that—call it the English law—has for its one great principle "to make business for itself" (548). Accordingly, the delays and remands that amount to an effective suspension of its declared end should not be seen to debilitate Chancery, but rather to allow one to take it seriously as—in Dickens's facetious phrase from *The Old Curiosity Shop* (1841)—"the long and strong arm of the law."[17]

In light of the fact that the novel about this long arm itself exercises a considerable reach—that the representation *of* length goes on *at* length too—we are invited to consider the extent to which the novel runs the risk of resembling the Chancery suit that it holds in despite. Certainly, the unfolding of the novel could be thought to parallel the elaboration of the suit insofar as it threatens an analogous failure to bring its ever more abundant materials to a proper or conceivably adequate summation. We already noted how the long novel foregoes "the immense benefit of *totality*" because it cannot be read at a single sitting; but even if we were to export to the nineteenth century the anachronism of a "speed-reader," Victorian practices of distributing the novel-product would still render the interruptedness of reading all but inevitable. Serial publication neces-

16. G. W. F. Hegel, *Phenomenology of Spirit*, trans. A. V. Miller (Oxford: Oxford University Press, 1977), p. 17.

17. Charles Dickens, *The Old Curiosity Shop* (Oxford: Oxford University Press, 1951), p. 553.

sarily barred the reader from having full physical possession of the text he was reading until he was almost done with it; and even once the novel was published in volume form as a "three-decker," the ordinary subscription to the circulating libraries (which provided the majority of readers with their access to it) allowed to a borrower only one volume at a time. These determinations are of course merely external, but they are fully matched by the compositional principles of discontinuity and delay that organize the form from within its own structure: not only in the formal breaks of chapters, installments, volumes, but also in the substantive shifts from this plot-line to that, or from one point of view or narration to another; and generally in the shrewd administration of suspense that keeps the novel always tending toward a denouement that is continually being withheld. In Dickens, of course, the fissured and diffused character of novel form is far more marked than in the work of any of his contemporaries, extending from the extraordinary multitude of memorably disjunct characters, each psychologically sealed off from understanding any other, to the series of equally disparate and isolated spaces across which they collide. And, like the larger structure of suspense, even individual sentences will frequently derive their effects from the lengths to which they will go in withholding predication.[18] No doubt, both as a system of distribution and as a text, the Victorian novel establishes a little bureaucracy of its own, generating an immense

18. For example: "Jostling against clerks going to post the day's letters, and against counsel and attorneys going home to dinner, and against plaintiffs and defendents, and suitors of all sorts, and against the general crowd, in whose way the forensic wisdom of ages has interposed a million of obstacles to the transaction of the commonest business of life—diving through law and equity, and through that kindred mystery, the street mud, which is made of nobody knows what, and collects about us nobody knows whence or how: we only knowing in general that when there is too much of it, we find it necessary to shovel it away—the lawyer and the law-stationer come to a Rag and Bottle shop" (135).

amount of paperwork and sending its readers here, there, backward and forward, like the circumlocutory agencies that Dickens satirizes. On this basis, it could be argued that, despite or by means of its superficially hostile attitude toward bureaucracy, a novel like *Bleak House* is profoundly concerned to train us—as, at least since the eighteenth century, play usually trains us for work—in the sensibility for inhabiting the new bureaucratic, administrative structures.

To say this, of course, is to neglect what Roland Barthes has identified as the "readerly" orientation of the traditional novel: the tendency of its organization to knit its discontinuities together by means of codes such as those ordering our perception of plot and suspense.[19] Although *Bleak House* baffles us in the first few hundred pages by featuring a profusion of characters who seem to have nothing to do with one another, a miscellany of events whose bearing on a possible plot is undecidable, and even two separate systems of narration that are unequal and unrelated, it simultaneously encourages us to anticipate the end of bafflement and the acquisition of various structures of coherence: in the revelation or development of relationships among characters; in the emergence of a plot whereby the mysteries of the text will be enlightened and its meanings fully

---

19. "To end, to fill, to join, to unify—one might say that this is the basic requirement of the *readerly*, as though it were prey to some obsessive fear: that of omitting a connection. Fear of forgetting engenders the appearance of a logic of actions; terms and the links between them are posited (invented) in such a way that they unite, duplicate each other, create an illusion of continuity. The plenum generates the drawing intended to 'express' it, and the drawing evokes the complement, coloring: as if the *readerly* abhors a vacuum. What would be the narrative of a journey in which it was said that one stays somewhere without having arrived, that one travels without having departed—in which it was never said that, having departed, one arrives or fails to arrive? Such a narrative would be a scandal, the extenuation, by hemorrhage, of readerliness" (Roland Barthes, *S/Z*, trans. Richard Miller [New York: Hill and Wang, 1974], p. 105).

named; and in the tendency of the two narrations to converge, as Esther's account comes to include characters and information that at first appeared exclusively in the anonymous one. In other words, the novel dramatizes the liabilities of fragmentation and postponement within the hopeful prospect that they will eventually be overcome. We consume the enormous length of a novel like *Bleak House* in the belief that it is eminently digestible—capable, that is, of being ultimately rendered in a readerly *digest*: a final abridgment of plot and character that stands for (and so dispenses with) all that came before it. From the standpoint of this promised end, the massive bulk of the novel will always have concealed the perfectly manageable and unmonstrous proportions of a much shorter, tauter form.

Yet however sustained, the mere promise of an ending, far from being sufficient to differentiate the novel from Chancery, would positively enlarge on the analogy between the novel's practices and those of the court, which also entices its subjects by means of promises, promises. We read the novel under the same assumption that Richard makes about the suit, that "the longer it goes on, ... the nearer it must be to a settlement"; and if the assumption is to be validated in the one case as it is discredited in the other, the novel is under obligation to make good its promise by issuing in judgments and resolutions. For even if we always know about the novel (as we do not about the suit) that its length is finite, involving only so many pages or installments, the vulgar evidence of an endpoint can never amount to the assurance of an *ending*: that is, the presence of a complex of narrative summations that would match or motivate the external termination of discourse with its internal closure. The suit, which attains an endpoint but no ending, embodies the distinction that the novel, to be different, will have to obliterate. Though the suit reaches a point at which it is correctly declared "over for good" (865), this point is determined extrinsically by the lack of funds that prevents the protracted, complex cause from being pursued to a proper conclusion of its own. "Thus the suit lapses and melts away" (867), instead of coming to the judgment that would have constituted a proper internal resolution. It is never known, for instance, whether the new will is a genuine document, and the project of finding out has been "checked—brought up suddenly" upon what Conversation Kenge retains sufficient professional finesse to term the "threshold" (866).

In a pointed and self-serving contrast, the novel brings its characters to judgment, its mysteries to solution, and its plots to issues that would make further narrative superfluous. Immediately following the end of the suit, as a sort of consequence and reversal of it, Richard's death illustrates the contrast. Insofar as this death is premature, of course, it may look as though Richard will merely reenact the abrupt check of the suit. Juridical discourse has ceased not because it has said what it wanted to say, but only for lack of funds to say it; and similarly, Richard's utterance is simply "stopped by his mouth being full of blood" (868). But what is staged on the scene of Richard's deathbed is in fact his full recovery. In the paradoxical logic of nineteenth-century novelistic closure, whereby one sums up by subtracting, Richard is purged of unsteadiness and suspicion and so made whole. Whereas the suit ends as up in the air as ever it was, Richard's end achieves a fundamental clarification: "the clouds have cleared away, and it is bright now" (869). His tearful recognition that John Jarndyce, whom he mistrusted, is "a good man" renders him once more a good man himself. And his desire to be removed to the new Bleak House ("I feel as if I should get well there, sooner than anywhere") announces the redemptive turn from public institutional involvements to the domestic haven. As a result, even his death— no longer premature, but occurring only *after* the resolution of his character has been attained—bears witness to the seriousness of his conversion by making it permanent, the last word possible about him.

Unlike Chancery, then, the novel is willing to reward the

patience that, like Chancery, it has required. The destiny of the long-suffering Esther is only the most obvious figure for the link the novel everywhere secures between the practice of patience and its payoff. In the reader's case, the link is affirmed each time he gets an answer to one of the questions or riddles he has endured; each time he enjoys the jubilation of recognizing a character who has appeared earlier; each time a new installment comes out to reward his month-long wait for it. It isn't Esther alone in *Bleak House* who is extraordinarily self-deprecating and diffident in the face of authority, be it the heavenly Father in whom "it was so gracious . . . to have made my orphan way so smooth and easy," or simply John Jarndyce, to whom she declares: "I am quite sure that if there were anything I ought to know, or had any need to know, I should not have to ask you to tell it to me. If my whole reliance and confidence were not placed in you, I must have a hard heart indeed" (27, 99). The novel puts every reader in an equally subservient position of reliance upon the author, who, if one waits long enough (as, given the nature of the readerly text, one cannot but do), will delight us with the full revelation of his design, offering the supreme example of those happy surprises that Dickens's benevolent father-figures are fond of providing for those they patronize. Still less obviously, the novel develops our trust in the machinery of distribution itself, which can, for instance, be counted upon to provide the next installment at exactly the interval promised. In short, the novel encourages a series of deferential cathexes—all the more fundamental for being unconscious—onto various instances of authority. What is promoted in the process is a paternalism that, despite the dim view the novel takes of the power structures of the British state, can only be useful in maintaining such structures. To submit to the novel's duration is already to be installed within an upbeat ethic of endurance. If, as we speculated above, the novel trains us to abide in Chancery-like structures—by getting us to wait, as it were, in its very long lines—it does this only insofar as it is organized as a *reformed* Chancery, a Chancery that can moralize its procrastinations in a practice of delayed gratification. Recklessly, the court demanded an attendance so futile that it inspired dangerously anarchistic fantasies of destruction. More prudently, the novel, urging us to wait, also promises (to use the very formula of prudence) that we shall wait *and see*.

VI

Though it goes to great lengths, *Bleak House* also goes to extremities to save these lengths from lapsing into mere unproductive extensions of the Chancery suit. Or rather, it saves them from such a fate *at* the extremities, or end-parts, in the production of a closure. Even so the novel cannot yet be considered to have won free of public, institutional attachments. For the very closure that secures a formal narrative difference between the novel and bureaucracy implicates the novel in a formal narrative resemblance to the institution that has played a sort of rival to the bureaucracy, the police. It is clear that the difference that obtains between Chancery and the novel applies equally in the relationship between Chancery and the police. In determining its own closure as revelation and fixed repose, the novel appears to have rejected the conception of termination proper to bureaucracy only to espouse the one proper to the police. The closural specimen that takes place, for example, at Richard's deathbed, even if it begins as though it will merely reflect the bureaucratic logic of lapse, achieves a permanent clarification of his character that rather subsumes the scene under the police model of closure as a double (cognitive and practical) apprehension. It can be further argued that, insofar as it arouses a desire for expeditious, conclusive solutions but only represents a single agency capable of providing them, the novel subtly identifies the reader's demand for closure with a general social need for the police, thus continuing (with only a considerable increase of cunning) the apologetics for the new forces of order that Dickens began as an essayist in *Household Words*.

The novel, however, is just as little eager to appear an agency of the police as it was to resemble a relay of the Chancery system. The relatively friendly treatment that *Bleak House* accords to the Detective Police is qualified by a number of reservations about the nature and effects of its power. Most of these, like the other aspects of the police, are carried in the characterization of Inspector Bucket. His black clothes, linking him sartorially with Tulkinghorn and Vholes, darken his character as well with an association to the court; and like the undertaker to whose costume this dress also makes allusion, Bucket induces an ambivalence even in those he works for. Depending on the regularity of corruption, his profession has the doubly offensive aspect of a speculation on human weakness that happens also to be invariably justified. Yet the grief betokened by "the great mourning ring on his little finger" (310) might as well take Bucket himself for its object as any of his clients. His nature subdued to what it works in, Bucket too may be counted among the victims of crime. "Pour bien faire de la police," Napoleon is supposed to have said, "il faut être sans passion." The moral horror of crime, which Dickens preserves (among other things) in his sensationalistic treatment of it, must be irrelevant—might even be counterproductive—to the professional dispassion required for the task of apprehending the criminal. This task may no doubt be considered itself a moral one. But the game function of detection thoroughly dominates whatever ethical ends it presumably serves; and, as Bucket himself can assure Sir Leicester, his profession has placed him utterly beyond the possibility of being scandalized: "I know so much about so many characters, high and low, that a piece of information more or less, don't signify a straw. I don't suppose there's a move on the board that would surprise *me*; and as to this or that move having taken place, why my knowing it is no odds at all; any possible move whatever (provided it's in a wrong direction) being a probable move according to my experience" (726). The ethical perspective survives only in the faint melancholy with which Bucket, truly the "modern prince" in this respect, appears to regret the necessity of his own pessimism; or in the personal ascesis that, when every consequence of desire proves criminal, is perhaps the only humane response remaining. Nonetheless, the melancholy is hardly sufficient to prevent him from eliciting the very weaknesses that are the object of its contemplation. The momentary collaboration between Skimpole and Bucket revealed at the end of the novel, an alliance of two species of moral indifference, throws no more discredit on the aesthete who delivers a dangerously ill child over to the police for no better reason than a bribe, than on the officer who extends the bribe for no better reason than to cover his client's prying. Even the ascesis surrenders its moral truth to the extent that it is the very evidence of Bucket's amoral professionalization. As Tulkinghorn's fate exemplifies, amateur detectives run amok because they are motivated by personal desires for possession. Renunciation is thus for the professional detective a positive qualification, much as what Bucket appears to lament as his barren marriage shows a clear profit as an amicable and highly efficient business partnership.

These reservations are most tellingly inscribed in the novel as a narrative difference, once again centering on the question of ending, between the novel and the detective story that it includes. According to what will later be codified as the "classical" model, the detective story in *Bleak House* reaches its proper end when Bucket, having provided a complete and provable account of her guilt, arrests Mademoiselle Hortense for Tulkinghorn's murder. In the classical model, one may observe, though the security of its preferred decor, the locked room, is regularly breached, it is also invariably recovered in the detective's unassailable *reconstruction* of the crime. And similarly, in this not yet quite classical example, Bucket's ironclad case against Hortense may be understood as the reparation of Tulkinghorn's tragically vulnerable chambers. Yet if one tradition, the detective story, violates its closed rooms only to produce better defended versions of them in the detective's closed cases, another tradition, let us call it the Novel, violates even these cases. In this latter tradition, to which *Bleak House* ultimately bears allegiance, there is no police case so flawless that a loophole cannot be found through which its claims to closure may be challenged. Here our vision of the loophole is supplied by Mademoiselle Hortense:

> "Listen then, my angel," says she, after several sarcastic nods. "You are very spiritual. But can you restore him back to life?"
>
> Mr Bucket answers, "Not exactly."
>
> "That is droll. Listen yet one time. You are very spiritual. Can you make an honourable lady of Her?"
>
> "Don't be so malicious," says Mr Bucket.
>
> "Or a haughty gentleman of *Him?*" cries Mademoiselle, referring to Sir Leicester with ineffable disdain. "Eh! O then regard him! The poor infant! Ha! ha! ha!"
>
> "Come, come, why this is worse Parlaying than the other," says Mr Bucket. "Come along."
>
> "You cannot do these things? Then you can do as you please with me. It is but the death, it is all the same. Let us go, my angel. Adieu you old man, grey. I pity you, and I des-pise you!" (743)

Hortense enumerates the various existential problems that, outlasting Bucket's solution, make it seem trivial and all but inconsequential. Her purely verbal qualification is soon worked into the actual plot when Bucket sets out in search of Lady Dedlock and finds her dead body instead. However skillfully prosecuted, the work of detection appears capable only of attaining a shell from which the vital principle has departed. Other closural moments in *Bleak House* similarly end by producing a corpse, as though the novel wanted to attest, not just the finality, but also the failure of a closure that, even as it was achieved, missed the essence of what it aspired to grasp. In its ostentatious awareness of this failure, the novel defines its relationship to the materials of police fiction that it has adopted. On one side of this relationship there would be a detective story whose shallow solution naively gratifies our appetite for closure; on the other, there would be a Novel that, insisting at the very moment of solution on the insoluble, abiding mysteriousness of human and literary experience, provides superior nourishment by keeping us hungry.[20] Not to be identified with Chancery, the novel contrasts the aimless suspension of the suit with the achievement of its own ending; but not to be confused with the police either, it counters the tidy conclusion of the case with a conspicuous recognition of all that must elude any such achievement. If in the first instance, the novel must affirm the possibility of closure, in the second it is driven to admit the *inadequacy* of this closure.

In the end, then—precisely there—the novel's attempt to differentiate its own narrative procedures from those of the institutions it portrays falters, and the effort to disentangle itself from one institution only implicates it in another. So the seemingly perverse pattern continues wherein the novel is eager to produce a sheltered space whose integrity it is equally willing

---

20. *Bleak House* is thus one of the first texts to adumbrate a position that with modernism becomes commonplace: namely, that a literature worthy of the name will respect mystery by keeping it inviolate. For a canonical allusion to the position, see Kafka's remarks on the detective story in Gustav Janouch, *Conversations with Kafka*, trans. Goronwy Rees, 2d ed. rev. (New York: New Directions, 1971), p. 133; and among recent rehearsals, see David I. Grossvogel, *Mystery and Its Fictions: From Oedipus to Agatha Christie* (Baltimore: Johns Hopkins University Press, 1979). Yet insofar as the modernist cult of the irresolvable is perfectly consistent with the efficient workings of the Court of Chancery, *Bleak House* is also one of the first texts to indicate the difficulties with this position, which advancing beyond cheap consolations, may only bind us more profoundly to a society that thrives on delayed and ever-incomplete satisfactions.

to endanger. We have seen how the novel establishes the opposition between the private-domestic and the social-institutional (1) within the representation, as the contrast between Esther's Bleak House and Chancery, and between the former and the police; (2) as a formal practice of consumption, in which the novel-reading subject shuttles to and fro between the home in which the novel is read and the world in which it is verified; and (3) at the intersection of the novel's own representational practice with the represented practice of institutions that it includes in its content. We have also seen how, in every instance, the opposition is accompanied by the possibility that it may be, or have been, nullified. At the same time as the existence of an "outside" to institutional power is affirmed, that very affirmation is undercut with doubt.

Yet to describe the novel's rhetorical operation in this way, as the work of destructuration and subversion, is to identify it wholly with what is in fact only its negative moment.[21] We

21. The moment exclusively occupies those two modes of literary criticism to which this essay may be thought to address itself: Marxism and deconstructionism. Contemporary Marxist criticism would construe the ambiguities we have noticed as the contradictions that inscribe the text's inevitable failure to make its domestic ideology cohere. By virtue of "internal distanciation," the literary text finds itself compelled to betray this ideology, if only in its hesitations, silences, discrepancies. Not altogether dissimilarly, deconstruction would take such ambiguities for the aporias in an allegory of the process and problems of signification itself. Intended meaning is always exceeded in the signifiers to which it commits its expression, since by their nature those signifiers defer meaning even as they differentiate it. The trace of such differentiation, furthermore, carrying over as a kind of residue from one signifier to another, undermines the integrity of each: so that, in the case of an opposition, one term will invariably prove to be contaminated with the term it is meant to oppose. Without insisting on the comparison, one might say that Marxist criticism, urgently putting under scrutiny the evidence of a text that thereby never fails to convict itself, proceeds rather like the Detective Police; whereas a deconstructive criticism, patiently willing to remain on the threshold of interpretation in the wisdom that every

need to envision the positivity of this operation too, for what is put in question has also by the same token been put in place, and can be put to use as well. The ideological dividends paid in the difference between the "inside" and the "outside" of power are clear. The "outside" gives the assurance of liberty

---

reading it might offer would be a misreading, behaves somewhat like the Court of Chancery. If only from *Bleak House*, however, we know that a practice claiming to resemble neither the bureaucracy nor the police merely uses this pretension to camouflage its alliances with both. For us, therefore, it cannot exactly be a matter of repudiating these critical modes, but rather of writing against them, as against a background. "Against" Marxism, then, we stress the positivity of contradiction, which, far from always marking the fissure of a social formation, may rather be one of the joints whereby such a formation is articulated. Contradiction may function not to expose, but to construct the ideology that has foreseen and contained it. And "against" deconstruction, we should urge (rather as did Hegel in confronting the nothingness of skepticism) that undecidability must always be the undecidability of *something in particular*. The trouble with the deconstructionist allegory of signification is not that it is untrue, but that, despite the deceptive "closeness" of the readings, it is abstract. Two things, I think, ought to remove the effects of undecidability and contradiction from the void in which deconstruction places them. For one, they have a history or genealogy that determines them and whose traces must be registered. It may be ultimately true, for instance, as J. Hillis Miller has said, that "*Bleak House* is a document about the interpretation of documents" (Introduction, p. 11), but the formulation elides the rivalrous differentiations among institutional practices through which the concern with interpretation comes to emerge (and then, not as a theme so much as the stakes in a contest). As a result, one misses seeing the extent of the novel's assumption that it is *not* a document like those it is about. For a second, these effects, once formed, are never left at large and on the loose to wreak havoc on discursive and institutional operations. On the contrary, the latter have always already drafted them into a service that takes its toll and whose toll, accordingly, needs to be assessed in turn. Thus, Miller's account keeps characteristic silence about what even *Bleak House* (for highly partisan reasons of its own, of course) is quite willing to publicize: that the hermeneutic problematic itself is an instrument in the legal establishment's will to power.

that makes tolerable the increasingly total administration of the "inside" and helps avoid a politicization of society as a whole. It also provides a critical space from which amendments and reforms useful to this administration can be effectively broached and imposed. As we began by observing, however, *Bleak House* troubles the straightforwardness of this difference, which it transforms into the question of a difference. What, then, are the ideological dividends paid in *bringing the difference in question*? A full answer would have to inquire into a whole range of practices whereby our culture has become increasingly adept in taking benefit of doubt.[22] But we can provide the syn-

22. At the level of subjective practices, a central and quite literal example would be the continuity noted by Max Weber between the religious ethos of Protestantism and the mental disposition of capitalism. The Calvinist subject's doubt as to his salvation engages him in intense worldly activity as a means to attain self-confidence. Such self-confidence is thus made to ride on restless, continuous work in a calling—a process that may surpass the moment of possession or remain on this side of it, but in any case never coincides with it. The task of proving one's election becomes as endless as the increase of capital that is the sign of its being successfully accomplished. Dickens is far enough from—or close enough to—this psychological structure to make it a prime target of his criticism, either in the spiritual bookkeeping of a Mrs. Clennam or the entrepreneurial pieties of a Bounderby. Yet the end of such criticism is not to repudiate the nexus between personal doubt and worldly duty, but rather to free its terms from their limiting specifications. This means, in effect, re-encoding it within the organization of the family. Weber's Protestant ethic is replaced by Freud's family romance, as a structure linking self-doubt with worldly ambition. When the specific doctrinal source of doubt (predestination) has been familialized as a problematic of the "orphan," uncertain both of his parents' identity and hence of his place in the world; when even the "calling" has been transferred from the primary capitalist sphere (where with the advent of industrialism its integrity had been seriously compromised) to the still-undisparaged domain of domestic economy, then Robinson Crusoe returns as Esther Summerson: both the doubt-ridden, self-effacing orphan, always on the verge of being overwhelmed by the question of her origin and the consequent problem of her destiny, and the "methodical" housekeeper (92) "with a

ecdoche of an answer by turning in conclusion to the specific practice that, though we have seen it continually emerge both as an effect of various institutions and as the term of sundry oppositions, we have stopped short of considering in itself. Yet it is the practice that *Bleak House* is most concerned to promote: the practice of the family.

VII

Even in what otherwise would be her triumph, when the recognition of her merit has assumed public proportions, Esther Summerson retains her modest blindfold: "The people even praise Me as the doctor's wife. The people even like Me as I go about, and make so much of me that I am quite abashed. I owe it all to him, my love, my pride! They like me for his sake, as I do everything I do in life for his sake" (880). And to Allan's affirmation that she is prettier than ever she was, she can only respond: "I did not know that; I am not certain that I know it now. But I know that my dearest little pets are very pretty, and that my darling is very beautiful, and that my husband is very handsome, and that my guardian has the brightest and most benevolent face that ever was seen; and that they can very well do without much beauty in me—even supposing—" (880). Just as earlier Esther could barely speak of Allan, or her desire for him, so now, at the moment this desire is returned, she can only stammer. With her unfinished sentence, *Bleak House* "ends." Though one easily supplies what Esther keeps from saying ("even supposing I have my beauty back"), the modesty that consigns this assertion to silence is, to the last, radically inconclusive. Like woman's work, which is the external means

---

fine administrative capacity" (597), who, admonishing herself "Duty, my dear!" shakes the keys of her kingdom to ring herself "hopefully" to bed (80).

to Esther's social recognition, the labors of modesty, its inner correlative, are never done.

What might be a matter for grief or grievance, however, as Esther's "neurotic" inability to relinquish her self-doubt in the hour of success, also means that the energy that has gone into consolidating and sustaining one Bleak House after another will not be dissipated in the complacency of enjoyment or relaxation. The text has posed the origin of Esther's self-doubt in the question of her proper place in a family structure (her illegitimacy), and this origin has shaped her tacit ambition to install herself securely within such a structure. Given a twist, however, by the psychology of modesty through which it is obliged to pass, the ambition attains a frustration that is exactly proportionate to its achievements. Esther never ceases to earn her place, as though, were she to do so, she might even at the end be displaced from it. Yet there is a twist to the frustration too, as Esther's endless modesty finds its nonneurotic social validation in the family that, no less precarious than her own sense of identity, requires precisely such anxious and unremitting devotion for its survival. Or, as these relations might be generally summarized: the insecurity of the family subject is indispensable to counter the instability of the family structure, of which it is an effect.

The instability of the family, therefore, is constitutive of its very maintenance. As Jacques Donzelot has shown, the nineteenth-century family develops within two registers, which he calls *contract* and *tutelage*. Contract indicates the free and easy family autonomy ensured through "the observance of norms that guarantee the social usefulness of [its] members"; whereas tutelage designates the system of "external penetration" of the family, transformed into an object of surveillance and discipline. The two registers are positive and negative dimensions of a single policy of incentive: if the family satisfactorily performs its social tasks, then it is granted the liberty and autonomy of contract; but should it fail to pay back the privileges thereby conferred upon it in the proper accomplishment of responsibilities, then it must fall back into the register of tutelage.[23]

With these two registers, one can correlate the two causes that Dickens's novels regularly ascribe to the faultiness of the family: on one hand, the external interference of institutions that (like the workhouse in *Oliver Twist*) dislocate and disjoin the family; and on the other, the internal dynamic that (as exemplified in *Oliver Twist* by Monks's oedipal and sibling rivalry) determines its own divisions and displacements. The first cause amounts to a demand for contract; the second is a concession to the necessity of tutelage. The theme of outside interference bears a message to society at large to reform its institutions in the interest of preserving the only natural and naturally free space within it. (The argument is never free from the utilitarianism that Dickens's sentimentality about the family rationalizes rather than resists. The novels continually imply the family's advantages over other agencies in producing acceptable citizens of the liberal state both in quantitative terms—as its greater economy—and in qualitative ones—as the superiority of the bonds between its members.) The theme of internal disruption, on the other hand, addresses its message to the family itself, which had better do its utmost to stay together or else face the misery of being dispersed or colonized by remedial institutions. In the first instance, Dickens advises society to police for the family, which would thereby be safeguarded as the home of freedom; in the second, he counsels the family to police itself, that it might remain free by becoming its own house of correction. The two apparently incompatible themes, informing the representation of the family throughout Dickens's work, are in fact complementary. Likewise, the "practical" rec-

23. Jacques Donzelot, *The Policing of Families*, trans. Robert Hurley (New York: Pantheon, 1979). The discussion of contract and tutelage that is paraphrased and cited here appears on pp. 82–95.

ommendations attached to each find their mutual coherence precisely in the way that they cancel one another out. For if society reformed itself so that state institutions would, if not wither away, become minimal and humane, then there would no longer exist an outside threat to consolidate the family in the face of its internal dangers; and to the extent that the family could successfully repress these dangers itself, it would only reproduce such institutions in their worst aspects. With the disappearance of social discipline, the emancipated family would prove in greater need of it than ever; and in the enjoyment of its unobstructed independence, it would restore the discipline from which it was meant as an asylum, either in its own practice or in that of the institutions that would inevitably make their reappearance upon its breakdown.

Neither the social nor the familial "policing of the family," therefore, can be carried very far without giving rise to the very regimentation it was supposed to curtail. In this respect at least, Dickens's vigorous reformism makes better sense as an undeclared defense of the status quo: the social recommendations would merely be the weights (like most weights, not meant to be carried very far) to preserve the family in its present delicate balance. For the family's freedom is founded in the possibility of its discipline, and thus to enjoy the former means to have consented to the latter. Esther's insecurity, we said, works to oppose the instability of the family structure from which it results. It supplies the constant vigilance wanted to keep the contractual family from lapsing into the subjection of tutelage. It is equally true, however, that Esther's insecurity *confirms* the family in its faultiness. In the same degree that it propagates the worry and anxiety needed to maintain the family, it keeps alive the ever-present danger of its fall. The novel everywhere publishes the same fear of falling and implies the same urgency about holding one's place. The "outside" of power regularly incurs the risk that it may be annexed—or worse, may already have been annexed—by the "inside." So, for instance, the family will sometimes be shown as only a slight modulation of Chancery bureaucracy (comfortably domesticated with the Jellybys), or of the police (one of whose different voices can be heard in Mrs. Pardiggle, the "moral Policeman" who regiments her own family in the same spirit she takes others "into custody" [107]). And the risk touches us more nearly than do these unadmirable characters, for even the excellent Bagnets rely on an explicitly military order, and Esther herself may be only better directed than Mrs. Jellyby when she sits at her desk "full of business, examining trademen's books, adding up columns, paying money, filing receipts, and . . . making a great bustle about it" (122). Envisioning the family now as a firm counterweight to social institutions, now as a docile function of them, here as the insuperable refuge from the carceral, there as the insufferable replica of it, the novel poses the question of the family, which it thereby designates as the object of struggle. Rather as Esther takes up this question as the necessity of founding and keeping Bleak House, so the novel extends the question to its readers, both as a principle of hope and an exhortation, as it were, to work at home. Mr. Bagnet's famous catchword formulates what is no less the objective than the condition of the family in Dickens's representation of it: "Discipline"—within the domestic circle as well as outside it—"must be maintained."

VIII

Queen Victoria confided to her diaries: "I never feel quite at ease or at home when reading a Novel."[24] *Bleak House* makes itself as anxiogenic and incomplete as the home with which it

24. Viscount Esher, ed., *The Girlhood of Queen Victoria: A Selection from Her Diaries 1832–40*, 2 vols. (London: J. Murray, 1912), 2:83, reprinted in Collins, *Dickens: The Critical Heritage*, p. 44. The citation comes from an entry for December 23, 1838.

identifies. For in an age in which productivity is valued at least as much as the product, the novel must claim no less the inadequacy than the necessity of closure. This inadequacy can now be understood—not in the old-fashioned way, as a failure of organic form, nor even in the new-fashioned way, as the success of a failure of organic form—but, in the broader context of institutional requirements and cultural needs, as the novel's own "work ethic," its imposing refusal of rest and enjoyment. Certainly, when reading this novel, though in the reasons of the hearth it finds its own reason for being, one never feels quite at home; perhaps, having finished it, one knows why one never *can* feel at home. For what now is home—not securely possessed in perpetuity, but only leased from day to day on payment of continual exertions—but a House? And what is this House—neither wholly blackened by the institutions that make use of its cover, nor wholly bleached of their stain—but (in the full etymological ambiguity of the word) irresolvably Bleak? "Bleak House has an exposed sound" (68).

FOUR

The Novel as Usual: Trollope's *Barchester Towers*

I

Where are the police in *Barchester Towers* (1857)? Since they are literally nowhere to be found, the question is bound to seem both insensitive (to what the novel most evidently has chosen to represent) and far too attentive (to what—the evidence is no less compelling—it has not so chosen). The question intrudes as roughly on this novel as might, were they ever to appear in it, the police themselves. So well do the novel's representational and tonal practices avert the question of the police that to a suspicious mind such averting might well amount to a policing of this very question. The suspicion is "paranoid" only if one fails to recognize how difficult it is to give Trollope's fiction, so to speak, another thought: a thought, I mean, that is not wholly determined by the successful operation of the effects of his own novelistic project or that does not simply continue to familiarize us with what is already a highly developed system of familiarizations. In much the same way as one drops into the easy chair that is still the most likely place to read Trollope, or sinks into that half-slumber in which his pages there may be safely skimmed, so one falls into the usual appreciation of his appreciation of the usual, and into the paired assumptions on which it is based: "Life is like this," and "Novels are like this, too." It might require nothing less than impertinence to render as such, and not merely repeat, the terroristic effects of the banality that Trollope, as a matter of principle and program, relentlessly cultivates.

Where, then, are the police in *Barchester Towers*? Though they are literally nowhere to be found, we find them elsewhere, in the exotic space of metaphor. Mr. Slope thrives on the desecration of the Sabbath that he finds useful to lament, "as policemen do upon the general evil habits of the community," and Mrs. Proudie calls him to account for his visits to the Signora Neroni "with the stern look of a detective policeman in the act of declaring himself."[1] Yet even here, the very archness of the comparisons advertises an irony that must also prevent us from taking them entirely seriously. Comically mixing registers, Trollope reaffirms the decorum that would ordinarily keep them well separate—at least for anyone except the two ill-mannered arrivistes who, as he lets us know, are this genteel novel's male and female devils (241). There may be worse or simply other aspects to the police than vulgarity, but to give the devils their due, of all the charges the police metaphor might be thought to bring against them, this is the only one that is finally allowed to stick. Blackshirts in the close are an infinitely remote possibility when, despite his vision of "wheels within wheels" (136), Slope's extraordinary greasiness is incapable of applying itself to the social machinery with any effect but the local acts of mischief that ultimately victimize only him. And by the end of the novel, even Mrs. Proudie, who after all wears the trousers only within the partriarchal radius of the strings on her husband's apron, does "not often" interfere in the arrangement of ecclesiastical affairs in Barchester (504).

In other words, if it is reassuring to know that the police are only a metaphor in the world of *Barchester Towers*, it is doubly

---

1. Anthony Trollope, *Barchester Towers*, The World's Classics (London: Oxford University Press, 1960), pp. 25 and 148. All subsequent references to this novel are to this edition and are cited parenthetically in the text by page number.

so to know that this metaphor is also a catachresis, a metaphor that literally cannot be borne. Not only are there no police in *Barchester Towers*, but also—the better to avert the question of their whereabouts—neither is there anyone who can successfully assume their function. The ecclesiastical hierarchy of course supposes just such a function, but at the very top of it, the bishop, etymologically as well as institutionally charged to "oversee" his diocese, is quickly reduced to a misnomer. In the tactics of his wife, his chaplain, and Dr. Grantly, he encounters three lines of resistance that effectively destroy the coherence of any personal power of regulation, including that of the tacticians who draw up the lines. And at the bottom of this hierarchy, the churchwardens at Mr. Arabin's new parish are simply "ignorant . . . of the nature of their authority, and of the surveillance which it was their duty to keep" over the vicar himself (204). In any case, there is that about Mr. Arabin which makes even the overbearing archdeacon feel that "it would be difficult to rebuke him with good effect" (458). Characters are scarcely more imposing in the role of what Trollope (in the case of Bertie Stanhope) calls the "social policeman" (405). Cowed by Arabin, Grantly is ready enough to threaten sanctions against Eleanor's presumed treachery with Slope, but—as though to show that the Church militant is no more triumphant in this respect than the Church suffering—when it comes to results, his outraged activism is as null as its opposite: the resigned quietism of Mr. Harding, who refuses even to question his daughter, much less admonish her. All such instances are generalized to the community as a whole at the Ullathorne "fête," where Mr. Plomacy must act "as a sort of head constable as well as master of the revels" (380), and secure the park entrance from intruders. Miss Thorne has already enjoined him not to be "too particular" (340), and her instructions are reinforced when Mr. Greenacre, in the only case of attempted eviction we witness, reminds him not to "stick at trifles" (382). Before the day is half over, even the little work that on such liberal principles remains for him to do is "found to be quite useless": "almost anyone who chose to come made his way into the park" (341).

What is celebrated at Ullathorne is a society that is not only impossible, but unnecessary to police as well. The anarchy that the absence of the police and the failure of their surrogates might commonsensically be assumed to invite is prevented by the autarchy of a world whose own free operation remains in perfect accord with the policing it therefore doesn't require. Something like Providence, at work in the most ordinary psychological processes and social interactions, arranges things so that even though everyone goes his or her own way, no one goes astray, and each comes to a place tolerable, if not positively gratifying, to all. Thus, Eleanor and Arabin prove finally as undeserving of the archdeacon's rebukes as she is, and he would be, unmindful of them. And the same ambition that inspires Slope's machinations in Barchester teaches him to continue them elsewhere, in London, where he marries a sugar-baker's widow. The whole comedy of errors issues in a "rightness" that is all the more impressive for being at once transcendent of any individual design, taken singly, and immanent in all such designs, taken together. When, so to speak, every uninvited plasterer admitted to Ullathorne Park only further cements the social order he finds there, then to negate the police means already to have subsumed them.

The paradox is quite at home in the bourgeois liberal tradition of thought that postulates "freedom" in one dimension (usually inner, spiritual, domestic), the better to accommodate "unfreedom" in another (usually, after the Revolution, social, political, institutional).[2] The absence of the police, together with any need for their controls, would thus seem to imply the familiar double register of middle-class discipline, in which a

2. See "A Study on Authority," in Herbert Marcuse, *From Luther to Popper* (London: New Left Books, 1972), pp. 49–155.

subject is entitled to freedom only on condition that he or she tactfully internalizes as "self-control" what would otherwise, to achieve the same results, have to appear as massive institutional intervention. Yet what we typically see in Trollope are not repressed characters sternly denying themselves in the interest of the social good that in return guarantees their own well-being, but rather characters who uninhibitedly desire what Trollope calls, in one of his favorite legitimizing phrases, "the good things of the world" (369). (Even Mr. Harding, who rejects these good things in the form of a deanship, appeals to no other ideal than comfort in doing so.) It is strange, therefore—far stranger than the invisible hand of classic bourgeois economics to which the phenomenon bears so strong an analogy—that such characters, severally pursuing a thoroughly worldly happiness, simultaneously contribute to the maintenance of a social order whose cohesiveness and stability make it unique in nineteenth-century fiction. The *sauve-qui-peut* of an individualism run wild, central in a novelist like Balzac, is here as marginal as the police whose absence threatens to engender it. One might dismiss all this as just another element in an almost charmingly naive social fantasy, if it did not also more interestingly suggest that social cohesion in Trollope is achieved along other lines of strategy than policial interdictions, whatever their source. Inasmuch as the police are a kind of placeholder for a notion of power as repression, then to grasp with any concreteness how the social field is determined in *Barchester Towers*, where the police literally and finally even metaphorically have no place to hold, we need to rely on a different conception of power that, while it may include policelike restraints, is in no way reducible to them. The police, I said, are negated in *Barchester Towers* only because they have already been subsumed, but what is the nature of that more comprehensive and efficacious polity which, with such few and feeble traces, has absorbed them?

II

The real justice of the peace in *Barchester Towers* is—what might appear to be most in need of one—war itself: not the war that, according to Clausewitz, is the continuation of politics "by other means," but the political power that, according to Foucault, is the continuation of war, also by other means. "If it is true that political power puts an end to war, that it installs, or tries to install, the reign of peace in civil society, this by no means implies that it suspends the effects of war or neutralizes the disequilibrium revealed in the final battle. The role of political power, on this hypothesis, is perpetually to reinscribe this relation through a form of unspoken warfare; to reinscribe it in social institutions, in economic inequalities, in language, in the bodies of each and every one of us."[3] Barely policed, the social world in Trollope is thoroughly polemicized, and while the impoverished metaphor of the police is capable of yielding only the abstraction of a society that gets along quite well without them, if we only knew how, the abundant metaphor of war pervades and organizes every dimension of the social field. It extends—beyond the "hard battles" fought between the Grantly and Proudie "forces" and the "mutiny in the camp" on either side—from the bedroom politics of Mrs. Proudie and the battle of the sexes implied in every marriage and courtship, to the divided selves of characters as diverse as Slope, Quiverful, and Harding. "War, war, internecine war" (42) is in the archdeacon's heart and—so routinely as to make

3. Michel Foucault, "Two Lectures," in *Power/Knowledge*, ed. Colin Gordon (New York: Pantheon Books, 1981), p. 90. Two other texts by Foucault also deserve mention for their bearing on my later discussion of the novelistic pastorate: "Omnes et Singulatim: Towards a Criticism of 'Political Reason,'" in *The Tanner Lectures on Human Value*, ed. S. M. McMurrin, 2 vols. (Cambridge: Cambridge University Press, 1980–81), 2:223–54; and "The Subject and Power," *Critical Inquiry* 8 (Summer 1982): 777–95.

further evidence merely tedious—in nearly everything else besides.

Yet the metaphor, everywhere present, is everywhere comic as well, as though Trollope were already drawing comfortably on the assurance of social stability that "war," as we will see, works to procure. When the archdeacon liberally celebrates Eleanor's marriage to Arabin, those who know him well understand that his lavish wedding gifts are his hymn of thanksgiving: "He had girded himself with his sword, and gone forth to the war; now he was returning from the field laden with the spoils of the foe. The cob and the cameos, the violoncello and the pianoforte, were all as it were trophies reft from the tent of his now conquered enemy" (504). The vocabulary of final and total victory is hyperbolically out of proportion to a situation in which Slope, like a cat, has fallen on his feet (494), and the cob and the cameos, even if they had been Slope's possessions and not the archdeacon's purchases, make a sorry objective correlative for "spoils." The same overblown quality regularly characterizes a metaphor that, far from establishing the homicidal violence of the Barchester community, reduces it to the innocuous fantasies with which this community (or Trollope speaking on its behalf) seeks to enliven its teapot tempests. Though the bishop might like his wife and Slope to "fight it out so that one should kill the other utterly, as far as diocesan life was concerned" (234), he knows as well as we do that this is wishful thinking. The mock-heroics of the war metaphor turn war into a war game, so diminished in its aspirations and consequences that no one sustains serious bodily harm (even the devils: Mrs. Proudie is merely tripped up, and Slope is only he who gets slapped) or serious harm of any kind. On the contrary, in the course of the long theological polemic conducted between Slope and Arabin, "each had repeatedly hung the other on the horns of a dilemma; but neither seemed to be a whit the worse for the hanging; and so the war went on merrily" (116). Perhaps one reason it can do so is that the "final battle," in which the essential power relations of society would be decided, has already and long ago taken place, with the conclusion of a sanguinary religious politics in England at the end of the seventeenth century. Like, in a different national history, Stendhal's "Restoration comedy," Trollope's merry war exists as a belated copy, petty and peaceable, of a belligerent and heroic original—with the difference of course that modern bloodlessness appears in Trollope's color scheme less black than rose. Thus seeming to retract its very tenor, the war metaphor would be as catachretic as that of the police, were it not for the fact that, while there does not appear to be much policing in *Barchester Towers*, there is a great deal of fighting. Accordingly, since it is a question of "war by other means," its displacement and reinscription, one cannot rest entirely assured that the war metaphor functions only to self-destruct: as though it could also be taken for granted that political struggles always bore world-historical freight; that social conflict, when it had ceased to deal death, did not continue to administer life; and that mere war games were incapable of inciting power plays.

"What is the use," then, we ask with Mrs. Grantly, "of always fighting?" (456). Her question is rhetorical not because there is no use, as she seems to think, but because—at least for the novel's major instance of fighting—Trollope has already answered it: "We are much too apt to look at schism in our church as an unmitigated evil. Moderate schism, if there may be such a thing, at any rate calls attention to the subject, draws in supporters who would otherwise have been inattentive to the matter, and teaches men to think upon religion" (169–70). This "moderate schism" in fact structures both the clerical infighting in *Barchester Towers* and the considerable institutional and social coherence accruing to it. "If there may be such a thing"? There can scarcely be anything else in the novel, where schism reaches neither the rupture nor the healing that are, alternatively, its promised ends. War is total inasmuch as victory never is. The controversies and power struggles that seem to throw such dishonor on the Church are not likely ever to be resolved, and only an outsider and parvenu like Slope is naive enough to harbor "a view to putting an end to schism in the diocese" (305). The rest, including the dominant Grantlyites, are practically willing to abide in that interminable state of compromise which is always part victory, part defeat. Yet as Franco Moretti has seen, the distinctive function of compromise is not "to make everybody happy"—or even, for that matter, to make anybody happy—but rather "to create a broad area with uncertain boundaries where polarized values come into contact, cohabit, become hard to recognize and disentangle."[4] Similarly, the "use" of fighting in *Barchester Towers* is not to resolve once for all the issues at hand, but to bind the combatants to the capacious institution that sponsors their disputes. To contend over introducing Sabbath-day schools, or intoning the Sunday service, is not just to advertise the supreme importance of the Church of England in the national life. Even better, it is to make this importance vital in the contending subjects themselves, whose conflicts (amounting to so many cathexes) attach them not only to "religion" but also to the general social condition of bondedness that not inaptly passes here under that name. The entelechy of a war game, therefore, is not, as with a war, to be over, but, as with a game, to secure a maximum of play. What matters most in this game is not whether you win or lose, or even how well you play it, but that you play it at all.

We begin to see why Trollope's fiction frequently turns on contemporary social, political, and legal "issues," but also why it is at the same time so relatively indifferent to their substance, and so little eager to take sides. Rarely more developed than Hitchcock's "Macguffin," the issues are at bottom only pretexts to mobilize the novelistic population for a merry war. Trollope

4. Franco Moretti, *Signs Taken for Wonders* (London: New Left Books, 1983), p. 243n.

inflects the "social problem novel" so that any "problem" is already part of a more fundamental social solution: namely, the militant constitution and operation of the social field as such. Thus, on one hand, *Barchester Towers* may be thought to be about the Oxford Movement, insofar as the latter provides a referential matrix for the controversies and struggles that the novel represents. Yet on another, *Barchester Towers* is only "about" the Oxford Movement in the sense of skirting around it. This is not a novel from which one hopes—for which one even needs—to learn much about the movement, except perhaps the somewhat cynical knowledge that very little finally was moved by it. The movement makes a strictly token appearance here: in the references to items like roods, waistcoats, and so forth, which—deprived of any theological rationale— seem merely partisan badges or personal tics. Just as he will later (in the Palliser novels) portray a Parliament that, for all its politicking, has no politics, so here Trollope creates a church without elaborating its theology. Indicatively, the volumes of this theology in the cathedral library are "not disturbed, perhaps, quite as often as from the appearance of the building the outside public might have been led to expect" (168), and though the polemic between Arabin and Slope is said to concern the apostolic succession, what either has to urge on the matter is never reported. In the formalism of power to which Trollope reduces his church, theology comes down to an ad hoc allusion or two, as though only in the most perfunctory fashion to motivate the device that is thereby laid bare.

The intellectual dearth of an explicit set of ideas about God, man, revelation, and so on, is more than matched by the affective absence of anything like spiritual intensity. We have only to think of the rendering of religious feeling in George Eliot, where major characters are compulsively and hysterically overcome by it, to appreciate how levelheadedly secular Trollope's priests and "priestesses" are. Eliot's kind of urgency has no place in this novel, and though Bertie Stanhope's many and silly conversions do, Arabin must already have passed through his more serious religious crisis before he is allowed entry, and then only to learn that "the greatest mistake any man ever made is to suppose that the good things of the world are not worth the winning" (369–70). The point that clergymen are no better than other men is fondly and repeatedly made: the archdeacon calculates his chances of a bishopric at his father's deathbed; Slope succumbs to a passion for a married signora; Dr. Stanhope idles in Italy; and Tom Staple drinks. As in the notable conversation over Sunday lunch at the Thornes, which admixes with "all manner of ecclesiastical subjects" generous amounts of guano (211–12), the sacred has only to put forth its claim and—like any other pretension in comedy—it is brought down to earth.

Barchester Towers thus doubly demystifies the institution-as-religion, which not only lacks a higher agenda than the need (via moderate schism) to maintain itself but is also manned by a very ordinary run of men. In either case, institutional power is portrayed quite apart from an official account of its workings. The ostensive issues that such power engages are revealed in all their inconsequence as merely the means to secure institutional consolidation, ramification, and tenure. And the agents of such power come quickly to be divested of the halo that those to whom they minister—or whom they administer—wrongly but not unnaturally suppose them to wear. Reducing religion to an institution like any other, the novel achieves a compelling insight into the typical ideological process that is thus reversed: the self-promotion of an institution to the status of religion. One might applaud the insight, were it not the basis for endorsing the very phenomenon it uncovers, and for comfortably transferring all the authority of religion to the social-institutional domain. Mr. Arabin, the novel's "intellectual," tells Eleanor:

Our contentions do bring on us some scandal. The outer world, though it constantly reviles us for our human infirmities, and throws in our teeth the fact that being clergymen we are still no more than men, demands of us that we should do our work with godlike perfection. There is nothing godlike about us: we differ from each other with the acerbity common to man—we triumph over each other with human frailty—we allow differences on subjects of divine origin to produce among us antipathies and enmities which are anything but divine. This is all true. But what would you have in place of it? There is no infallible head for a church on earth. This dream of believing man has been tried, and we see in Italy and in Spain what has come of it. Grant that there are and have been no bickerings within the pale of the Pope's Church. Such an assumption would be utterly untrue; but let us grant it, and then let us say which church has incurred the heavier scandals. (195)

Much as, in late twentieth-century America, unseemly political activity against imperialist wars or for various civil rights is opportunistically converted into the very evidence of the "free society" that this activity is in fact trying to bring about, or a scandal like Watergate comes to vindicate a system that, even so severely tried, still triumphantly "works," so the bickering in Trollope's Church and the fallibility of its ministers are all to the good. They confer on this church its liberal Anglican identity, in contradistinction to the authoritarian Church of Rome. More than a simple mechanism or function, "moderate schism" is a supreme value and one whose religious implications easily gradate into political and social ones. With his comparisons to Italy and Spain, Arabin might almost be referring to the merits of a bicameral legislature or a two-party system (as Prime Minister Palliser actually will), or even to economic productivity. It is no less clear in the case of the all-too-human clergy that Trollope's disabused treatment of religion is only a subtler means of valorizing the social order that religion serves. Fond as he is of showing that clergymen are no more than men, Trollope is even fonder of showing that most of them, at any rate, are no less than gentlemen, with the civility and tolerance of such. The clergy are not debunked so much as brought under a wider and more generous set of social norms, as though religion itself were the old dispensation and "the social" the new. These norms—the novel's truly operative ethical criteria—still condemn Slope's advances to the signora (though as more inept than immoral), but they perfectly accommodate Dr. Gwynne's gout.

Necessarily, then, the demystifications stop short of impugning the category of the sacred from which the Church draws its institutional authority, for it is a matter of broadening this authority, not blasting it. "I may question the infallibility of the teachers, but I hope that I shall not therefore be accused of doubt as to the thing taught" (45). This is sufficiently pious to allow the demystifications to proceed without scandal even to the legendarily proper sensibilities of the middle-class mid-Victorian reader, who does not seem to have protested that "the thing to be taught" is as little specified as the teachers' doctrinal disputes (which do, however, necessarily shadow it in "doubt"). Abstractly upholding the claims of religion, the novelist's disclaimer promotes their concrete secularization: doctrinally vacant, Trollope's piety amounts to no more—but also to no less—than throwing a general transcendent aura over socially current norms of decent behavior. Similarly, his occasional but conspicuous gesture of blanking out the sacred from the novel has a double valence. At the same time that it piously retains the "prestige" of the sacred, it slyly neutralizes any otherness that might prevent the sacred from being assimilated to the way we live now. "It would not be becoming were I to travestie a sermon, or even to repeat the language of it in the pages of a novel" (45). It is a moot point whether what inspires the censorship here is a religious injunction, as against graven images (of which the printed fiction one calls a novel would be the most recent example), or a social protocol that determines the norm of what is or is not "becoming." In the very act of separating the sacred from the profane, the two are only further entangled. In Trollope sometimes to omit the sacred in its orthodox form is—not least by this very means—always to include it as the social order itself.

To this one must add that if religion is thus diffused as social schismatics, then diffused along with it is a certain structure of hegemony. Certainly, Arabin's theory of moderate schism, echoing and elaborating Trollope's own, implies the necessity of pluralism, dialogue, the universal embrace of various divergent views even as one militates for one such view in particular. Yet it also matters that it is Arabin who advances this theory, which therefore issues from the ideological wing of the party most "in power." Consider this pair of contrasts. Mr. Slope means "to rule without terms" (237), "conceives it to be his duty to know all the private doings and desires of the flock entrusted to his care" (28), and finds it expedient "that there should be but one opinion among the dignitaries of the diocese" (305). But as long as those around Dr. Grantly "fully and freely admitted the efficacy of Mother Church, [the archdeacon] was willing that that mother should be merciful and affectionate, prone to indulgence, and unwilling to chastize" (27): "He liked to give laws and be obeyed in them implicitly, but he endeavoured that his ordinances should be within the compass of the man, and not unpalatable to the gentleman" (28). And again: while Mrs. Proudie, "habitually authoritative to all," "stretches her power over all [her husband's] movements, and will not even abstain from things spiritual," Mrs. Grantly "values power, and has not unsuccessfully striven to acquire it; but she knows what should be the limits of a woman's rule" (20). The case for pluralism, or for the separation and distribution of powers, is never made by the outsiders, who might seem to secure themselves a hearing thereby, but who are instead—in a familiar pattern that extends far beyond Barchester—characterized as shrilly authoritarian. It may only be a measure of the constraint implied in the system of liberal tolerance that the characterization, also as usual, is all too plausible. For what Slope and Mrs. Proudie implicitly contest is, more than mere "positions," the very ground on which positions may be contested (or at least, this is how it must always appear when such ground virtually coincides with the "high and dry Church" party that occupies it). His demand for "but one opinion" in the diocese rejects the very principle that makes the game possible, just as her will to participate in what is strictly a man's game represents an unthinkable change in the rules. They are therefore defeated not *in* so much as *by* the game, which is too well entrenched not to be played in any case, even when players refuse to cooperate. Dissenting from the game itself, Slope is made to speak a fascist discourse that only further discredits his play in it. And if in the end Mrs. Proudie fares better than the self-exiled Slope, this is only because she is saved by the inconsistency that is, Trollope would tell us, a woman's privilege. In practice she must be more tolerant— more submissive to the limits of a woman's rule—than her evident intentions ever quite recognize: the same patriarchy that makes outrages like hers inevitable also makes their consequences minimal. While the outsiders, then, talk a totalitarianism that, to the extent an attempt is made to practice as well as preach it, only keeps them outside, insiders like Arabin and Grantly eloquently defend and practically cultivate a pluralism that stands thus revealed as not just a mechanism of social consolidation but also and coincidentally an ideology of social dominance. What matters most about the war game is that it continue to be played, since it is the game itself that most fundamentally ensures partisan privileges and social imbalances. Small wonder, then, that at Oxford Arabin "talked jovially over his glass of port of the ruin to be anticipated by the Church, and of the sacrilege committed daily by the Whigs" (173): the merry war is not a free-for-all.

III

The formal name for "moderate schism" would no doubt be plot—except that moderate schism, even extended to include all instances of fighting in *Barchester Towers*—does not quite amount to what ordinarily grips us under that term. It is odd that a narrative declaring itself "war" should be so open to charges of blandness. The frequent observation that "nothing happens" in Trollope, absurd if one is counting up narrative incidents, is true enough in the sense that these incidents occur in the absence of that strong teleology which, elsewhere in Victorian fiction, would allow them to gain point (as major climax or minor anticipation, in the beginning, middle, or end). Geared primarily to its own self-sustenance, moderate schism is useless in calling a halt or even giving much direction to the narrative, which as a result seems underplotted: more a meandering succession of episodes than a dynamic progression en route to Aristotelian catharsis or Freudian working-through. It is not that a novel like *Barchester Towers* quite deserves to be called "open-ended," though like very few nineteenth-century English novels, it both has and is a sequel. But even as the traditional closural chords are touched (the settlement of the good, the banishment or silencing of the bad), Trollope offers them as little more than expedients in the business of turning out products for the novel market. The end of a salable novel, like the end of a children's party, requires such "sweetmeats and sugar-plums" (502). When the text commodifies itself at such points, moreover, the item for sale is surely not just closure but its ironical negation as well. In any case, market considerations are not confined to determining Trollope's archly conventional closures. They determine none the less those loose and casual plots whose refusal to elaborate structures of secrecy or suspense is, in the Victorian context, the least conventional aspect of his fiction. For while a strong sense of an ending may get the novels sold, it is a weak sense of one—the condition for Trollope's un-equalled productivity among his contemporaries—that gets them written in lucrative quantities. Like a builder working under a slack construction code, Trollope may erect the houses of his fiction rapidly and all over the tract. Yet the evident cynicism of the artist-as-entrepreneur is rehabilitated in the happy marriage of convenience, celebrated throughout Trollope's work, between the Novel and the social order that (in more than one way) it represents. What at the phase of novel production is the superior efficiency of relaxing teleological construction (the endings are now detachable parts, for swifter assembly) shows up in the finished novel-product as the viability of a social order that, bound together in perennial militancy, no more foresees a resolution to the "problems" that in fact sustain it than it envisions its own coming-to-an-end. If closure does not carry much conviction in Trollope, it doesn't need to: the social security that traditional closure means to establish has been displaced into the tensions, differences, and disequilibriums that engender or motivate the narrative processes themselves.

"But the novelist has other aims than the elucidation of his plot," and the sheer readiness with which Trollope, in his own public relations, concedes his imperfections in this branch of work notifies us that he bases his claims to our attention elsewhere. "The novelist has other aims than the elucidation of his plot. He desires to make his readers so intimately acquainted with his characters that the creations of his brain should be to them speaking, moving, living, human creatures. . . . And as, here in our outer world, we know that men and women change,—become worse or better as temptation or conscience may guide them,—so should these creations of his change, and every change should be noted by him. . . . If the would-be novelist have aptitudes that way, all this will come to him without much struggling;—but if it do not come, I think he can only make novels of wood."[5] Rather in the way that a given sociopolitical issue provides only a pretext to set the plot going, so it is implied that plot itself need be no more than a makeshift for the primordial exhibition of character. Plot seems to exhaust its only valid function in educing, along with certain general truths about human nature, certain specific truths about its varieties, inasmuch as these are the real burden of representation. Concomitantly, the motivations of plot (in social schismatics) tend to be all but dismissed as so many local or contingent occasions permitting the display of such truths. The priority that Trollope accords the category of character thus belongs to the "depoliticizing" ambition of his fiction, as does the indifference of this fiction to the polemics that it at once excites and refuses to be excited by. As, formally speaking, character takes precedence over plot, which merely affords an opportunity for rendering it, so, in a thematic dimension, the human agent stands above the social fray to which he or she can never be reduced.

Yet even as Trollope foregoes the elaboration of plot for the exposition of character, he hardly thereby remits the workings of merry warfare, which are rather displaced into the constitution of the subject who wages it. For what does the well-advertised complexity of his characters come to if not the simple effect, almost gimmicky in its insistence, of showing that they have "mixed motives"? Trollopean man, like Trollopean woman, is every bit as much a "moderate schism" as the social disputes in which he contends. Thus, the archdeacon, committed to upholding the Church, likes to broadcast his enjoyment of "the good things of this world" (27). Arabin loves Eleanor, but as he also knows, he loves her money too (323). Mr. Quiverful is anxious for means to quiet his butcher, but equally anxious to be right with his own conscience (218). "In

5. Anthony Trollope, An Autobiography, The World's Classics (London: Oxford University Press, 1953), pp. 199–200.

his indecision, his weakness, his proneness to be led by others,"
Mr. Harding—who on occasion, however, can show resolution
enough—is "very far from being perfect" (154). An unsexed
virago whose milk has been exchanged for a not entirely Shake-
spearean gall, Mrs. Proudie proves herself so far a woman as to
be "touched" by Mrs. Quiverful's unquiet desperation (241).
And so on. Even Mr. Slope is not in all things a bad man: "His
motives, like those of most men, were mixed, and though his
conduct was generally very different from that which we would
wish to praise, it was actuated perhaps as often as that of the
majority of the world by a desire to do his duty" (123). Characters are at war within themselves no less than they are at war
with one another, and the implied politics of subjectivity are
both isomorphic and continuous with the politics of the social
that, as we will see, they underwrite. Tellingly, it is the fascist
Slope who is most willing to rationalize himself into pure,
single-minded will, as though the despot's first conquest were
of necessity over himself. "He had early in life devoted himself
to works which were not compatible with the ordinary pleasures of youth, and he had abandoned such pleasures not without a struggle" (124). If what undoes Slope politically is his
refusal to recognize an already (and solidly) constituted party
system, what undoes him psychologically is his repression of
the passional drives that, willy-nilly, return to humiliate even
his own sense of ethics. Sex in this guardian of morality has
been buried alive, and its reemergence from the vault is cor-
respondingly violent. "Mr. Slope tried hard within himself to
cast off the pollution with which he felt that he was defiling
his soul" (254), but insofar as to cast off or emit a pollution is
precisely what pollution entails, the energy of resistance is already the compulsiveness of surrender: "He could not help
himself. Passion, for the first time in his life, passion was too
strong for him" (245–46). By contrast, Arabin, whose "weakness" it has ever been "to look for impure motives for his own
conduct" (323), sits far more comfortably in his skin. Person-

ality begins to resemble a parliamentary democracy, appertaining to multiple constituencies, and any attempt to deny this structure—which in this version appears no less than ontologically grounded—seems only to confirm its existence to the discomfort of the usurping member. Like the war game that is always on, most of all when it is the game itself that is being contested, so the heterogeneity of the subject invariably triumphs over every effort to purify it.

There is—or would be, if Trollope ever went to extremes— a paradox in his conception of character, in the sense that precisely what is alleged to make character interesting—its variability—also risks undermining the coherence that allows character to flourish as a valid category in the first place. What besides a proper name could hold the self together once it were radically split into discontinuities? Yet for all the shades of difference within the characters in *Barchester Towers*, what they shade is an eminently recognizable unit of self-identity: a totality that compels into integration the parts that thereby "compose" it. It is as though each character were governed by a principle of majority rule that necessitates diversity and simultaneously dominates it. Like the moderate schism of Trollope's sociology, the moderate schizophrenia of his psychology organizes divergent motives according to an ethical dominant—as it were, a moral majority—that in the last analysis (and therefore even in the first) determines their play. This dominant founds a character's coherence and continues to subject him or her to the moral judgments that Trollope, like most of his fellow Victorian novelists, has no wish to abandon. (If his judgments are more nuanced than is usual in Victorian fiction, it is because they too are structured around a dominant that imposes itself through its willingness to "tolerate" that which it dominates.) Thus, for all his mixed motives, Slope remains fundamentally repellent, and despite his imperfections, Harding generally wins our admiration. The archdeacon, a more complicated instance, may dare to ask himself whether he covets a bishopric whose price is his father's life, but: "the question was answered in a moment. The proud, wishful, worldly man, sank on his knees by the bedside, and taking the bishop's hand within his own, prayed eagerly that his sins might be forgiven him" (3–4). It does not much matter that no sooner has the father died than the son angles to succeed him in the palace, for the essential moral demonstration—the worldling draws the line at selling his soul—has been made. The parliamentary structure of personality thus "calls for a division" in a double sense: the same organization that allows all disputants to speak also periodically compels them to vote, and thus to determine which party holds sway.

We are now in a position to address a key question that the notion of moderate schism inevitably raises—namely, what keeps it moderate? What prevents the differences of opinion and sentiment that constitute the social field from reaching an intensity at which they constitute a threat to it? It will be recalled from *The Warden* (1855) that one of the founding gestures of Trollope's work is the derision it casts on the precursive achievement of Dickens—a derision that specifically targets the Dickensian forms of institution and character. In "The Almshouse," by Mr. Popular Sentiment, an absurdly one-dimensional institution given over to pure exploitation recruits exploiters and exploited alike from a population of absurdly one-dimensional human subjects. The carceral uniformity of the institution entails the impermeability of the subject (or vice versa) as a container of undiluted good or evil. Trollope's real rejoinder to Dickens, however, comes in the oeuvre that goes beyond satire to offer its own alternative treatment of the same concerns. The institutional landscape, for instance, is no more pervasive in Dickens than in Trollope, who is in fact the only Victorian novelist to rival him in the amount of attention he pays to institutional phenomena (not just the Church and Parliament, but also the school, the civil service, the law). This landscape is, in fact, ubiquitous in Trollope, where there is no place—like home in Dickens—to retreat from it. It is as though Trollope had liberated from its characteristic Dickensian confinement the institution that is consequently at large to traverse and structure the entire social field. Yet if flight is now impossible, neither is there the same need to flee, since what is stifling about institutions in Dickens is aerated in Trollope's representation of them. No longer the melodramatically enclosed site of a monolithic and homogeneous oppression, the institution has become—no doubt, more plausibly—a wide, highly variegated network, with multiple and mutually correcting jurisdictions. Thus, in *Barchester Towers*, if the bishop may appoint the warden of Hiram's Hospital, it is the archdeacon who is entitled to fill the living at St. Ewold's, and neither has any authority to select the dean. And just as the dean and chapter have the right to exclude Slope from the cathedral pulpit, so Harding may resign the wardenship or refuse the deanship. Dickens's insight into the institution-as-confinement induces a claustrophobia so exasperating that the only proper political response to it seems to be "a direct attack on the whole system,"[6] but in Trollope's vision of the institution-as-"schism," resistance follows the usual bureaucratic instructions to apply elsewhere, in another department. Mediated by numerous overlapping and realigning divisions of power, social warfare is kept from lapsing into a single and sustained binary opposition, or from aggregating the intensities that drive it forward into mass movements. Not only are there always more than two sides in this war; they are reapportioned in every skirmish as well.

The system is further complicated—moderated—by being anchored in a subject whose own internal schisms likewise atomize the intensities they generate. The "sides" of war are thus

6. Anthony Trollope, *The Warden*, The World's Classics (London: Oxford University Press, 1961), p. 186.

doubly distributed: between different subjects across an imbri-
cated social-institutional surface, and within the same subject,
who is simultaneously attached to more than one point on this
surface. By virtue of one set of commitments, for example,
Harding belongs to the Grantlyite party, but through another,
he does not hate the chaplain as the archdeacon does (154) and
so countenances Slope's courtship of Eleanor. Similarly, though
Slope sees at once the necessity of "open battle against Dr.
Grantly and all Dr. Grantly's adherents" (43), he also develops
an interest in Dr. Grantly's sister-in-law, which he tries to promote by getting her father the wardenship, even at the risk of
alienating his only ally, Mrs. Proudie. His sexuality, moreover,
compelling him to the side of Signora Neroni's couch, undermines all these projects, much as a certain loyalty to her sex
ultimately tempers the signora's own designs on Arabin. All in
all, the political commotion occasioned by Bishop Grantly's demise seems scarcely less fortuitous as it develops than the tim-
ing of his death. Trollope is positively eager to feature a politics
that stems not from meditated strategy (or even from the dialectic that will always have its reasons), but from the happen-
stance and "comic" conjunction of events, persons, motives belonging to radically different series. In the matter of the
wardenship, Slope finds himself working to realize the desires
of his enemy, and in the case of the deanship, whatever Grantly
thinks, "not he, but circumstances, had trampled on Mr.
Slope" (497). Yet if politics is thus conspicuously devoid of the
coherence that its self-appointed directors have planned, it does
not lack coherence of another kind. Whether the subject is the
effect of the internalized social schism or whether this schism
is the collective projection of a psychological structure, in
either case, the continuity between the social order and the subject who relays it makes for a supremely steady State, unstag-
gered by the militancy that, in the very act of diffusing, they
collaborate to defuse.

IV

The subsumption of religion under the social alerts us to the novel's own inherence in the latter category, which alone entitles (and is entitled to) representation. It may not be becoming to repeat the language of a sermon in the pages of a novel, but it is taken for granted that the novel has a right to rehearse the social interactions that have traditionally been the proper object of its imitation of life. Yet the system Trollope calls moderate schism is not just a fact about the social world that he elects to describe; nor is it even just a fact about the social world that he does his best to valorize. Far more immediately and concretely than either its representation as theme or its designation as value, the system operates in the novel's own representational technology and in the reading practice that this determines. As we will see, it is too simple to say that Trollopean narration merely doubles thematic structures with its own more or less analogous forms. But even if this were all it did, it would always be doing more than this, in positing as an incontestable readerly "experience" the ideological propositions that, even when eventually stated as such, have therefore already won a fundamental assent. The spiritual exercise of reading the novel catches us in confirming that which we might wish to bring into question, even before we quite know what this involves. Accordingly, whatever dissent we do manage is likely to remain within the bounds of moderation, since we have already put into practice some of the basic tenets of what gets preached. At best, a character like Arabin, even when he is being used as the novelist's mouthpiece, can only make a virtue of necessity, throwing a system that operates in any case into the flattering half-light of ideology. But the novelist can go him one better and make a necessity of virtue, embedding his political values in a specific course of formal operations to which any reader of his novel, including the most hostile, is inevitably subject. Perhaps the best instance of how technique drills us in doctrine concerns the virtue that is the very ethos of moderate schism, a virtue without which it is quite simply impossible to read Trollope: tolerance.

In the warring world of *Barchester Towers*, tolerance is the moral consciousness that allows partisans to transcend the one-sided particularity of their cause. Through tolerance, characters acknowledge and uphold the general polity that submits their aims to varying degrees of compromise and even defeat. That the winners in the merry war are notably more tolerant than the losers no doubt owes something to the sentimental Victorian stipulation that only the meek shall inherit the earth; but it owes more, we have seen, to the hegemonic structure that is to be tolerated. One might even point to the practical advantages that tolerance—as the foundation of a realpolitik—gives in maneuvering. "It will be unseemly of us to show ourselves in a bad humour," advises Dr. Gwynne after the bishop's appointment of Quiverful; "moreover, we have no power in this matter, and it will therefore be bad policy to act as though we had" (420). Having downplayed his power here, however, Gwynne is able to exercise it the more successfully later on, when he is instrumental not only in "representing in high places the claims which Mr. Harding had upon the Government," but also in "getting the offer [of the deanship] transferred to Mr. Arabin" (495). Yet tolerance, though always an objective state of affairs in Barchester, is not often a subjective state of mind among the Barchester warriors—for the good reason that, were it wholly to engross consciousness, it might undermine the beliefs that must remain sufficiently unsuspended to be worth fighting for. Combatants must know they are right, and such conviction as militancy requires easily blinds them to the irreducibility of other "sides." Conversely, insofar as a tolerant appreciation of these other sides tends to transform beliefs into the mere system of differences that makes a game possible, then the players of such a game cannot be counted on to be quite so hard at play. Psychologically speaking, too much tolerance is as debilitating in the merry war as too little, and the intolerant Slope no more misses his mark than the all-too-tolerant Bertie Stanhope, whose halfhearted schemes are plagued with futility from the outset. Arabin and Grantly are careful to promote tolerance only before a battle has begun, or after it is over, or during a lull in the hostilities. Less careful, the unceasingly tolerant Harding is so unfit for war that his weakness takes the socially alarming form of a refusal to fight at all. The same social engineering that makes tolerance an indispensable formal condition of moderate schism makes it equally indispensable that the schismatizers largely forget this fact.

The narration, however, embodies the tolerant consciousness more amply and consistently than the characters ever can. One notices, for instance, that Trollope's prescriptions for the sympathetic depiction of characters as "living, human creatures," are somewhat belied by the evenhanded detachment of his actual treatment of them. At whatever point the novelist must learn to hate his characters and to love them, "must argue with them, quarrel with them, forgive them, and even submit to them,"[7] by the time of composition he has also evidently learned to moderate the degree of his affective involvement in them. At the heart of our reading of most other Victorian fiction lies an affective schema as adolescent as the protagonists who command our attention therein: those whom we love struggle with those whom we hate, against a background of those to whom we are largely indifferent. The schema is grounded, of course, in the imaginary, specular relationship that the novelist's own partiality encourages us to form with one character in particular—usually the one we call the hero. This primary identification determines a host of secondary ones—with the hero's allies, against the hero's enemies—in what amounts overall to an exclusive and hierarchical organization of

7. Trollope, *Autobiography*, p. 200.

affect. The jubilation of my identification with David Copperfield, for example, entails my unequivocal acceptance of Peggotty, the nice variations in my response to Betsey Trotwood and Steerforth, my amused lack of concern for the Micawbers, and my peremptory rejection of the Murdstones. Even George Eliot's programmatic attempt to compensate for the effects of this single (or singularly intense) emotional focus is not quite the same thing as abandoning it, and her narrator's periodic gesturing to, say, Casaubon's point of view only succeeds in reinforcing our initial sympathy for Dorothea's—as though the decisive proof of Casaubon's repulsiveness were that he remained chilling even after benefit of so remarkably generous an apology. One might almost make the case that the high or simply Philistine moral insistence of most Victorian novels exonerates what is in fact a kind of emotional bigotry. Trollope, however, plays so fair in this regard that he can freely admit to liking one character (Eleanor) and disliking another (Slope), as novelists who play favorites never do. This is primarily a matter of limiting, in both extent and depth, the affective intensity that his narration brings to focus on a character. On the one hand, it would be difficult even to identify, much less identify with, the "hero" of *Barchester Towers*, so evenly and dispassionately does the novelist's shifting attention circulate among all his characters. And on the other, even when his preferences are declared, they never impede a cool and constant appraisal of imperfections, so that no great discrepancy in either tone or treatment separates likable characters from unlikable ones. For all of Trollope's emphasis on rendering a character in the fullness of his or her particularity, it is from an enmiring attachment to this particularity that Trollopean narration regularly takes flight. Instead of loving this character and hating that one, Trollope is at once charmed and irritated by them all, thus cultivating a pluralistic appreciation of the value—as well as the limitations—that each in one context or another proves to have. In contradistinction to George Eliot, Charlotte Brontë, or

Dickens, whose sometimes ruthless emotional simplifications are but one step removed (what reader has not taken the step?) from a Stalinist wish that large segments of the novelistic population be purged, Trollope gives structure to an accommodating perception that it truly takes all kinds to make a world.

What facilitates the affective detachment from characters, however, is the novelist's minute and sustained moral appraisal of them, from which none escapes in any condition to be the object of an idealizing overinvestment. The very excuses made for characters are often the best evidence of the accusations implied against them. "Our archdeacon was worldly—who among us is not so?" (9). Yet were we all so, the worldliness would scarcely be worth observing in the first place, or the observation worth repeating on almost every occasion the archdeacon appears. Eleanor's "devotion to her late husband was fast fading" under the pressure of Arabin and Bertie Stanhope: "Will anyone blame my heroine for this?" (214, 215). Perhaps no one would, but for the blame that the exoneration presupposes. Poverty had had an effect on Mr. Quiverful "not beneficial either to his spirit, or his keen sense of honour": "Who can boast that he would have supported such a burden with a different result?" (217–18). All the same, the fact that we might have behaved similarly never shakes our conviction that Quiverful's spirit is as tremulous as his sense of honor is dull. Trollope's tolerance thus includes an acute consciousness of all that needs to be tolerated. It requires—or better, requisitions—the stuff on which to exercise itself, and this involves, in addition to the humane impulse to understand, mitigate, and accept shortcomings, a less evident commitment to finding them out. Trollope's generosity toward his characters regularly depends on what ought to be equally notorious: his carping attention to even their least moral failings, which he never ceases to hold in view. The paradox of his tolerance is that it is willing to overlook only that which it has closely looked over: it accepts "regardless" what in fact has been put under careful and critical scrutiny. It is thus a mild manner of promoting such scrutiny, as though subjects could be brought all the more frequently before a tribunal whose sentences are so lenient. Like the clergymen, the novelist of *Barchester Towers* has his own cure of souls: that congregation of characters whose little vagrancies he untiringly tracks down in his concern for the welfare of each and all. In fact, Slope's wish "to know all the private doings and desires of the flock entrusted to his care" (28) would be far better satisfied in the position of the omniscient Victorian novelist, who must know whether his charges be true or false, "and how far true, and how far false."[8] And Slope's reflections on the superiority of "spiritual" over "temporal" modalities of power are no less pertinent to the novelist than to the priest whose pastorate the novelist appears in any case to have largely taken over: "The temporal king, judge, or gaoler can work but on the body. The spiritual master, if he have the necessary gifts and can duly use them, has a wider field of empire. He works upon the soul. If he can make himself be believed, he can be all powerful over those who listen" (27). From this perspective, all that distinguishes Slope's ambition from Trollope's practice—though it quite suffices to scapegoat the chaplain as a monster of intolerance—is the end to which pastoral power is solicited. Inasmuch as Slope aims to impose "but one opinion" on the diocese, such knowledge of differences as he is intent on acquiring would support a program of repressing them. Repression, however, is just what Trollope's nice account of the number, degree, and extent of his characters' weaknesses stops short of inviting. His tolerance follows fascism up to the point of marshaling the data for a case that, departing from fascism, it never prosecutes. Instead, it dissipates its findings by assimilating individual delinquencies to the general ways of humankind: "Which of us has not . . . ?" We would call this generosity, as many have done, if it did not always underline how

8. Ibid.

much was owing to it—or if, far from effacing the normative grid that determines delinquencies, it did not extend the grid all the way to "us" and our own self-perception. Thus, if the easygoing Trollope foregoes some of his customary aplomb in presenting Slope, he needs to surrender almost as much when it comes to introducing the Stanhopes, who represent an opposite, but complementary, threat to tolerance. Whereas Slope refuses to accept differences, the Stanhopes tend not even to recognize them, mainly or altogether ignoring the value discriminations in which tolerance finds its footing. Of course, what Trollope rebukes most sharply in this clerical family is the want of religious principle. The father manifests no belief in the Church he laxly serves; the daughters are the one "a pure freethinker" (66) and the other a devotee of "latitudinarian philosophy" (70); and the son flirts indifferently with Jesuits and Jews. But to the extent that "religion" merely names the transcendent status conferred on community bonding and on "becoming" norms of conduct, it is the social atheism of the Stanhopes that is the real target of censure. Though "they bore and forebore" (64), there is no basis in conviction, value, or norm from which forebearance proceeds. Bertie's indifference to religion, for example, extends pointedly to value-criteria of any kind, whether moral ("no virtue could charm him, no vice shock him"), social ("he had no respect for rank, and no aversion to those below him"), economic (the "prudence" of the scheme to catch Eleanor is "antagonistic to his feelings"), or even aesthetic (his art gravitates naturally toward the carnivalesque genre of caricature). "All people were nearly alike to him. He was above, or rather below, all prejudices" (73–74). What will finally require the Stanhopes' departure from Barchester (only shortly before Slope's) is precisely their inferiority to those "prejudices" which tolerance not only works by invoking but also, in the process, works to invoke.

If tolerance is thus a mode of normalization, normalization is equally a mode of tolerance. For the norms "secreted" in Trollope's narration (as gradually as secretions, as inferentially as secrets) are not concerned to determine behavior as such, which is on the contrary avidly gathered under them in all its variety. What these norms do determine, however, is our consciousness of behavior, and whatever diversity appears in the characters' lives never exceeds the ordinating power of the far more consistent perspective from which they are viewed. Normalization necessarily tolerates the way we live now, but only to call vigilantly to mind the way we ought to. The current notion of a "dark" Trollope—insofar as it is anything more than a marketing ploy—only measures the depth of his assumption that, for basic purposes of socialization, a deontology is enough: the standards of a normalizing narration need not always or even often be incarnate in the narrative, since "deviant" data, too, pay tribute to the norm that saturates them with its values. Yet it is no less clear that any attempt to explicate these standards as so many injunctions (on the model of a legal code or an etiquette manual) must belie their textual status. Normalization in Trollope never issues from a single or constant source, but is rather floated across the text on a number of unlike supports, with none of which is it actually identified. It speaks variously in the voice of the novelist, of characters, of the fictive reader (not to mention the "dual voice" of *style indirect libre*), and in a mode that may be hyperbolic, direct, understated, or ironic. These multiple and overlapping instances contest, qualify, and reinforce one another—rather in the manner of moderate schism—to promote norms whose vagueness of origin and even of content helps make them ubiquitous. What emerges from the process are not commandments, but problem areas, in which behaviors are not so much judged as worried.

When Eleanor boxes Slope's ears, for example, it is an occasion for considerable fretting on the part of narrator and narratee alike. The well-bred reader, the writer fears, will now throw down the book in disgust. "She is a hoyden, one will say. At any rate she is not a lady, another will exclaim. I have suspected her all through, a third will declare; she has no idea of the dignity of a matron; or of the peculiar propriety which her position demands." The writer himself holds to a more scrupulous and nuanced view of the matter: Eleanor "cannot altogether be defended; and yet it may be averred that she is not a hoyden." And yet again, "It were to be wished devoutly that she had not struck Mr. Slope on the face. In doing so she derogated from her dignity and committed herself." Still, as far as Slope is concerned, "the slap on the face that he got from Eleanor was . . . the fittest rebuke which could have been administered to him." "But nevertheless, she should not have raised her hand against the man. Ladies' hands, so soft, so sweet, so delicious to the touch, so grateful to the eye, so gracious in their gentle doings, were not made to belabour men's faces" (389–90). All this, moreover, remains for real readers to fret about further. Both parties to the narrative contract (one will say) agree that a sin against propriety has been committed: the only question is whether the sin be mortal or venial, and it is easily answered, since Eleanor's own sense of guilt confirms the writer's defense of her against the well-bred reader's exaggerations. Yet (another will rejoin) Slope's rebuke is so clearly deserved that Trollope's treatment of the episode, including his remarks on ladies' hands, must be meant ironically to win our applause for Eleanor's spunk. What grounds, however, are there for speaking of irony (a third will demur) when Eleanor's "independence" is qualified here and elsewhere as "a feeling dangerous for a young woman" (390)? *E così via*—the game is afoot. On the one hand, the incident (ironic, or not, or ironic and not) is ordained to be the locus of a certain, albeit minor, controversy. On the other, even if its "moral" were agreed to be that "ladies' hands . . . were not made to belabour men's faces," this would be much less important than the prior consensus implied in the fuss that has put the incident under intensive moral consideration in the first place. That fuss, of course, situates Eleanor's gesture within a familiar code of propriety, on the

Victorian-bourgeois horizon of class and gender expectations. Whatever we may think of her gesture, in order to think of it at all we cannot but keep in mind the code that inscribes it. And whatever we may think of this code—at least so long as we are readers of *Barchester Towers*—we can scarcely avoid thinking in it. Even when we subject it to various refinements and perversions, we remain caught in the closure of its own terms, which are thus perpetuated and revitalized. What Trollope describes in *Barchester Towers* is a world whose specific social problems are part of the general social solution that requires just such agitation to secure its consistency. What Trollope may be said to practice in *Barchester Towers* is a similarly socializing art of controversy, an art whose very interrogation of "problematic" behavior answers the need—where a police force is hardly feasible—for a common ground.

V

Since this common ground always doubles for a specific social organization, it is far from arbitrary which kinds or aspects of behavior are brought into question to support it. In this light, we might pursue the question of a woman's position—or rather the larger question of sexual difference that encompasses it. At its simplest (say, in the Grantly menage), sexual difference in *Barchester Towers* is posed as a variant of moderate schism, in which each uniquely determined sex makes love and war with the other, and both sexes cooperate accordingly to produce and reproduce the social. The asymmetries of power that the practice of moderate schism rehearses would here take the accumulated form of "patriarchy." Yet on the face of it, this basic structure is plagued with a major complication: the lines in the battle of the sexes are so frequently crossed (by virile females, by effeminate males) that Miss Thorne is not altogether implausible when she declares that "now-a-days the gentlemen were all women, and the ladies all men" (335). In fact, however, the phenomena she observes are such regular effects of the structure that they scarcely render it unintelligible. The Anglican Church, in contrast to either Roman Catholicism (whose priests are forbidden to marry) or early Methodism (where women were allowed to preach), provides Trollope with a lucid institutional model of patriarchy and its intrinsic discontents. Only men may occupy, solicit, and assign positions of power in this church; at the same time, the men so entitled are all but made to share their lives with women, who are thus debarred from power even as they apparently need to be distributed throughout its organization. Part of women's patriarchal mission, this suggests, is to absorb a just dose of the homosocial affect required between men to maintain the institution: not so much of it, of course, that none is left over for its purpose, but neither so little of it that—as homosexuality, for instance—it unprofitably exceeds its function.[9] Patriarchal organization thus incurs two impediments to its own smooth functioning: the "strong" woman (who would be more than the socializing medium in the exchange and transfer of power between men) and the "weak" man (who, falling under the spell of such a woman, would imperil male bonding; or who, alternatively, fixated on male bonding per se, would endanger its social vocation).

In a liberal patriarchy, these figures must be tolerated; they would in any case be hard to eliminate from a social order that systematically produces them. But they are tolerated only insofar as they are immobilized as perennial "problem-types," sites of a critical concern so habitual that it can afford to be relaxed and amused. The gentleman-woman and the lady-man

9. Eve Kosofsky Sedgwick would frankly call this homosocial affect *desire*, and thus insist on "the potential unbrokenness of a continuum between homosocial and homosexual—a continuum whose visibility, for men, in our society, is radically disrupted" (*Between Men: English Literature and Male Homosocial Desire* [New York: Columbia University Press, 1985], pp. 1–2).

in Trollope are not symptoms of a patriarchy in disarray; nor do they imply a critique of the established gender code or an invitation to transsexual experimentation. Rather, they are the raw material for that massive stereotyping which, turning them into reminders of the gender norms they seem to transgress, makes radical transgression impossible. The virago, the siren, the "independent" woman (Mrs. Proudie, Signora Neroni, Eleanor) are roles in the patriarchal image-repertory as stock as the ladies' man, the henpecked husband, the feckless father (Slope, Bishop Proudie, Harding). Trollope develops these roles with an easy confidence—as though it were not an emergency measure, but the routine task of liberal patriarchy to contain therein the dynamic that might otherwise issue in female "feminism" and male "homosexuality." In other words, if such terms are "anachronistic" applied to Trollope, it is because he is part of his culture's general effort to make them so. (*Encore un effort*: the terms remain utopian even in our day, when the groups they designate must still confront the difficulty of determining what their "own" discourse might be.)

It is easy to see, for example, that a standard of the "feminine" pervades the presentation of Mrs. Proudie, the signora, and Eleanor, measuring whether, in what way, and to what degree they do or do not conform to it. The feminine, moreover, is not just an external norm, imposed on female characters like an oppression by a narration in which they necessarily have no say, or by other, male characters whose opinions may be supposed to be biased. It is also psychologically anchored in woman herself, at a point—all the more fitting if it is her "weak point"—where the "nature" she may try to avert returns to claim its rights and establish her truth. Thus, in her compassion for Mrs. Quiverful, Mrs. Proudie has "proved herself a woman" (241), and thereby for once wins our sympathy. The signora, Trollope's chastened version of the self-sacrificing prostitute of continental literature, generously withdraws from competition "to give up Mr. Arabin to the woman whom he loved" (375)—as though she had perfectly absorbed from her reading of French novels the lesson of Balzac, Dumas, and Sue, that the only good "girl" is the one who knows she is bad. She condemns herself in the same *bien-pensant* terms her life only seems given over to mocking: "What would I not give to be loved by such a man [as Arabin]," she tells Eleanor, "that is, if I were an object fit for any man to love!" (446). And Eleanor herself—"the widow Bold"—comes to desire nothing better than to lose that appellation (which her baby-worship has never rendered very convincing): "She would give up the heavy burden of independence, and once more assume the position of a woman, and the duties of a trusting and loving wife" (478).

Yet perhaps these characters submit most deeply to patriarchy not when they acknowledge their latent femininity, but when they succeed in repressing it. For their only alternative to a femininity thoroughly circumscribed by its patriarchal determination seems to be a perverse identification with an oppressive masculinity equally and likewise circumscribed. Eleanor's decision to surrender her independence indicates, besides the extent to which she has been bought off, her understandable distaste for the world to which her independence has introduced her ("My name," she tells Arabin, "should never have been mixed up in your hostilities" [285]). Unlike her, of course, Mrs. Proudie embraces domination without scruple. Though the bishop may not be able to command her affections, they are altogether captivated by the male power game that she merely wants to play too. Her "petticoat government" only rather more successfully realizes the tyrannical fantasies of those who govern in trousers. Her ideal is as authoritarian as Slope's, and her character as macho as Dr. Grantly's. In a different register, the signora's siren act is also a willing assumption of the male power fantasies that have been literally pounded into her. Made by male violence to figure as the castrated woman ("maimed, lame, and . . . married" [253]), she returns the favor by playing to the hilt the role's other face: the castrating woman, with "dreadful eyes to look at" (69), and who, though lacking a leg, "is as full of mischief as tho' she had ten" (359). She positively cultivates the phallocentrism that determines her as the incomplete object of unfulfilled desire, as though she were cynically past caring that this rendered her the incomplete subject of unfulfilled desire as well. The "good-natured act" that "for once in her life" she resolves to perform (375) ought not to come as a surprise. Smitten once by a man's power, she is well prepared to be smitten a second time by a man's truth— by "the very spirit of truth" in which Arabin speaks to her (374). If the "feminist" is an impossible figure in *Barchester Towers*, it is because she has always already been seduced, by her own femininity, or—what comes to the same—by the male power and truth that determine it.

The trouble with a woman like Eleanor who boxes a man's ears is that, we recall, "she cannot altogether be defended." But if, having derogated from a proper feminine role, she cannot be defended, she must also have diminished a proper masculine role, which includes taking up her defense. The norm of femininity thus always presupposes a norm of masculinity, and the male characters in *Barchester Towers* are held to as stringent a gender ideal as the female. Slope's "broad chest and wide shoulders" (25), for instance, do not square the rap he takes for being (in the full ambiguity of the phrase) a ladies' man. Serenading "the softer sex" with "a soft word" and "that low silky whisper which he had always specially prepared for feminine ears" (24, 56), he becomes so soft himself that when "the priestly charmer" (28) meets his match in another, "Italianised charmer" (122), he cannot manfully defend against her wiles, but yields to passion in the best feminine style. The implied accusation of effeminacy is not far removed from the charge of "latent homosexuality" that it will become a tradition to lay at the door of the Don Juan. And what better partner with whom to arraign Slope on these grounds than the emasculated bishop, "the little man" (125) so diminutive that Dr. Grantly, if he liked, might pat him on the head (486)?

[The bishop's] little idea of using Mr. Slope as a counterpoise to his wife had well nigh evaporated. He had all but acknowledged the futility of the scheme. If indeed he could have slept in his chaplain's bed-room instead of his wife's, there might have been something in it. But——. (304)

If the "feminist" needs to be seduced, the "homosexual" needs to be abandoned—to the derision of Trollope's joke, and worse, to the impossibility of its "But——." The comfortable, clubby wit is just what is required, since it is the comfort of the club that might otherwise have been at stake. The euphoric moment in the normative experience of homosocial patriarchy comes not simply when "the ivy has found its tower" (477), and Eleanor accepted Arabin, but after Arabin has communicated the news to another man. "It's just as I would have it," says Grantly, holding Arabin "fast by the hand."

And as he finished speaking, a tear might have been observed in each of the doctor's eyes.

Mr. Arabin warmly returned the archdeacon's grasp, but he said little. His heart was too full for speaking, and he could not express the gratitude which he felt. Dr. Grantly understood him as well as though he had spoken for an hour.

"And mind, Arabin," said he, "no one but myself shall tie the knot." (487)

The "fast" hand holding, the unfallen tears, the tacit expression of gratitude—all such details indulge the affect of male bonding even as they overcome the femininity with which it must never be confused—or at least not until the bonding subjects, like the odd, loving couple formed by Harding and Bishop Grantly, are old enough to have already performed their social functions.

VI

When I read Trollope, it is all I can do not to be bored. All I can do, because Trollope always seems a little bored himself. What produces this impression is his habitual manner of making the stuff of his fiction matter of course, of dressing it in an ever-familiar uniform. "A morning party is a bore" (401). We may not have known this before, but if we know it now, we know it too well: in the mode, not of an insight owing to the novelist's penetration, but of a truism that he merely passes along. From the boredom of a world whose phenomena are universally sedated in the routinized perception of them "as usual" derives the comfort that Trollope is known to administer. But boredom, as the example of pornography perhaps best illustrates, overtakes not what is intrinsically dull, but what is "interesting" to excess. Far from the simple reflex-response to banality, boredom hysterically converts into yawning affectlessness what would otherwise be outright panic. When I read Trollope—when, in other words, the individual subject reads the generality that abolishes him—it is all I can do to refuse my impending boredom: to convert it back into the anxiety that it is meant to bind, to insist on the shock that it is the attempt to meet and parry. And should one recognize Trollope for the proper name of a cultural strategy that is still "boring" us, boring through us (though the Novel is no longer the primary site or instrument of the drill), the shock would only widen.[10]

10. Paul de Man would have been the last to claim that puns are personal property, but that what painfully wearies may also no less painfully pierce was suggested to me by a remark he once made on Baudelairean ennui.

FIVE

Cage aux folles: Sensation and Gender in Wilkie Collins's *The Woman in White*

I

Nothing "boring" about the Victorian sensation novel: the excitement that seizes us here is as direct as the "fight-or-flight" physiology that renders our reading bodies, neither fighting nor fleeing, theaters of neurasthenia. The genre offers us one of the first instances of modern literature to address itself primarily to the sympathetic nervous system, where it grounds its characteristic adrenalin effects: accelerated heart rate and respiration, increased blood pressure, the pallor resulting from vasoconstriction, and so on. It is not, of course, the last, and no less current than the phenomenon is the contradictory manner in which, following in the Victorians' footsteps, we continue to acknowledge it.[1] On the one hand, a vulgar salesmanship unblinkingly identifies hyperventilation with aesthetic value, as though art now had no other aim or justification than its successful ability to rattle what the French would call, with anatomical precision, our *cage*. That the body is compelled to automatism, that the rhythm of reading is frankly addictive— such dreary evidence of involuntary servitude is routinely marshaled in ads and on back covers to promote entertainments

1. A valuable survey of Victorian responses to sensation fiction may be found in Elizabeth K. Helsinger, Robin Lauterbach Sheets, and William Veeder, *The Woman Question: Society and Literature in Britain and America, 1837–1883*, 3 vols. (New York: Garland, 1983), 3:122–44.

whose Pavlovian expertise has become more than sufficient recommendation. On the other hand, an overnice literary criticism wishfully reassures us that these domineering texts, whose power is literally proved upon our pulses, are beneath notice. By a kind of Cartesian censorship, in which pulp-as-flesh gets equated with pulp-as-trash, the emphatic physicality of thrills in such literature allows us to hold them cheap. Accordingly, the sensation novel is relegated to the margins of the canon of approved genres, and on the infrequent occasions when it is seriously discussed, "sensation"—the modern nervousness that is as fundamental to this genre as its name—is the first thing to be dropped from the discussion.[2] What neither view of sensation fiction questions—what both views, it might be argued, become strategies for not questioning—is the natural immediacy of sensation itself. The celebration of sensation (as a physical experience to be enjoyed for its own sake) merely *receives* it; the censure of sensation (granting to it the obviousness of something about which there is nothing to say) refuses to *read* it. In either case, sensation is felt to occupy a natural site entirely outside meaning, as though in the breathless body signification expired.

To be sure, the silence that falls over the question of sensation seems first enjoined by the sensation novel itself, which is obsessed with the project's finding meaning—of staging the suspense of its appearance—in everything except the sensations that the project's unfolding excites in us. Yet in principle the sensation novel must always at least imply a reading of these sensations, for the simple reason that it can mobilize the sym-

---

2. The omission is well exemplified in a recent article by Patrick Brantlinger entitled "What Is 'Sensational' About the Sensation Novel?" *Nineteenth-Century Fiction* 37 (June 1982): 1–28. Having posed the crucial question, the author elides its most obvious answer—namely, the somatic experience of sensation itself—by at once proceeding to considerations of "content" (murder, adultery, bigamy) and generic "mixture" (domestic realism, Gothic romance, and so on).

pathetic nervous system only by giving it something to sympathize with. In order to make us nervous, nervousness must first be represented: in situations of character and plot that, both in themselves and in the larger cultural allusions they carry, make the operation of our own nerves significant in particular ways. The fiction elaborates a fantasmatics of sensation in which our reading bodies take their place from the start, and of which our physiological responses thus become the hysterical acting out. To speak of hysteria here, of course, is also to recall the assumption that always camouflages it—that what the body suffers, the mind needn't think. "So far as my own sensations were concerned, I can hardly say that I thought at all."[3] The efficacy of psychosomatisms as "defenses" presupposes a rigorously enforced separation in the subject between *psyche* and *soma*, and hysteria successfully breeches the body's autonomy only when this autonomy is felt to remain intact. Reading the sensation novel, our hystericized bodies "naturalize" the meanings in which the narrative implicates them, but in doing so they also nullify these meanings. Incarnate in the body, the latter no longer seem part of a cultural, historical process of signification but instead dissolve into an inarticulable, merely palpable self-evidence. Thus, if every sensation novel necessarily provides an interpretation of the sensations to which it gives rise in its readers, the immediacy of these sensations can also be counted on to *disown* such an interpretation. It may even be that the nonrecognition that thus obtains between our sensations and their narrative thematization allows the sensation novel to "say" certain things for which our culture—at least at its popular levels—has yet to develop another language.

Wilkie Collins's *The Woman in White* (1860)—of all sensation novels the best known, and considered the best—seems at

---

3. Wilkie Collins, *The Woman in White*, ed. Julian Symons (Harmondsworth: Penguin, 1974), p. 47. Subsequent references to the novel are to this edition and are cited parenthetically in the text by page number.

any rate an exemplary text for making this case. For what "happens" in this novel becomes fully clear and coherent only, I think, when one takes into account the novel's implicit reading of its own (still quite "effective") performative dimension and thus restores sensation to its textual and cultural mediations. For the reason given above, the attempt to do so must be prepared to seem rather "forced"—as unprovable as a connotation and as improbable as a latency—but it is worth undertaking for more than a better understanding of this particular text. The ideological valences with which sensation characteristically combines in the novel do not of course absolutely transcend the second half of the Victorian period in which they are elaborated—as though the social significance of nervousness (itself a historical construct) were fixed once for all; but neither are they restricted to this period. Collins's novel continues to be not just thoroughly readable but eminently "writable" as well. If it is still capable of moving readers to the edge of their seats (and how sharp a sense of this edge may be is suggested when one character starts from his own seat "as if a spike had grown up from the ground through the bottom of [his] chair" [41]), this is because its particular staging of nervousness remains cognate with that of many of our own thrillers, printed or filmed. It thus offers a pertinent, if not exhaustive, demonstration of the value, meaning, and use that modern culture—which in this respect has by no means broken radically with Victorian culture—finds in the nervous state.

Without exception, such a state affects all the novel's principal characters, who are variously startled, affrighted, unsettled, chilled, agitated, flurried. All sooner or later inhabit the "sensationalized" body where the blood curdles, the heart beats violently, the breath comes short and thick, the flesh creeps, the cheeks lose their color. No one knows what is the matter with Mr. Fairlie, but "we all say it's on the nerves" (61), and in widely different ways his niece Laura is "rather nervous and sensitive" (63). The "nervous sensitiveness" (127) of her double and half-sister Anne Catherick, the Woman in White, issues in the aneurism that causes her death. Characters who are not constitutionally nervous become circumstantially so, in the unnerving course of events. Unsettled by the mystery surrounding Anne, fearful that Laura may be implicated in it, suspecting that he is himself being watched, Walter Hartright develops a "nervous contraction" about his lips and eyes (178), which he appears to have caught from Laura herself, whose "sweet, sensitive lips are subject to a slight nervous contraction" (75). At first "perfect self-possession" (209), Sir Percival Glyde degenerates after his marriage to Laura into "an unsettled, excitable manner . . . a kind of panic or frenzy of mind" (417). And Marian Halcombe, Laura's other half-sister, has already lost the "easy inborn confidence in herself and her position" (60) that initially characterized her by the time of the first anxious and "sadly distrustful" extract (184) from her diary. In the course of keeping that diary, of gathering the increasingly less equivocal evidence of a "plot" against Laura, she literally writes herself into a fever. It is a measure of Count Fosco's control over these characters that he is said to be "born without nerves" (376), though his "eternal cigarettes" (252) attest that even here nervousness is not so much missing as mastered, and mastered only insofar as its symptoms are masked in the banal practices of civilized society.

Nervousness seems the necessary "condition" in the novel for perceiving its real plot and for participating in it as more than a pawn. The condition is not quite sufficient, as the case of the willfully ignorant Mr. Fairlie shows, but otherwise those without the capacity to become nervous also lack the capacity to interpret events, or even to see that events require interpreting. The servants, for instance, also called (more accurately) "persons born without nerves" (69), are uniformly oblivious to what is or might be going on: the "unutterably tranquil" governess Mrs. Vesey (72), the maid who "in a state of cheerful stupidity" grins at the sight of Mrs. Catherick's wounded dog (229), the housekeeper Mrs. Michelson, whose Christian piety prevents her from advancing "opinions" (381). It is not exactly that the novel uses nervousness to mark middle-class status, since the trait fails to characterize the "sanguine constitution" of Mr. Gilmore, the family lawyer, who "philosophically" walks off his "uneasiness" about Laura's marriage (159) [Rather the novel makes nervousness a metonymy for reading, its cause or effect.] No reader can identify with unruffled characters like Gilmore or Mrs. Michelson, even when they narrate parts of the story, because every reader is by definition committed to a hermeneutic project that neither of these characters finds necessary or desirable. Instead we identify with nerve-racked figures like Walter and Marian who carry forward the activity of our own deciphering. We identify even with Anne Catherick in her "nervous dread" (134), though she is never capable of articulating its object, because that dread holds at least the promise of the story we will read. Nervousness is our justification in the novel, as Mrs. Michelson's faith is hers, insofar as it validates the attempt to read, to uncover the grounds for *being* nervous.

The association of nervousness with reading is complicated—not to say troubled—by its coincident, no less insistent or regular association with femininity. However general a phenomenon, nervousness is always gendered in the novel as, like Laura's headache symptom, an "essentially feminine malady" (59). Of the novel's three characters who seem "born" nervous, two are women (Anne and Laura) and the third, Mr. Fairlie, an effeminate. "I am nothing," the latter pronounces himself, "but a bundle of nerves dressed up to look like a man" (370). No one, however, is much convinced by the drag, and Walter's first impression—"He had a frail, languid-fretful, over-refined look—something singularly and unpleasantly delicate in its association with a man" (66)—never stands in need of correction. Even in the less fey male characters, nervousness remains a signifier of femininity. At best it declares Walter still "unformed," and Sir Percival's imposture—that he is not, so to speak, the man he is pretending to be—is already in a manner disclosed when Mrs. Michelson observes that "he seemed to be almost as nervous and fluttered . . . as his lady herself" (403). Fosco too, Marian informs us, "is as nervously sensitive as the weakest of us [women]. He starts at chance noises as inveterately as Laura herself" (242).

The novel's "primal scene," which it obsessively repeats and remembers ("Anne Catherick again!") as though this were the trauma it needed to work through, rehearses the "origins" of male nervousness in female contagion—strictly, in the woman's touch. When Anne Catherick, in flight from the asylum where she has been shut away, "lightly and suddenly" lays her hand on Walter Hartright's shoulder, it brings "every drop of blood in [his] body . . . to a stop" (47). Released from—and with—the Woman, nervousness touches and enters the Man: Anne's nervous gesture is at once sympathetically "caught" in Walter's nervous response to it. Attempting to recover himself, Walter tightens his fingers round "the handle of [his] stick," as if the touch—"from behind [him]" (47)—were a violation requiring violent counteraction, and what was violated were a gender identification that needed to be reaffirmed. Yet Anne Catherick impinges on him again: "The loneliness and helplessness of the woman touched me" (49). His formulation hopefully denies what is happening to him—Anne's weak femininity is supposed to evince *a contrario* his strong masculinity—but the denial seems only to produce further evidence of the gender slippage it means to arrest. Even in his classic gallantry, Walter somehow feels insufficiently manly, "immature": "The natural impulse to assist her and spare her got the better of the judgment, the caution, the worldly tact, which an older, wiser, and colder man might have summoned to help him in this strange emergency" (49). He is even "distressed by an uneasy sense of having done wrong" (54), of having betrayed his sex: "What had I done? Assisted the victim of the most horrible of all false imprisonments to escape; or cast loose on the wide world of

London an unfortunate creature, whose actions it was my duty, and every man's duty, mercifully to control?" (55). Walter's protection has in fact suspended the control that is "every man's duty" to exercise over the activity of the neuropathic woman. Thanks to his help, Anne eludes a manifold of male guardians: the turnpike man at the entry gate of the city; the two men from the asylum including its director; the policeman who, significantly, is assumed to be at their disposal; and even Walter himself, who puts her into a cab, destination unknown. "A dangerous woman to be at large" (177): the female trouble first transmitted to Walter will extend throughout the thick ramifications of plot to excite sympathetic vibrations in Laura and Marian, and in Sir Percival and even Fosco as well. And not just in them. "The reader's nerves are affected like the hero's," writes Mrs. Oliphant in a contemporary review of the novel; in what I have called the novel's primal scene, this means that "the silent woman lays her hand upon our shoulder as well as upon that of Mr. Walter Hartright."[4] As the first of the novel's sensation effects *on us*, the scene thus fictionalizes the beginning of our physiological experience of the sensation novel as such. Our first sensation coincides with—is positively triggered by—the novel's originary account of sensation. Fantasmatically, then, we "catch" sensation from the neuropathic body of the Woman who, no longer confined or controlled in an asylum, is free to make our bodies resonate with—like—hers.

Every reader is consequently implied to be a version or extension of the Woman in White, a fact that entails particularly interesting consequences when the reader is—as the text explicitly assumes he is—male.[5] This reader willy-nilly falls vic-

4. Mrs. [Margaret] Oliphant, "Sensation Novels," *Blackwood's Magazine* 91 (May 1862), reprinted in Norman Page, ed., *Wilkie Collins: The Critical Heritage* (London: Routledge and Kegan Paul, 1974), pp. 118–19.
5. For example, Walter, the master narrator who solicits the others' narratives and organizes them into a whole, speaks of Laura to the reader: "Think of her as you thought of the first woman who quickened the

tim to a hysteria in which what is acted out (desired, repressed) is an essentially female "sensation." His excitements come from—become—her nervous excitability; his rib cage, arithmetically Adam's, houses a woman's quickened respiration, and his heart beats to her skittish rhythm; even his pallor (which of course he cannot see) is mirrored back to him only as hers, the Woman in White's. This reader thus lends himself to elaborating a fantasy of *anima muliebris in corpore virili inclusa*—or as we might appropriately translate here, "a woman's breath caught in a man's body." The usual rendering, of course, is "a woman's soul trapped . . . ," and it will be recognized as nineteenth-century sexology's classic formulation (coined by Karl Ulrichs in the 1860s) for male homosexuality.[6] I cite it not

---

pulses within you" (76). The same identification is also sustained implicitly, as in the equation between the reader and a judge (33). As Veeder documents, Victorian discussion emphasized the dangers that sensation fiction posed to the *female* reader, as though a perilous natural affinity linked sensation to her all-too-excitable body. Positing a male reader, *The Woman in White* has the advantage of allowing us to show what ulteriorly determined the Victorian concern with protecting "the woman" from "her" own susceptibilities.

6. See Jeffrey Weeks, *Coming Out: Homosexual Politics in Britain, From the Nineteenth Century to the Present* (London: Quartet Books, 1977), pp. 26–27. It does not seem altogether a historical "irony" that this intrinsically ambiguous notion—so useful to the apologists for homosexuality in the late nineteenth and early twentieth centuries—should popularly survive today as part of the mythological rationale for "vulgar" homophobia, which draws on an equally vulgar misogyny to oppress gay men. It may also be pertinent here to note that turn-of-the-century sexology almost universally agreed on "a marked tendency to nervous development in the [homosexual] subject, not infrequently associated with nervous maladies" (Edward Carpenter, *The Intermediate Sex* [1908], in *Selected Writings* [London: Gay Men's Press, 1984], 1:209). Criticizing Krafft-Ebing for continuing to link homosexuality with "'an hereditary neuropathic or psychopathic tendency'—*neuro(psycho)-pathische Belastung*," Carpenter remarks that "there are few people in modern life, perhaps none, who could be pronounced absolutely free from such a *Belastung*!" (210). His

just to anticipate the homosexual component given to readerly sensation by the novel, but also, letting the phrase resonate beyond Ulrichs's intentions, to situate this component among the others that determine its context. [For if what essentially characterizes male homosexuality in this way of putting it is the woman-in-the-man, and if this "woman" is *inclusa*, incarcerated or shut up, her freedoms abridged accordingly, then homosexuality would be by its very nature homophobic: imprisoned in a carceral problematic that does little more than channel into the homosexual's "ontology" the social and legal sanctions that might otherwise be imposed on him.] Meant to win a certain intermediate space for homosexuals, Ulrichs's formulation in fact ultimately colludes with the prison or closet drama—of keeping the "woman" well put away—that it would relegate to the unenlightened past. And homosexuals' souls are not the only ones to be imprisoned in male bodies; Ulrichs's phrase does perhaps far better as a general description of the condition of nineteenth-century women, whose "spirit" (whether understood as intellect, integrity, or sexuality) is massively interned in male corporations, constitutions, contexts. His metaphor thus may be seen to link or fuse (1) a particular fantasy about male homosexuality; (2) a homophobic defense against that fantasy; and (3) the male oppression of women that, among other things, extends that defense. All three meanings bear pointedly on Collins's novel, which is profoundly about enclosing and secluding the woman in male "bodies," among them institutions like marriage and mad-

---

ostensible point—that nervous disorders are far too widespread in modern life to be the distinctive mark of homosexuals, whose "neuropathic tendency" would bespeak rather a social than a metaphysical fatality— is still (mutatis mutandis) worth making. Yet in a discursive formation that insistently yokes male homosexuality and neuropathology (in the femininity common to both), his observation might also be taken to conclude that this homosexuality *too* (if principally in its reactive, homophobic form) is a general modern phenomenon.

houses. And the sequestration of the woman takes for its object not just women, who need to be put away in safe places or asylums, but men as well, who must monitor and master what is fantasized as the "woman inside" them.

II

Like *The Moonstone*, *The Woman in White* accords itself the status of a quasi-legal document.

If the machinery of the Law could be depended on to fathom every case of suspicion, and to conduct every process of inquiry, with moderate assistance only from the lubricating influences of oil of gold, the events which fill these pages might have claimed their share of the public attention in a Court of Justice. But the Law is still, in certain inevitable cases, the pre-engaged servant of the long purse; and the story is left to be told, for the first time, in this place. As the Judge might once have heard it, so the Reader shall hear it now. . . . Thus, the story here presented will be told by more than one pen, as the story of an offence against the laws is told in Court by more than one witness—with the same object, in both cases, to present the truth always in its most direct and most intelligible aspect. (33)

The organizational device is a curious one, since nothing in the story ever appears to motivate it. Why and for whom does this story need to be thus told? At the end of the novel—after which Walter Hartright presumably gathers his narratives together— neither legal action nor even a paralegal hearing seems in the least required. And it is of course pure mystification to preface a mystery story with a claim to be presenting the truth "always in its most direct and most intelligible aspect." But the obvious gimmickry of the device offers only the crudest evidence of the limited pertinence of the legal model that the text here invokes. On the face of it, despite its conventionally bitter references to oil of gold and the long purse, the text is eager to retain the law—the juridical model of an inquest—for its own narrative. It simply proposes to extend this model to a case that it wouldn't ordinarily cover. The explicit ideal thus served would be a law that fathomed every case of suspicion and conducted every process of inquiry. But what law has ever done this, or wanted to? Certainly not the English law, which like all non-totalitarian legal systems is on principle concerned to limit the matters that fall under its jurisdiction. The desire to extend the law as totally as the text utopically envisions—to *every* case of suspicion and *every* process of inquiry—would therefore supersede the legal model to which, the better not to alarm us, it nominally clings. For the project of such a desire makes sense only in a world where suspicion and inquiry have already become everyday practices, and whose affinities lie less with a given legal code or apparatus than with a vast, multifaceted network of inquests-without-end. Under the guise of a pedantic, legalistic organization, the novel in fact aligns itself with extra-, infra-, and supralegal modern discipline.

Not, of course, that *The Woman in White* represents the world of discipline in the manner of either *Bleak House* or *Barchester Towers*. Its most important relationship to this world, at any rate, does not come at the level of an "objective" portrayal, either of institutions (like Court of Chancery and the Detective Police in Dickens) or of less formal means of social control (like "moderate schism" and the norm in Trollope). It would be quite difficult to evolve a sociological understanding of Victorian asylums from Collins's novel, which, voiding a lively contemporary concern with the private madhouse, describes neither its structure nor the (medicinal? physical? psychological?) therapies that may or may not be practiced within it.[7] Anne never says, and Laura finds it too painfully confusing

---

7. See William Ll. Parry-Jones, *The Trade in Lunacy: A Study of Private Madhouses in England in the Eighteenth and Nineteenth Centuries* (Toronto: University of Toronto Press, 1972).

to recall, what goes on there. The asylum remains a very black "black box," the melodramatic site of "the most horrible of false imprisonments," where the sane middle class might mistakenly be sent. The asylum, in short, is available to representation mainly insofar as it has been *incorporated*: in Walter's "unsettled state" when he first learns that Anne is a fugitive from there, in Anne's nervous panic at the very word, in the difference between Laura's body before she enters the place and after she leaves, in the way we are invited to fill in the blank horror of what she cannot remember with the stuff of our own nightmares. What the example may be broadened to suggest is that the novel represents discipline mainly in terms of certain general isolated effects on the disciplinary *subject*, whose sensationalized body both dramatizes and facilitates his functioning as *the subject/object of continual supervision.*

These effects, together with the juridical metaphor under which they are first inscribed, are best pursued in the contradiction between the judge and the reader who is supposed to take his place. "As the Judge might once have heard [the story], so the Reader shall hear it now." The pronouncement, of course, confers on the latter role all the connotations of sobriety and even serenity attached to the former. That "wretches hang that jurymen may dine" will always give scandal to our Western mythology of justice, in which the judge—set above superstition, prejudice, "interest" of any kind—weighs the evidence with long and patient scruple before pronouncing sentence. Nothing, however, could be less judicial, or judicious, than the actual hermeneutic practice of the reader of this novel, whose technology of nervous stimulation—in many ways still the state of the art—has him repeatedly jumping to unproven conclusions, often literally jumping at them. Far from encouraging reflective calm, the novel aims to deliver "positive personal shocks of surprise and excitement" that so sensationalize the reader's body that he is scarcely able to reflect at all.[8] The novel's

8. Mrs. Oliphant, in Page, *Wilkie Collins*, p. 112.

only character with strictly judicial habits of mind is the lawyer Gilmore, who judges only to misjudge. Hearing Sir Percival's explanation of his dealings with Anne Catherick, he says: "My function was of the purely judicial kind. I was to weigh the explanation we had just heard . . . and to decide honestly whether the probabilities, on Sir Percival's own showing, were plainly with him, or plainly against him. My own conviction was that they were plainly with him" (155). Characters who rely on utterly unlegal standards of evidence like intuition, co-incidence, literary connotation get closer to what will eventually be revealed as the truth. In her first conversation with Walter, Anne Catherick nervously inquires about an unnamed baronet in Hampshire; Walter later learns that Laura is engaged to a baronet in Hampshire named Sir Percival Glyde. "Judging by the ordinary rules of evidence, I had not the shadow of a reason, thus far, for connecting Sir Percival Glyde with the suspicious words of inquiry that had been spoken to me by the woman in white. And yet, I did connect them" (101). Similarly, when after Sir Percival's explanation Gilmore wonders what excuse Laura can possibly have for changing her mind about him, Marian answers: "In the eyes of law and reason, Mr. Gilmore, no excuse, I dare say. If she still hesitates, and if I still hesitate, you must attribute our strange conduct, if you like, to caprice in both cases" (162). The competent reader, who does not weigh evidence so much as he simply assents to the ways in which it has been weighted, fully accepts the validity of such ungrounded connections and inexcusable hesitations: they validate, among other things, the sensations they make him feel. And this reader is capable of making what by the ordinary rules of evidence are comparably tenuous assumptions of his own. We can't know, just because Sir Percival's men are watching Somebody, and Walter may be being watched, that Walter is that Somebody, and yet we are convinced that we do know this. Or again, the loose seal on the letter that Marian recovers from the post-bag after she has seen Fosco hovering about it does not establish the fact that Fosco has opened and resealed her letter, but we take it firmly for granted none-theless. Our judgments are often informed by no better than the silliest folk wisdom. When Laura's pet greyhound shrinks from Sir Percival, Gilmore considers it "a trifle" (156), though Nina later jumps eagerly enough into his own lap: in the strange court of justice over which we preside, her discrimination is unimpeachable evidence. Yet neither adhering to or-dinary rules of evidence nor inhering in a decisive institutional context (except of course that provided by the conventions of this kind of novel), such "acts of judgment" are in fact only entitled to the considerably less authoritative status of *suspi-cions*, whose "uncertainty" in both these senses makes it easy to discredit them. Walter is the first to refer his hypotheses to their possible source in "delusion" and "monomania" (101, 105). Like the characters who figure him, the reader becomes—what a judge is never supposed to be—paranoid. From trifles and common coincidences, he suspiciously infers a complicated structure of persecution, an elaborately totalizing "plot."

What a judge is never supposed to be? Yet the most famous paranoid of modern times *was* a judge: the German jurist Dan-iel Paul Schreber, whose *Memoirs of My Nervous Illness* provided Freud's theory of paranoia with its major and most lurid ex-ample. Schreber's paranoia, we recall, was triggered precisely when, at Dresden, he entered on his duties as Senatspräsident. His case suggests that paranoia is "born" at the moment when the judge, without ceasing to be judge, has also become the accused, when he is both one and the other. It was, more than anything else, his homosexuality that put Schreber in this in-stitutionally untenable position, since the law he was expected to administer would certainly include, as Guy Hocquengham has pointed out, interdictions against homosexuality itself.[9] Schreber's delusion does nothing so much as elaborate the par-

9. Guy Hocquengham, *Homosexual Desire*, trans. Daniella Dangoor (Lon-don: Allison and Busby, 1978), pp. 42–43.

adoxical aspect of his actual situation as a judge who might well
have to judge (others like) himself. The Rays of God, he hal-
lucinates, having constituted his monstrosity (literally: by feminizing his constitution via the nerves), taunt him with it thus:
"So *this* sets up to have been a Senatspräsident, this person who
lets himself be f——d!"[10] In *The Woman in White*, another case
of feminization via the nerves, Mrs. Michelson's article of un-
suspecting faith—"Judge not that ye be not judged" (381)—
postulates an inevitable slippage between subject and object
whenever judgment is attempted. The slippage is in fact far
more likely to occur when judgment, no longer governed by an
institutional practice with established roles and rules of evidence, has devolved into mere suspicion. Unlike legal judgment, suspicion presupposes the reversibility of the direction
in which it passes. The novel abounds with suspicious characters, in the telling ambiguity of the phrase, for what Anne,
Walter, and Marian all suspect is that *they are themselves suspected.*
Why else would Anne be pursued, Walter watched, Marian's
correspondence opened? They are suspected, moreover, precisely *for being suspicious.* For Walter to notice that Anne's manner is "a little touched by suspicion" is already to suspect her,
as she instantly recognizes ("Why do you suspect me?" [48]).
Hence the urgency, as well as the futility, of the suspicious
character's obsessive desire *not to excite suspicion* (260, 275, 293,
311, 325), since the act of suspecting always already implies
the state of being suspect. The whole vertiginous game (in
which I suspect him of suspecting me of suspecting him) is
meant to ward off—but only by passing along—the violation
of privacy that it thus at once promotes and resists. In what
Roland Barthes would call the novel's symbolic code, this violation connotes the sexual attack whose possibility "haunts"

10. Quoted in Sigmund Freud, "Psycho-Analytic Notes on an Autobio-
graphical Account of Paranoia," in *The Standard Edition of the Complete
Works of Sigmund Freud*, ed. James Strachey, 24 vols. (London: Hogarth
Press and the Institute of Psycho-Analysis, 1953–74), 12:20.

the novel no less thoroughly than the virginal presence—insistent like a dare—of the Woman in White. What stands behind the vague fears of Anne and Walter during their first encounter; what subtends Mr. Fairlie's malicious greeting ("So glad to possess you at Limmeridge, Mr. Hartright" [66]); what Sir Percival sadistically fantasizes when he invites his wife to imagine her lover "with the marks of my horsewhip on his shoulders" (283); and what Fosco finally accomplishes when he reads Marian's *journal intime*—is virtual rape. We might consider what is implied or at stake in the fact that the head game of suspicion is always implicitly transcoded by the novel into the body game of rape.

Perhaps the most fundamental value that the Novel, as a cultural institution, may be said to uphold is privacy, the determination of an integral, autonomous, "secret" self. Novel reading takes for granted the existence of a space in which the reading subject remains safe from the surveillance, suspicion, reading, and rape of others. Yet this privacy is always specified as the freedom to read about characters who oversee, suspect, read, and rape one another. It is not just that, strictly private subjects, we read about violated, objectified subjects but that, in the very act of reading about them, we contribute largely to constituting them as such. We enjoy our privacy in the act of watching privacy being violated, in the act of watching that is already itself a violation of privacy. Our most intense identification with characters never blinds us to our ontological privilege over them: they will never be reading about *us*. It is built into the structure of the Novel that every reader must realize the definitive fantasy of the liberal subject, who imagines himself free from the surveillance that he nonetheless sees operating everywhere around him.

The sensation novel, however, submits this panoptic immunity to a crucial modification: it produces repeated and undeniable evidence—"on the nerves"—that we are perturbed by what we are watching. We remain unseen, of course, but not untouched: our bodies are rocked by the same "positive personal shocks" as the characters' are said to be. For us, these shocks have the ambivalent character of being both an untroubled pleasure (with a certain "male" adventurism we read the sensation novel in order to *have* them) and a less tame and more painful *jouissance* (with a certain "female" helplessness we often protest that we can't *bear* them, though we do when they keep on coming). [The specificity of the sensation novel in nineteenth-century fiction is that it renders the liberal subject the subject of a *body*, whose fear and desire of violation displaces, reworks, and exceeds his constitutive fantasy of intact privacy.] The themes that the liberal subject ordinarily defines himself against—by reading *about* them—are here inscribed into his reading body. Moreover, in *The Woman in White* this body is gendered: not only has its gender been *decided*, but also its gender identification is an active and determining *question*. The drama in which the novel writes its reader turns on the disjunction between his allegedly masculine gender and his effectively feminine gender identification (as a creature of "nerves"): with the result that his experience of sensation must include his panic at having the experience at all, of being in the position to have it. In this sense, the novel's initial assumption that its reader is male is precisely what cannot be assumed (or better, what stands most in need of "proof"), since his formal title—say, "a man"—is not or not yet a substantial entity—say, "a real man."

By far the most shocking moment in the reader's drama comes almost in the exact middle of the novel when the text of Marian's diary, lapsing into illegible fragments, abruptly yields to a postscript by the very character on whom its suspicions center. Not only has Count Fosco read Marian's "secret pages" (240), he lets her know it, and even returns them to her. In a fever that soon turns to typhus, Marian is in no condition even to take cognizance of this revelation, whose only immediate register is the reader's own body. Peter Brooks articulates our state of shock thus: "Our readerly intimacy with Marian is violated, our act of reading adulterated by profane eyes, made secondary to the villain's reading and indeed dependent on his permission."[11] It is not only, then, that Marian has been "raped," as both the Count's amorous flourish ("Admirable woman!" [258]) and her subsequent powerless rage against him are meant to suggest. We are "taken" too, taken by surprise, which is itself an overtaking. We are taken, moreover, from behind: from a place where, in the wings of the ostensible drama, the novelist disposes of a whole plot machinery whose existence—so long as it didn't oblige us by making creaking sounds (and here it is as "noiseless" as Fosco himself [242])—we never suspected. (We never suspected, though the novel has trained us to be nothing if not suspicious. Surprise—the recognition of what one "never suspected"—is precisely what the paranoid seeks to eliminate, but it is also what, in the event, he survives by reading as a frightening incentive: he can never be paranoid enough.) To being the object of violation here, however, there is an equally disturbing alternative: to identify with Fosco, with the novelistic agency of violation. For the Count's postscript only puts him in the position we already occupy. Having just finished reading Marian's diary ourselves, we are thus implicated in the sadism of his act, which even as it violates our readerly intimacy with Marian reveals that "intimacy" to be itself a violation. The ambivalent structure of readerly identification here thus condenses—as simultaneous but opposite renderings of the same powerful shock—homosexual panic and heterosexual violence.

This is the shock, however, that, having administered, the novel (like any good administration) will work to absorb. The shock in fact proves the point of transition between what the narrative will soothingly render as a *succession*: on one side, a passive, paranoid, homosexual feminization; on the other, an

11. Peter Brooks, *Reading for the Plot* (New York: Knopf, 1984), p. 169.

active, corroborative, heterosexual masculine protest. Marian
alerts us to this succession ("Our endurance must end, and our
resistance must begin" [321]), but only toward the end of her
narrative, since the moment of "resistance" will need to be effectively sponsored not just by a male agent but by an indefec-
tibly composed male discourse as well. The master narrator and
actor in the second half of the novel is therefore Walter: no
longer the immature Walter whose nerve-ridden opening narrative seemed—tonally, at any rate—merely continued in Marian's diary, but the Walter who has returned from his trials in
Central America "a changed man": "In the stern school of ex-
tremity and danger my will had learnt to be strong, my heart
to be resolute, my mind to rely on itself. I had gone out to fly
from my own future. I came back to face it, as a man should"
(427). Concomitantly, the helpless paranoia of the first half of
the novel now seeks *to prove itself*, as Walter aggressively attempts to "force a confession" from Sir Percival and Fosco "on
[his] own terms" (470). Shocks decline "dramatically" in both
frequency and intensity (our last sensation: its absence) as characters and readers alike come to get answers to the question that
sensation could never do more than merely pose of the event
occasioning it—namely, "What did it mean?" (99)[Foremost
on the novel's agenda in its second half is the dissolution of
sensation in the achievement of decided meaning] What the
narrative must most importantly get straight is, from this perspective, as much certain sexual and gender deviances as the
obscure tangles of plot in which they thrive. In short, the novel
needs to realize the normative requirements of the heterosexual
menage whose happy picture concludes it.

This conclusion, of course, marks the most banal moment
in the text, when the sensation novel becomes least distinguish-
able from any other kind of Victorian fiction.[Herein, one
might argue, lies the "morality" of sensation fiction, in its ultimately fulfilled wish to abolish itself: to abandon the gro-
tesque aberrations of character and situation that have typified

its representation, which now coincides with the norm of the Victorian household. But the project, however successful, is nothing here if not drastic. In *Barchester Towers*, by contrast, the normative elements of heterosexual coupling—the manly husband, the feminine wife—are ready-to-hand early on, and the plot is mainly a question of overcoming various inhibitions and misunderstandings that temporarily prevent them from acknowledging their appropriateness for one another. In *The Woman in White*, however, these elements have to be "engendered" in the course of the plot through the most extreme and violent expedients. The sufficiently manly husband needs to have survived plague, pygmy arrows, and shipwreck in Central America, and the suitably feminine wife must have been schooled in a lunatic asylum, where she is half cretinized. Such desperate measures no doubt dramatize the supreme value of a norm for whose incarnation no price, including the most brutal aversion therapy, is considered too high to pay. But they do something else besides, something that Victorians, in thrall to this norm, suspected when they accused the sensation novel of immorality and that we, more laxly oppressed than they, are perhaps in a better position to specify. This is simply that, re-contextualized in a "sensational" account of its genesis, such a norm risks appearing *monstrous*: as aberrant as any of the abnormal conditions that determine its realization.

III

"It ended, as you probably guess by this time, in his insisting on securing his own safety by shutting her up" (557). Male security in *The Woman in White* seems always to depend on female claustration. Sir Percival not only shuts up Anne in the asylum but successfully conspires with Fosco to shut up Laura there as well. In a double sense, he also shuts up Anne's mother, whose silence he purchases with a "handsome" allowance and ensures by insisting she not leave the town where she has been shamed and where therefore "no virtuous female friends would tempt [her] into dangerous gossiping at the tea-table" (554–55). Thanks to "the iron rod" that Fosco keeps "private" (224), Madame Fosco, who once "advocated the Rights of Women" (255), now lives in a "state of suppression" that extends to "stiff little rows of very short curls" on either side of her face and "quiet black or grey gowns, made high round the throat" (238–39). She walks in a favorite circle, "round and round the great fish pond" (290)—the Blackwater estate is in any case already "shut in—almost suffocated . . . by trees" (220)—as though she were taking yard exercise. The novel does not of course approve of these restraining orders, which originate in unambiguously criminal depravity, but as we will see it is not above exploiting them as the stick with which to contrast and complement the carrot of a far more ordinary and acceptable mode of sequestration.

Sandra M. Gilbert and Susan Gubar have argued that "dramatizations of imprisonment and escape are so all-pervasive in nineteenth-century literature by women that . . . they represent a uniquely female tradition in this period." Male carceral representations, "more consciously and objectively" elaborated, tend to be "metaphysical and metaphorical," whereas female ones remain "social and actual."[12] Yet at least in the nineteenth-century novel, the representation of imprisonment is too pervasive to be exclusively or even chiefly a female property, and too consistent overall to be divided between male and female authors on the basis of the distinctions proposed. On the one hand, Dickens's carceral fictions refer pointedly to actual social institutions, and there is little that is metaphysical in Trollope's rendering of social control: what little there is, in the form of "religion" or "Providence," merely sanctions the

---

12. Sandra M. Gilbert and Susan Gubar, *The Madwoman in the Attic* (New Haven: Yale University Press, 1979), pp. 85–86.

social mechanisms concretely at work. On the other hand, Charlotte Brontë's "dramatizations of imprisonment" do not deal with literal prisons at all, as Gilbert and Gubar themselves demonstrate. Insofar as these critics endorse a familiar series of oppositions (masculine/feminine = abstract/concrete = conscious/unconscious = objective/subjective) that, even graphically, keeps women behind a lot of bars, their attempt to isolate the essential paradigm of female writing unwittingly risks recycling the feminine mystique. We are nonetheless indebted to them for posing the question of the specific historical configuration, in the nineteenth-century English novel, of what might be called the "feminine carceral." As they plausibly show, this configuration centers on the representation, in varying degrees of alienation, of the "madwoman," and if this representation is not a uniquely female tradition, one readily grants that it is dominantly so. *The Woman in White*, however, with impressive ease incorporating the story of female "imprisonment and escape" (again, *anima muliebris inclusa*), suggests that there is a radical ambiguity about the "madwoman" that allows the feminist concerns she often voices to have already been appropriated in antifeminist ways. To the extent that novelists (or critics) underwrite the validity of female "madness" as virtually the only mode of its subject's authenticity, they inevitably slight the fact that it is also her socially given *role*, whose quasi-mandatory performance under certain conditions apotheosizes the familiar stereotypes of the woman as "unconscious" and "subjective" (read: irresponsible) that contribute largely to her oppression. The madwoman finds a considerable part of her truth—in the corpus of nineteenth-century fiction, at any rate—in being implicitly juxtaposed to the male *criminal* she is never allowed to be. If, typically, *he* ends up in the prison or its metaphorical equivalents, *she* ends up in the asylum or *its* metaphorical equivalents. (As a child perusing the shelves of a public library, I thought *The Woman in White* must be the story of a nurse: it at least proves to be the story of various women's subservience to "the doctor," to medical domination.) The distinction between criminal men (like Sir Percival and Fosco) and innocently sick women (like Anne and Laura) bespeaks a paternalism whose "chivalry" merely sublimates a system of constraints. In this light, the best way to read the madwoman would be not to derive the diagnosis from her social psychology ("Who wouldn't go crazy under such conditions?") but rather to derive her social psychology from the diagnosis: from the very category of madness that, like a fate, lies ever in wait to "cover"—account for and occlude—whatever behaviors, desires, or tendencies might be considered socially deviant, undesirable, or dangerous.

The achievement of blowing this cover belongs to *Lady Audley's Secret* (1862), the novel where, writing under the ambiguous stimulus of *The Woman in White*, Mary Elizabeth Braddon demonstrates that the madwoman's primary "alienation" lies in the rubric under which she is put down. Not unlike Anne Catherick, "always weak in the head" (554), Lady Audley appears to have been born with the "taint" of madness in her blood. She inherits the taint from her mother, whose own madness was in turn "an hereditary disease transmitted to her from her mother, who died mad." Passed on like a curse through—and as—the woman, madness virtually belongs to the condition of being female. But the novel is not so much concerned to conjoin madness and femininity, each the "truth" of the other, as to display how—under what assumptions and by what procedures—such a conjunction comes to be socially achieved. For in fact the text leaves ample room for doubt on the score of Lady Audley's "madness." Her acts, including bigamy, arson, and attempted murder, qualify as crimes in a strict legal sense, and they are motivated (like crime in English detective fiction generally) by impeccably rational considerations of self-interest. When her nephew Robert Audley at last detects her, however, he simply arranges for her to be pronounced "mad" and imprisoned accordingly in a *maison de santé* abroad. The "secret"

let out at the end of the novel is not, therefore, that Lady Audley is a madwoman but rather that, *whether she is one or not*, she
must be treated as such. Robert feels no embarrassment at the
incommensurability thus betrayed between the diagnosis and
the data that are supposed to confirm it; if need be, these data
can be dispensed with altogether, as in the findings of the doctor ("experienced in cases of mania") whom he calls in for an
opinion:

"I have talked to the lady," [the doctor] said quietly, "and we understand each other very well. There is latent insanity! Insanity which
might never appear; or which might appear only once or twice in a
lifetime. It would be a *dementia* in its worst phase, perhaps; acute
mania; but its duration would be very brief, and it would only arise
under extreme mental pressure. The lady is not mad; but she has the
hereditary taint in her blood. She has the cunning of madness, with
the prudence of intelligence. I will tell you what she is, Mr. Audley.
She is dangerous!"[13]

The doctor's double-talk ("the cunning of madness, with the
prudence of intelligence") will be required to sanction two contradictory propositions: (1) Lady Audley is criminal, in the
sense that her crimes must be punished; and (2) Lady Audley
is not criminal, in the sense that neither her crimes nor her punishment must be made public in a male order of things. ("My
greatest fear," Robert tells the doctor, "is the necessity of any
exposure—any disgrace.") "Latent insanity, an insanity which
might never appear" nicely meets the requirements of the case.
At the same time that it removes the necessity for evidence (do
Lady Audley's crimes manifest her latent insanity? or is it, quite
independent of them, yet to make its appearance?), it adduces
the grounds for confining her to a madhouse. Lady Audley is
mad, then, only because she must not be criminal. She must

13. Mary Elizabeth Braddon, *Lady Audley's Secret* (New York: Dover, 1974),
    p. 249.

not, in other words, be supposed capable of acting on her own diabolical responsibility and hence of publicly spoiling her assigned role as the conduit of power transactions between men.[14] Whatever doubts the doctor entertains in pronouncing her mad do not affect his certainty that she is, at all events, dangerous, and this social judgment entirely suffices to discount the ambiguities that the properly medical one need not bother to resolve.

Lady Audley's Secret thus portrays the woman's carceral condition as her fundamental and final truth. The novel's power as a revision of *The Woman in White* consists in its refusal of the liberal dialectic whereby the latter thinks to surpass this truth. Up to a certain point—say, up to the success of the conspiracy to confine Laura—Collins's novel is willing to tell the same story as Braddon's: of an incarceration whose patriarchal expediency takes priority over whatever humane considerations may or may not be invoked to rationalize it. (Anne's mental disorder, though real enough, is only a plausible pretext for confining her on other grounds, and Laura's confinement has no medical justification whatsoever.) But unlike Lady Audley, Lady Glyde *escapes* from her asylum, and fortunately has somewhere else to go. The asylum has an "alibi" in Limmeridge House (twice called an "asylum" in the text [367, 368]), where in the end Laura settles happily down with Walter. Whereas in the first movement of the novel the woman is shut up, in the

14. A Victorian reviewer, W. Fraser Ray, criticizes the characterization of Lady Audley thus: "In drawing her, the authoress may have intended to portray a female Mephistopheles; but if so, she should have known that a woman cannot fill such a part"; "Sensation Novelists: Miss Braddon," *North British Review* 43 (1865), quoted in Veeder, *The Woman Question*, p. 127. Ray might have spared himself the trouble (not to mention, in our hindsight, the embarrassment of failing to read the text that nonetheless proves quite capable of reading him), since his objection merely rehearses the same principle that, within the novel, Robert Audley victoriously carries in having Lady Audley confined.

second she is liberated, and it is rather the "feminine carceral" that is put away instead. Laura thus follows a common itinerary of the liberal subject in nineteenth-century fiction: she takes a nightmarish detour through the carceral ghetto on her way *home*, to the domestic haven where she is always felt to belong. Yet while her history plainly dichotomizes carceral and liberal spaces, the asylum that keeps one inside and the "asylum" that keeps others out, it also gives evidence of continuities and over-lappings between them. If her situation as Mrs. Hartright throws domesticity into relief as relief indeed from the brutal-ities of the asylum, her state as Lady Glyde (at Sir Percival's "stifling" house [227]) merely anticipates the asylum, which in turn only perfects Sir Percival's control over her. The difference between the asylum-as-confinement and the asylum-as-refuge is sufficiently dramatic to make a properly enclosed domestic circle the object of both desire and—later—gratitude, but ev-idently it is also sufficiently precarious to warrant—as the means of maintaining it—a domestic self-discipline that must have internalized the institutional control it thereby forestalls. The same internment that renders Laura's body docile, and her mind imbecile, also fits her to incarnate the norm of the sub-missive Victorian wife. (Sir Percival might well turn in his grave to see his successor effortlessly reaping what, with noth-ing to show but acute frustration, *he* had sown.) Collins makes Laura's second marriage so different from her first that he has no reason to conceal the considerable evidence of its resem-blance to what can be counted upon to remain its "opposite."

   This evidence comes as early as when, virtually at first sight, Walter falls in love with Laura. "Think of her," he invites the reader who would understand his feelings, "as you thought of the first woman who quickened the pulses within you" (76). As here, so everywhere else his passion declares itself in the lan-guage of sensation: of thrill and chill (86); of pang and pain (96); of "sympathies" that, lying "too deep for words, too deep almost for thoughts," have been "touched" (76). Concomitantly, in the associative pattern we have already established, his sensationalized body puts him in an essentially feminine position. His "hardly-earned self-control" (90) is as completely lost to him as if he had never possessed it, and "aggravated by the sense of [his] own miserable weakness" (91), his situation becomes one of "helplessness and humiliation" (92)—the same hendiadys that Marian will apply to herself and Laura at Blackwater Park (272). This is all to say that, notwithstanding Walter's implication, Laura Fairlie is *not* the first woman to quicken his pulses but rather the object of a repetition compulsion whose origin lies in his (sensationalizing, feminizing) first encounter with the Woman in White. Walter replays this primal trauma, however, with an important difference that in principle marks out the path to mastering it. He moves from an identification with the woman to a desire for her, heterosexual choice replacing homosexual surprise. The woman is once more (or for the first time) the other, and the man, who now at least "knows what he wants," has to that extent taken himself in charge.

Yet the sensational features of Walter's desire necessarily threaten to reabsorb it in the identification against which it erects itself as a first line of defense. Something more, therefore, is required to stabilize his male self-mastery, something that Walter does *not* know that he wants. "Crush it," Marian counsels him, "Don't shrink under it like a woman. Tear it out; trample it under foot like a man!" (96). But the eventual recipient of this violence will be as much the object of Walter's passion as the passion itself. From the very beginning of his exposure to it, Laura's "charm" has suggested to him "the idea of something wanting":

At one time it seemed like something wanting in *her*; at another, like something wanting in myself, which hindered me from understanding her as I ought. The impression was always strongest in the most contradictory manner, when she looked at me, or, in other words, when I was most conscious of the harmony and charm of her face, and yet, at the same time, most troubled by the sense of an incompleteness which it was impossible to discover. Something wanting, something wanting—and where it was, and what it was, I could not say. (76–77)

This is not (or not just) a Freudian riddle (Q.: What does a woman want? A.: What she is wanting), though even as such it attests the particular anxiety of the man responsible for posing it: who desires Laura "because" (= so that) she, not he, is wanting. For shortly afterward, with "a thrill of the same feeling which ran through [him] when the touch was laid upon [his] shoulder on the lonely highroad," Walter comes to see that the "something wanting" is "[his] own recognition of the ominous likeness between the fugitive from the asylum and [his] pupil at Limmeridge House" (86). Laura's strange "incompleteness" would thus consist in what has made this likeness imperfect—namely, that absence of "profaning marks" of "sorrow and suffering" which alone is said to differentiate her from her double (120). Accordingly, the Laura Walter most deeply dreams of loving proves to be none other than the Anne who has been put away. It is as though, to be quite perfect, his pupil must be taught a lesson: what is wanting—what Laura obscurely lacks and Walter obscurely wishes for—is her sequestration in the asylum.

Courtesy of Sir Percival and Fosco, the want will of course be supplied, but long before her actual internment Laura has been well prepared for it at Limmeridge House, where—on the grounds that her delicacy requires protection—men systematically keep their distance from her. Rather than deal with her directly, Sir Percival, Mr. Gilmore, Mr. Fairlie, Walter himself all prefer to have recourse to the mannish Marian, who serves as their intermediary. "I shrank," says Walter at one point, "I shrink still—from invading the innermost sanctuary of her heart, and laying it open to others, as I have laid open my own"

(90). His many such gallant pronouncements entail an unwillingness to *know* Laura, the better to affirm without interference
the difference between him and her, man and woman. ("Me
Tarzan, you Jane": notice how male solipsism overbears the very
opposition that guarantees male difference. Laura is a closed
sanctuary / Walter is an open book, but it is Walter here who
empowers himself to decide, by his shrinking reticence, what
Laura shall be.) More than anything else, this "respect" is responsible in the text for rendering Laura—even in terms of a
genre that does not specialize in complex character studies—a
psychological cipher. (An English translation of the French
translation of the novel might be entitled, precisely, *The Woman
as Blank*.) From turbid motives of her own, Marian is more
than willing to do her part in drawing round Laura this *cordon
sanitaire*. Like an efficient secretary in love with her boss, she
spares Laura all troublesome importunities, and she is no less
aggressive in forbidding an interview between Laura and Anne
("Not to be thought of for a moment" [131]) than in dispatch-
ing Walter from Limmeridge House "before more harm is
done" (95). Laura's subsequent experience of the asylum only
further justifies the imperative to isolate her. "The wrong that
had been inflicted on her . . . must be redressed without her
knowledge and without her help" (456). And now a self-
evident opposition between parent and child is available to
overdetermine what had been the all-too-doubtful difference
between man and woman. "Oh, don't, don't, don't treat me
like a child!" Laura implores, but Walter immediately takes
the plea for more evidence of her childishness and accordingly
gives her some pretend-work to do. When she asks him "as a
child might have" whether he is as fond of her as he used to
be, he reassures her that "she is dearer to [him] now than she
had ever been in the past times" (458). His profession carries
conviction, and no wonder, since his passion for her, now become a part-parental, part-pedophilic condescension, no longer
makes him feel like a woman. Though the text takes perfunc-

tory notice of "the healing influences of her new life" with Walter (576), these have no power to produce a Laura who in any way exceeds men's (literal or "liberal") incarcerating fantasies about her. It is not just, as the text puts it, that the mark of the asylum is "too deep to be effaced" but that it has always already effaced everything else.

The same could not be said of Marian Halcombe, whose far more "interesting" character represents the only significant variation on business-as-usual in the novel's gynaeceum. As the conspicuously curious case of a woman's body that gives all the signs of containing a man's soul, Marian figures the exact inversion of what we have taken to be the novel's governing fantasy. Yet we must not conceive of this inversion standing in opposition to what it inverts, as though it implied not just the existence of a rival set of matching *female* fears and fantasies but also the consequent assurance that, in the love and war between the sexes, all at least is fair: *così fan tutte*, too. No less than that of the woman-in-the-man, the motif of the man-in-the-woman is a function of the novel's anxious male imperatives ("Cherchez, cachez, couchez la femme") that, even as a configuration of resistance, it rationalizes, flatters, and positively encourages. Thus, however "phallic," "lesbian," and "male-identified" Marian may be considered at the beginning of the novel, the implicit structuring of these attributes is precisely what is responsible for converting her—if with a certain violence, then also with a certain ease—into the castrated, heterosexualized "good angel" (646) of the Victorian household at the end.

Our memorable first view of her comes in the disappointed appraisal of Walter's idly cruising eye:

The instant my eyes rested on her, I was struck by the rare beauty of her form, and by the unaffected grace of her attitude. Her figure was tall, yet not too tall; comely and well-developed, yet not fat; her head set on her shoulders with an easy, pliant firmness; her waist, perfection in the eyes of a man, for it occupied its natural place, it filled out its natural circle, it was visibly and delightfully undeformed by stays. She had not heard my entrance into the room; and I allowed myself the luxury of admiring her for a moment, before I moved one of the chairs near me, as the least embarrassing means of attracting her attention. She turned towards me immediately. The easy elegance of every movement of her limbs and body as soon as she began to advance from the far end of the room, set me in a flutter of expectation to see her face clearly. She left the window—and I said to myself, The lady is dark. She moved forward a few steps—and I said to myself, The lady is young. She approached nearer—and I said to myself (with a sense of surprise which words fail me to express), The lady is ugly!

Never was the old conventional maxim, that Nature cannot err, more flatly contradicted—never was the fair promise of a lovely figure more strangely and startlingly belied by the face and head that crowned it. The lady's complexion was almost swarthy, and the dark down on her upper lip was almost a moustache. She had a large, firm, masculine mouth and jaw; prominent, piercing, resolute brown eyes; and thick, coal-black hair, growing unusually low down on her forehead. Her expression—bright, frank, and intelligent—appeared, while she was silent, to be altogether wanting in those feminine attractions of gentleness and pliability, without which the beauty of the handsomest woman alive is beauty incomplete. To see such a face as this set on shoulders that a sculptor would have longed to model— to be charmed by the modest graces of action through which the symmetrical limbs betrayed their beauty when they moved, and then to be almost repelled by the masculine form and masculine look of the features in which the perfectly shaped figure ended—was to feel a sensation oddly akin to the helpless discomfort familiar to us all in sleep, when we recognize yet cannot reconcile the anomalies and contradictions of a dream. (58–59)

Though the passage develops all the rhetorical suspense of a striptease, in which, as Barthes has written, "the entire excitation takes refuge in the hope of seeing the sexual organ," the place of the latter seems strangely occupied here by Marian's "head and face."[15] What Barthes calls the "schoolboy's dream" turns into a far less euphoric "sensation" of "helpless discomfort" when, at the climactic moment of unveiling, the woman's head virtually proves her a man in drag. Banal as this kind of revelation has become in our culture (where it is ritualized in a variety of spectacles, jokes, and folkloric anecdotes), it never ceases to be consumed, as here, "with a sense of surprise." The surprise would perhaps better be understood as a stubborn refusal to recognize how unsurprising it is that an obsessively phallocentric system of sexual difference, always and everywhere on the lookout for its founding attribute (if only in the case of women to make sure it isn't there), should sometimes, as though overcome by eyestrain, find this attribute even in its absence. Yet Walter's sense of surprise exceeds the more or less conscious ruse that serves to divorce his quasi-heterosexual identity from its quasi-homosexual genealogy. Surprise is also the text's figure for the violence of that double metamorphosis which overtakes this identity and thus calls for such a ruse. Marian's sudden transformation from the object that Walter looks at into the subject whose "piercing" eyes might look back at him—look at his back—simultaneously entails the reverse transformation in him. In a context, then, where the positions of subject and object are respectively gendered as male and female, and where the relation between them is eroticized accordingly, the nature of Walter's surprise, "which words fail [him] to express," may go without saying. Necessarily, his recovery has recourse to the affect of *repulsion*, which will reinstate the distance that surprise has momentarily abolished between him and the amphibolous figure of the "masculine woman." Walter's recoil carries the "instinctive" proof—more than welcome after his unnerving encounter with the Woman in

15. Roland Barthes, *The Pleasure of the Text*, trans. Richard Miller (New York: Hill and Wang, 1975), p. 10.

White—both of his competence in a male code of sexual signs (which Marian's monstrosity, far from compromising, offers the occasion for rehearsing and confirming) and of his own stable, unambiguous position in that code (as a man who judges with "the eyes of a man"). On such a basis, he succeeds in containing his potentially disturbing vision within the assured comic effects ("The lady was ugly!") of a worldly raconteur to whom Marian's sexual anomalousness presents no threat of contagion.

For Marian's "masculine look" may be seen in two ways, not just as what poses the problem she embodies but also as what resolves it. Precisely in her "masculinity" she incarnates that wit which men familiarly direct against women who are "altogether wanting in those feminine attractions of gentleness and pliability." We notice, for a characteristic example of such wit, that someone—an erring Nature, if not the anxious drawing master who faithfully copies Nature's work—*has drawn a moustache on her*. However perturbed Walter may be that Marian lacks the lack, he is also plainly gratified to take inventory of the numerous phallic signs on her person, as though these could finally only mock the absence of the penile referent. The well-known anxiety attaching to male jokes about the "masculine woman" in no way extenuates the strategy that it energizes: which is to render the woman who is their target external to the system of sexual difference that gets along quite well without her. Unable to compete (when the chaps are down), she cannot be "male"; unable to attract (as though the derisive signs remained persuasive after all), neither can she be "female." What is thereby neutralized, in the root as well as derived sense of the word, is any sexuality—female and/or male—that cannot be reduced to either term of a phallic binarism.

Yet Walter's aggressive indifference to Marian as a relevant sexual counter is eventually belied when Count Fosco—who is as helpful in acting out the implications of Walter's fantasy here as he is in the case of Laura—takes a pronounced, even violent erotic interest in her. How does this ugly, neutered woman come to be targeted for what, as we have seen, the novel encodes as "rape"? We notice that Walter's portrait of Marian, though it abounds in phallic *signs*, nowhere offers a phallic *symbol:* only later, too late, will the novelist hand her "the horrid heavy man's umbrella" (235). Where, then, *is* the phallus so bountifully signified? If it isn't *on* Marian, whose unimpeachably curvilinear body (like the perfect waist that is its synecdoche) is "visibly and delightfully undeformed by stays," then it must be *in* her, the iron in the soul that manifests itself only through the soul's traditional windows: those "prominent, piercing, resolute brown eyes" with their "masculine look." (Even her moustache suggests that the masculine signs defacing her body have pushed through from within.) Psychoanalysis and the male adolescent alike are familiar with the castration fantasy in which (act one) the penis gets "locked" in the vagina during intercourse and (act two) having broken off, remains inside the female body. *Anima virilis in corpore muliebri inclusa*: Marian is not just the "dog" that no self-respecting male adolescent would be "caught with"; she is also—the "evidence" for act one of course being canine—the dog that he would not be caught *in*.[16] As the focus of fears of *male* incarceration, Marian's

16. The novel's elaborate canine thematics more than justify this slang usage, which of course postdates it. Marian's first lesson at Blackwater Park, for instance, involves being instructed in the destiny of dogs there. A housemaid thus accounts to her for the wounded dog found in the boathouse: "Bless you, miss! Baxter's the keeper, and when he finds strange dogs hunting about, he takes and shoots 'em. It's keeper's dooty, miss. I think that dog will die. Here's where he's been shot, ain't it? That's Baxter's doings, that is. Baxter's doings, miss, and Baxter's dooty" (229). "Baxter's" doings indeed: if the keeper is little more than a name in the novel, the name nonetheless contains almost all the elements in the novel's representation of female containment. For one thing, the suffix -ster originally designates a specifically feminine agency (in Old English a *baxter* means a female baker): whence perhaps Baxter's violence, as though he were protesting the femininity latently inscribed in his name. For another, in the context of the novel's insistence on "the touch

body becomes the operational theater for the two tactics of "men's liberation" that usually respond to these fears. She is firmly abandoned by Walter's erotic interest and forcibly seduced by Fosco's. The two tactics cohere in a single strategy, since perhaps the most important fantasy feature of rape is the reaffirmation of the rapist's unimpaired capacity to withdraw, the integrity of his body (if not his victim's) recovered intact. (Fosco, we recall, returns to Marian the journal he has indelibly signed, and she, evidently, is stuck with it.)[17] As its sexual variant, seduction-and-abandonment would thus in both senses of the word "betray" the constitutive myth of the liberal (male) subject, whose human rights must include the freedom, as he pleases, to come and go.

The meaning of Marian's "rape" is of course further determined by another, better-known figure of the *anima virilis*: the lesbian. "She will be *his* Laura instead of mine!" (207), writes Marian of the bride of Limmeridge—having taken the precaution, however, of promoting rather this faint-hearted marriage to Sir Percival than the obvious love match with Walter, as if already anticipating the consolation that an unhappy Lady Glyde will not fail to bring to her closet: "Oh, Marian! . . . promise you will never marry, and leave me. It is selfish to say so, but you are so much better off as a single woman—unless—unless you are very fond of your husband—but you won't be very fond of anybody but me, will you?" (235). Important as it is not to censor the existence of erotic feeling between wom-

---

from behind," the name would also signify the person who handles (its gender inflection keeps us from quite saying: man-handles) the hinder part of the body.

17. In this context one must read Fosco's dandiacal lament after the episode where—"to the astonishment of all the men" who watch him—he successfully intimidates "a chained bloodhound—a beast so savage that the very groom who feeds him keeps out of his reach": "Ah! my nice waistcoat! . . . Some of that brute's slobber has got on my pretty clean waistcoat!" (243–44).

en in the text (in any of the ways this can be done, including a certain way of acknowledging it),[18] it is perhaps more important to recognize that what would also get absorbed here under the name of lesbianism is a woman's unwillingness to lend her full cooperation to male appropriations of her, as though Marian's "gayness" were the only conceivable key to passages like the following: "Men! They are the enemies of our innocence and our peace—they drag us away from our parents' love and our sisters' friendship—they take us body and soul to themselves, and fasten our helpless lives to theirs as they chain up a dog to his kennel. And what does the best of them give us in return? Let me go, Laura—I'm mad when I think of it!" (203). In general, the "lesbianism" contextualized in *The Woman in White* amounts mainly to a male charge, in which the accusation is hard to dissociate from the excitation. In particular, the novel most effectively renders Marian "lesbian" in the sense that it makes her suffer the regular fate of the lesbian in male representations: who defiantly bides her time with women until the inevitable and irrevocable heterosexual initiation that she, unlike everyone else, may not have known that she always wanted. One recalls this exchange from *Goldfinger*, after James Bond has seduced Pussy Galore: "He said, 'They told me you

18. For example: "Does [Marian] . . . have Lesbian tendencies?" the editor of the Penguin edition boldly speculates, before prudently concluding that "it is doubtful whether such thoughts were in Collins's mind" (15). The response, which rationalizes its titillation as a sophisticated willingness to call things by their names and then rationalizes its disavowal of that titillation (and of those names) as scholarly caution, typifies the only acknowledgment that homoeroticism, female or male, is accustomed to receive in the criticism of nineteenth-century fiction. Here it does little more than faithfully reproduce—"Mind that dog, sir!" (243)—the novel's own equivocal structuring of the evidence for Marian's lesbianism. One may observe in passing how a similar fidelity entails that the editor who can mention lesbianism must fall entirely silent on the *male* homoerotics of the novel (see p. 184 below for why this should be so).

only liked women.' She said, 'I never met a man before.' "[19] Not dissimilarly, Marian's "half-willing, half-unwilling liking for the Count" (246)—what in a rape trial would be called her "complicity"—provides the novel's compelling, compulsive proof of the male erotic power that operates even and especially where it is denied. "I am almost afraid to confess it, even to these secret pages. The man has interested me, has attracted me, has forced me to like him" (240). Fosco's eyes "have at times a clear, cold, beautiful, irresistible glitter in them which forces me to look at him, and yet causes me sensations, when I do look, which I would rather not feel" (241, repeated almost verbatim on 287). Like Pussy Bonded, Marian Foscoed (hearing the metathesis in the name of the "wily Italian" [264], we need not even consider resorting to what Freud called Schreber's "shamefaced" elision) is a changed woman. If it is not her ultimate destiny to roll up the Count's endless cigarettes "with the look of mute submissive inquiry which we are all familiar with in the eyes of a faithful dog" (239), as she abjectly fantasizes, he has nonetheless well trained her to be another man's best friend. "What a woman's hands *are* fit for," she tells Walter, whom she entrusts with her avengement, "early and late, these hands of mine shall do. . . . It's my weakness that cries, not me. The house-work shall conquer it, if *I* can't" (453–54). The old signs of Marian's "masculinity"—the hands that were "as awkward as a man's" (253), the tears that came "almost like men's" (187)—now realize what had always been their implied potential to attest a "weakness" that (like the housework she takes on "as her own right") refeminizes her. In the novel's last image, almost exactly according to the proper Freudian resolution of *Penisneid*, Marian is able to "rise" only on condition that she "hold up" Walter's son and heir "kicking and crowing in her arms" (646). Almost exactly, but not quite, since the

19. Ian Fleming, *Goldfinger* (1959; New York: Berkley Books, 1982), p. 261.

child is not of course her own. It is as though the woman whom Fosco "rapes" and the woman whom Walter "neuters" prove finally one and the same odd thing—as though, in other words, a woman's heterosexuality ("hetero-" indeed) were no sexuality of hers.

Even as the victim of terrific male aggression, however, Marian is simultaneously the beneficiary of considerable male admiration. Walter aptly imagines that she "would have secured the respect of the most audacious man breathing" (60), and apart from Fosco, who eventually embodies that hypothetical man, apart even from Walter, who at once finds in the ugly lady an old friend (59), the novelist himself unexceptionally portrays Marian as a "positive," immensely likable character. Demonstrably, then, *The Woman in White* accords a far warmer welcome to the fantasy of the man-in-the-woman (which, fully personified, the novel works through to a narrative resolution) than to the apparently complementary fantasy of the woman-in-the-man (which, as we have seen, the novel only broaches obscurely, in the blind spot of "nonrecognition" between textual thematics and male reading bodies). This is doubtless because the *anima virilis* includes, in addition to the aspects aforementioned, a male identification. "I don't think much of my own sex," Marian admits to Walter on their first meeting; "No woman does think much of her own sex, though few of them confess it as freely as I do" (60). As though misogyny were primarily a female phenomenon and as such justified the male phenomenon that ventriloquially might go without saying, Marian's voice becomes the novel's principal articulation of that traditional code according to which women are quarrelsome, chattering, capricious, superstitious, inaccurate, unable to draw or play billiards. For all the pluck that it inspires, Marian's male identification consistently vouches for her female dependency. Thus, determined "on justifying the Count's opinion of [her] courage and sharpness" (340), she bravely makes her night-crawl onto the eaves of the house at Blackwater to overhear Fosco's conversation with Sir Percival. But—perhaps because, as the male-identified woman necessarily comes to think, her "courage was only a woman's courage after all" (341–42)—this determination obliges her to remove "the white and cumbersome parts of [her] underclothing" (342) and so to prepare herself for the violation that, on one way of looking at it, follows soon afterward but that, on another, has already succeeded. If the woman-in-the-man requires his *keeping her* inside him, the man-in-the-woman takes for granted her *letting him* inside her. The sexual difference that the former endangers, the latter reaffirms: by determining a single view of women—men's—to which women accede in the course of constructing a male-identified femininity. Fosco "flatters" Marian's vanity "by talking to [her] as seriously and sensibly as if [she were] a man" (245), and she more than returns the favor by addressing Fosco, Walter, and the male reader on the same premise, reassuring all concerned that even the woman who speaks as "freely" as a man remains the prolocutor of a masculist discourse that keeps her in place. Finally, therefore, Marian may be taken to suggest how the novel envisions that *female* reader whom, though it nominally ignores, it has always taken into practical account. For the same sensation effects that "feminize" the male reading body also (the quotation marks are still indispensable) "feminize" the female: with the difference that this feminization is construed in the one case to threaten sexual identity and in the other to confirm it. Implicitly, that is, the text glosses the female reader's sensationalized body in exactly the terms of Marian's erotic responsiveness to Fosco: as the corporal confession of a "femininity" whose conception is all but exhausted in providing the unmarked term in opposition to a thus replenished "masculinity." If only on its own terms (though, when one is trembling, these terms may be hard to shake), the sensation novel constitutes proof of women's inability, as Marian puts it, to "resist a man's tongue when he knows how to speak to them" (278) and especially, we might add with Marian emblematically in mind, when he knows how to speak through them.

IV

Precisely insofar as it does not fail, the project of confining or containing the woman cannot succeed in achieving narrative quiescence or closure. Safely shut up in the various ways we have considered, women cease being active participants in the drama that nonetheless remains to be played out (for over a hundred pages) "man to man." For when the text produces the configuration of incarcerated femininity, it simultaneously cathects the congruent configuration of phobic male homoeroticism: thus, for instance, its "paradoxical" rendering of Fosco, who is at once "a man who could tame anything" (239) and "a fat St. Cecilia masquerading in male attire" (250). Accordingly, the novel needs to supplement its misogynistic plot with a misanthropic one, in which it will detail the frightening, even calamitous consequences of unmediated relations between men, thereby administering to its hero an aversion therapy calculated to issue in a renunciation of what Eve Kosofsky Sedgwick has called "male homosocial desire," or in a liberation from what—with a more carceral but no less erotic shade of meaning—we might also call male bonds.[20] After Sedgwick's demonstration that men's desire for men is the very motor of patriarchally given social structures, it might seem implausible even to entertain the possibility of such a renunciation or liberation, which would amount to a withdrawal from the social *tout court*. Yet this is apparently what the endings of many

20. Readers of Eve Kosofsky Sedgwick's *Between Men: English Literature and Male Homosocial Desire* (New York: Columbia University Press, 1985) will recognize how nearly its concerns touch on those of this chapter.

nineteenth-century novels paradigmatically stage: the hero's thoroughgoing disenchantment with the (homo)social, from which he is resigned to isolate himself. By and large, nineteenth-century fiction is no less heavily invested than Sedgwick's analysis of it in luridly portraying the dysphoric effects—particularly on men—of homosocial desire, and this fact must raise the question of the status of such effects within the general rhetorical strategy of the fiction that cultivates them. If, for example, *The Woman in White* obligingly constitutes a "pathology" of male homosocial desire, this is not because the novel shares, say, Sedgwick's ambition to formulate a feminist/gay critique of homophobically patriarchal structure; but neither is it because the novel so naively embraces this structure that it recounts-without-counting its psychological costs. Rather, as we will see, the novel puts its homosocial pathology in the service of promoting a homosocial cure: a cure that has the effect of a renunciation of men's desire for men only because, in this treated form, and by contrast, such desire exists in a "normal" or relatively silent state.

The novel's most obvious specimen of an abnormal male homosocial *Bund*—the one it adduces at the end, as though at last to consolidate the freely floating homoerotics of the text and thus to name and contain them—is that secret Italian political association which (Walter is quite correct in saying) is "sufficiently individualized" for his purposes if he calls it, simply, "The Brotherhood" (595). The novel tolerates this exotic freemasonry on two ideological conditions, which, if they were not so inveterately combined in a policy of quarantine, might otherwise strike us as incompatible. On the one hand, The Brotherhood owes its existence to the political adolescence of Italy (595–96), to which, in case the point is lost, Pesca correlates his own immaturity when he became a member (597). The advanced nation as well as the enlightened parent may rest assured imagining that The Brotherhood is only a phase that in the normal course of political or personal development will be superseded. Yet on the other hand, no possible course of development can retrieve someone once he has been admitted into this society of fellows and bears its "secret mark," which, like his membership, lasts for life (596). Strange as it may be for Walter to learn that some one of his best friends belongs to the secret fraternity, the revelation occasions no alarm (lest, for instance, an attempt be made to initiate *him*), since the pathos of Pesca's case is well cultivated by Pesca himself, who admits to suffering still from those youthful impulses ("I try to forget them—and they will not forget *me*!" [642]), which forever condemn him to consort in such dubious company. (In the usual distribution of roles, Walter's mother, but not his sullenly nubile sister, has welcomed Pesca into the household.) A congenial point is borne in the activities of The Brotherhood itself, whose in-house purges are the "outside" world's best protection against it. Walter's sword need never cross with Fosco's—a mercy given the impressive estimates we are invited to make of the "length" of the latter (611)—in the duel that "other vengeance" has rendered unnecessary (642). The Brotherhood has mortally called the Count to "the day of reckoning" (642)—not for his offenses against Walter but for his all-too-promiscuous fraternizing within and without its organization. The wound struck "exactly over his heart" (643) hints broadly at the "passional" nature of the crime in which—for which—Fosco is murdered. Thus, at the exhibition of his naked and knifed corpse (the former "Napoleon" [241] now, as it were, the dead Marat, and the rueful Parisian morgue, also as it were, the gayer continental baths), we hear the curator's familiarly excited double discourse, in which a flushed moralism never quite manages to pacify the sheer erotic fascination that hence remains available to incite it: "There he lay, unowned, unknown, exposed to the flippant curiosity of a French mob! There was the dreadful end of that long life of degraded ability and heartless crime! Hushed in the sublime repose of death, the broad, firm, massive face and head fronted us so grandly that the chattering Frenchwomen about me lifted their hands in admiration, and cried in shrill chorus, 'Ah, what a handsome man!' " (643).

"And all men kill the thing they love": what is often taken for Wilde's gay depressiveness (though in Reading Gaol, what else is left to intelligence but to read its prison?) provides a not-so-oddly apt formula for the novel's pathology of male bonds, whose godforsaken expression coincides with its providential punishment in death. (Besides the murder of Fosco, we may cite the "suicide" of his boon companion: it is no accident that, having locked himself in the vestry, Sir Percival accidentally sets it on fire.) A couple of reasons obtain for bringing out, as I have pseudo-anachronistically been doing, the continuities between the novel's representation of "brotherhood" and our media's no less sensational staging of male homosexuality. One would be to begin measuring the extent to which nineteenth-century culture has contributed to the formation of the context in which an uncloseted gayness is popularly determined. (Thus, the homophobic virulence that dispreads in response to AIDS is "only" the most recent, extreme, and potentially catastrophic figure of an interpretative framework that has preceded the disease by well over a century.) Another would be to recognize that if our culture can only "think" male homosexual desire within a practice of aversion therapy, this is because—for a long while and with apparently greater efficiency—it has routinely subjected male homosocial desire to the same treatment.

Representationally, this treatment consists of a diptych in which the baleful images of homosocial apocalypse on one panel confront a comparatively cheering family portrait on the other. The fact that Fosco and Sir Percival are both married is far from making them what *The Woman in White* understands by family men. For as the novel's final tableau makes abundantly clear, what is distinctively cheering about the family portrait is less the connection between husband and wife (Marian, not Laura, holds up his son to Walter's charmed gaze) than the bond between father and son. Thus, the aim of what we have called aversion therapy is not to redirect men's desire for men onto women but, through women, onto boys: that is, to privatize homosocial desire within the middle-class nuclear family, where it takes the "normal" shape of an oedipal triangle. Yet the twinned projects whose achievement the novel makes *precede* the establishment of a family curiously correspond to what, at least since Freud's summation of nineteenth-century culture, we may recognize as the family's own defining injunctions: (1) shut up the woman—or, in the rivalry between father and son of which she is the object, keep mother from becoming the subject of a desire of her own; and (2) turn from the man—or, in that same rivalry, develop an aversion therapy for home use. The foundation of the Hartright family, therefore, cannot put an end to the brutalities of its prehistory, nor will these brutalities have dialectically prepared the way for a civilizing familialism, since the violent workings of an oedipal family organization (Sir Percival is a much older man than Walter, and so forth) have implicitly generated the narrative that this organization is explicitly constituted to conclude. At the end, then, the novel has merely discovered its beginning, in the family matrix where such violence has acquired its specific structure and whence it has made its fearful *entrée dans le monde*. "And there is more where that came from," if only because where that came from is also where that eventually returns. As though refusing to cease shocking us, even where it least surprises us, *The Woman in White* "ends" only by recurring to that family circle which will continue to relay—with no end in sight—a plot that still takes many people's breath away.[21]

21. Like the woman's, or the homosexual's, or (for she has figured in both roles) Marian's: "Let Marian end our Story" (646), but—these are the text's last words, as well as Walter's—what follows is dead silence.

V

A note on the author's body: shortly after I began writing this essay, the muscles on my shoulders and back went into spasm. Referring this pain to other matters (excessive working out, an affair of the heart) than the work on which it continually interrupted my progress, I consulted physical and psychological therapists. Only when the former at last pronounced that a rib was out of place (which may have been what the latter was getting at when he diagnosed, on the insurance form, a personality disorder), was I willing to entertain the possibility that I had become, in relation to my own writing, an improbably pat case of hysteria. Now that a practiced hand has put the fugitive rib back into its cage, my spine tingles to have borne out my assumption of that "nonrecognition" which evidently also obtains between the somatics of writing and what is written about. I am less pleased (though still thrilled) to understand that, on the same assumption, what dumbfounds me also lays the foundation for my dumbness: too stupid to utter what has already been said in the interaction between body and text, and in the traces of that interaction within body or text; and too mute to do more than designate the crucial task of identifying in this writing the equivocal places where "sensation" has gone, not to say love.

SIX

Secret Subjects, Open Secrets

I

"And who's this shaver?" said one of the gentlemen, taking hold
of me.

"That's Davy," returned Mr Murdstone.

"Davy who?" said the gentleman.[1]

For a moment in *David Copperfield* (1850), the text raises the
possibility that David might be any David; for a moment, it so
happens, it invites me to imagine that he might be myself. Assuming that autobiographical representation is replete with
such narcissistic lures, sites where the reader's own subjectivity
comes to be invoked and identified, even without benefit of a
namesake, why not begin with myself? Why not begin by recounting the insertion of my own person into a novel that I read
and reread as a child, "in those tender years," Virginia Woolf
called them, "when fact and fiction merge"? Why not anthol-
ogize those all-too-affecting passages in the novel through
which David's story—I mean the other one's—became hope-
lessly entangled with my own? Why not admit, by the way,

1. Charles Dickens, *David Copperfield* (Harmondsworth: Penguin Books,
1966), p. 72. I depart from my practice of citing Dickens in the Oxford
Illustrated Dickens, which does not contain the original preface to *David
Copperfield*. All further page references to the Penguin edition will be
made parenthetically in the text.

how readily everything else in this novel flees from my memory—rather, how peremptorily everything else is dismissed
from it: much as the other David admits, sitting by the fire,
that "there was nothing real in all that I remembered, save my
mother, Peggotty, and I" (165)? And why not gloss those figures in the novel who have signified and predicted my sentimental education: from the Mother who fondled me, saying
"Davy, my pretty boy! my poor child!" (162); the (step-) Father whose unfeeding hand I rabidly bit; the Friend who,
though Mr. Sharp and Mr. Mell were notable personages in my
eyes, was to them what the sun was to two stars (144); and the
(second) Wife, center and circle of my life, in whom I might
have inspired a dearer love (938, 902); down to David himself,
cognate and first cognition of myself, who, of a summer evening, the boys at play in the churchyard, sat on my bed, reading as if for life (106)?

But as I eagerly put these questions, in the arrogant rhetorical form that waited for no reply, but already did what it pretended to ask permission for, I was also obliged to recognize
why, "subduing my desire to linger yet" (950), I must not pursue such a confession. For we are all well acquainted with those
mortifying charges (sentimentality, self-indulgence, narcis-
sism) which our culture is prepared to bring against anyone
who dwells in subjectivity longer or more intensely than is necessary to his proper functioning as the agent of socially useful
work. (It is bad enough to tell tales out of school, but to tell
them in school—or what comes to the same, in a text wholly
destined for the academy—would be intolerable.) And those
envious charges have at least this much truth in them, that the
embarrassing risk of *being too personal* all too often comes to coincide with its opposite in the dismal fate of banality, of *not
being personal enough*. Nothing, for instance, is more striking
than the disproportion between the embarrassed subject and
the occasion of his embarrassment: while the former imagines
his subjectivity on conspicuous and defenseless display, the

latter has usually been rendered all but invisible by its sheer mundaneness, its cultural or physiological predictability. Rarely does anyone even think to watch the spectacle we assumed we were making of ourselves. We say truly, "I could have died of embarrassment," but nearer than one's fantasized murder at the hands (the eyes, the tongues) of the others is the danger lest such worldly homicide prove embarrassingly unnecessary, the subject who fears extinction having already died out on his own. The painfulness of embarrassment, which at least ought to have guaranteed its subject's vitality, instead betokens a mountainously agitated subjectivity that refuses to acknowledge its mousy stillbirths. Accordingly, what could whatever "embarrassed" revelations I might make about my intimacy with *David Copperfield* amount to, except a particularly cathected paraphrase of an already written text? What could I—presumptively unique, private subject of unique, private desires—finally signify in such revelations, but a character in a novel so familiar that no one, it is said, can even remember reading it for the first time?

Let me not, then, speak of myself, but let my seduction by *David Copperfield* stay a secret. Yet is my secrecy any less paradoxical than the embarrassment that I thereby seem to avoid? It almost goes without saying that, though I conceal the details of this seduction, they would not be very difficult to surmise: no more esoteric, perhaps, than Oedipus and his commonplace complex. For I have had to intimate my secret, if only *not to tell it*; and conversely, in theatrically continuing to keep my secret, I have already rather *given it away*. But if I don't tell my secret, why can't I keep it better? And if I can't keep it better, why don't I just tell it? I can't quite tell my secret, because then it would be known that there was nothing really special to hide, and no one really special to hide it. But I can't quite keep it either, because then it would not be believed that there *was* something to hide and someone to hide it. It is thus a misleading common sense that finds the necessity of secrecy in the "special" nature of the contents concealed, when all that revelation usually reveals is a widely diffused cultural prescription, a cliché. A character in Oscar Wilde is closer to the truth when he observes of secrecy that "it is the one thing that can make modern life mysterious and marvellous. The commonest thing is delightful if one only hides it."[2] More precisely, secrecy would seem to be a mode whose ultimate meaning lies in the subject's formal insistence that he is radically inaccessible to the culture that would otherwise entirely determine him. I cannot, therefore, resolve the double bind of a secrecy that must always be rigorously maintained in the face of a secret that everybody already knows, since this is the very condition that entitles me to my subjectivity in the first place. But the double bind is not at all the same thing as a dead end, and if I cannot speak of myself without losing myself in the process, I can keep myself secret and—"so to speak"—change the subject: convinced of my indeterminability in the safety of silence, as I speak of— and seek to determine—somebody or something else. Were not the personal rewards for good behavior in the administered society so readily accepted, it might seem strange that I can best establish myself as a private subject only in the dutiful performance of the professional obligation that it profits nothing to put off any longer: to speak of *David Copperfield*.

We begin, then, not with myself, but with the first paragraph of Dickens's text, which falls in his preface:

I do not find it easy to get sufficiently far away from this Book, in the first sensations of having finished it, to refer to it with the composure which this formal heading would seem to require. My interest in it, is so recent and strong; and my mind is so divided between pleasure

2. Oscar Wilde, *The Picture of Dorian Gray* [1890]; in *The Portable Oscar Wilde* (Harmondsworth: Penguin Books, 1977), chap. 1, p. 143. Appropriately, the character in question, Basil Hallward, affirms the value of secrecy in virtually the same breath as he violates it, in telling Lord Henry what he didn't intend to tell him: the name of Dorian Gray.

and regret—pleasure in the achievements of a long design, regret in the separation from many companions—that I am in danger of wearying the reader whom I love, with personal confidences and private emotions. (45)

Strongly hinting at the intimate and specular nature of his relationship to *David Copperfield*, Dickens nonetheless courteously refrains from elaborating on it. Yet it is fair to wonder how "wearying" the personal confidences and private emotions could possibly be, when something very like them has been appetizingly promised on the title page of the very book that Dickens is presenting: "The Personal History, Adventures, Experience, & Observation of David Copperfield . . . (Which He never meant to be Published on any Account)." And if we do not fully believe in their wearisomeness, neither can we quite credit the "love" for the reader on whose account they are suppressed: the concern for the burdened reader is surely more defensive than protective. In any event, no sooner is Dickens's subjectivity put before us than it is also put away: made to vanish in the act of proffering the Book itself: "All that I could say of the Story, to any purpose, I have endeavoured to say in it." Unwilling to speak of himself, Dickens instead points to his story of the other, in which C.D., authorial signature, will be inverted—or rather, extroverted—into D.C., sign of a character who is also, as though to indicate his purely verbal existence, sign of a book.

While it may be the usual task of a preface to manage such transitions from author to text, from subjectivity to its eclipse in the object at hand, here, at any rate, the business is not just routine. For the gesture made in Dickens's preface is repeated within the novel by David himself, who regularly and almost ritually "secretes" his subjectivity at precisely what would appear to be its determining moments. For example, when David returns home on holiday from school, he has the more than pleasant surprise of finding his mother alone nursing her newly delivered child:

> I spoke to her, and she stared, and cried out. But seeing me, she called me her dear Davy, her own boy! and coming half across the room to meet me, kneeled down upon the ground and kissed me, and laid my head down on her bosom near the little creature that was nestling there, and put its hand to my lips.
>
> I wish I had died. I wish I had died then, with that feeling in my heart! I should have been more fit for Heaven than I ever have been since. (162)

The supreme importance of the incident seems to depend wholly on the intensity of an affect that, though cited, is never specified. No doubt we could be more precise than David about the nature of that feeling in his heart, whose principal component it would not be hard to nominate: the bliss of recovering the mother in a relationship that has been unexpectedly de-triangulated not only by Murdstone's absence, but also by the presence of the new sibling, a minorized third who is more David's surrogate at the maternal breast than his rival. To which one could add the unholy excitement at seeing the mother who abandoned him for another abjectly repentant at his feet, along with the already pitiable infant by whom he might have been supplanted a second time; and finally, the consequent guilt that accedes to conscience only as the self-satisfied wish to have died in such a state of grace. Yet what matters more than the availability of these determinations is the fact that, even in this ample autobiography, intended for no one's eyes but his own (671), David only alludes to the feeling whose decisiveness he nevertheless advertises. And much as, in the preface, Dickens managed his own fraught subjectivity by introducing the novel in its place, so David, shortly after this episode, finds himself in his room, "poring over a book" (171).

The same pattern is enacted in Steerforth's bedroom, to
which David "belongs" (137), at Salem House:

> The greater part of the guests had gone to bed as soon as the eating
> and drinking were over; and we, who had remained whispering and
> listening half-undressed, at last betook ourselves to bed, too.
>
> "Good night, young Copperfield," said Steerforth. "I'll take care
> of you."
>
> "You're very kind," I gratefully returned. "I am very much obliged
> to you."
>
> "You haven't got a sister, have you?" said Steerforth yawning.
>
> "No," I answered.
>
> "That's a pity," said Steerforth. "If you had had one, I should think
> she would have been a pretty, timid, little, bright-eyed sort of girl.
> I should have liked to know her. Good night, young Copperfield."
>
> "Good night, sir," I replied.
>
> I thought of him very much after I went to bed, and raised myself,
> I recollect, to look at him where he lay in the moonlight, with his
> handsome face turned up, and his head reclining easily on his arm.
> He was a person of great power in my eyes; that was, of course, the
> reason of my mind running on him. No veiled future dimly glanced
> upon him in the moonbeams. There was no shadowy picture of his
> footsteps, in the garden that I dreamed of walking in all night. (140)

Here again a powerful affect is evoked, but evacuated of any
substantial content. *What* did David think of Steerforth as he
looked at him where he lay in the moonlight, his handsome face
turned up? In one sense, the question scarcely merits an answer,
so eloquently here does the love that dare not speak its name
speak its metonyms (the "whispering and listening half-
undressed," and so on). Yet in another sense, such an answer is
positively averted, since David lapses into distractingly cryptic
reverie at just the point where but for the veil of "no veiled
future" the classic erotics of the scene would have become manifest. And once again, the affect is soon displaced in an experience of fiction: in lieu of the nocturnal sexual episode that—
as David might say—"of course" does not take place between

him and Steerforth, they organize the institution of bedtime stories, in which David recounts to Steerforth from memory the novels he has read at home. As in the scene with his mother, David's reticence here may be largely "unconscious," but the distinction is secondary to a pattern that is also capable of being rehearsed quite consciously, as when David is forced to do manual labor at Murdstone and Grinby's warehouse. "I never said, to man or boy, how it was that I came to be there, or gave the least indication that I was sorry I was there. That I suffered in secret, and that I suffered exquisitely, no one ever knew but I. How much I suffered, it is . . . utterly beyond my power to tell" (218). The importance of this secret suffering—not just for David, but for Dickens, too, with his own traumatically secreted *déclassement* in Warren's Blacking Factory as a child— is in no danger of being underrated. It only loses the privilege that we are accustomed to accord to it by displaying the common structure of all such important moments in the novel: first the allusion ("how much I suffered"), then the elision ("is beyond my power to tell"), and finally the turn to the novelistic, as David attempts to entertain his fellow workers "with some results of the old readings."

The pattern that thus recurs in David's life, however, finds its most extensive embodiment in his life-story. We notice, for instance, that the gestures of secretiveness are made, not just then, at the time of the narrative ("That I suffered in secret, no one ever knew"), but now as well, at the time of its narration ("How much I suffered, it is beyond my power to tell"). The diffidence of this narration obviously perpetuates the same fears of discipline that inhibited David with the Murdstones, at Salem House (even Steerforth is likened to a magistrate [136]), and in the warehouse. But the narration of this diffidence also perpetuates the turn to (reading, recounting, writing) stories that was David's regular escape from these fears. The manuscript to which, in his own phrase, he *commits his secrets* (713), is precisely that: the place where he encrypts them. The manuscript to which, in his own phrase, he commits his secrets, *if he knows them* (713), is rather the place where he encrypts them so as neither to know them nor to make them known.[3] Writing the self, then, would be consistently ruled by the paradoxical proposition that the self is most itself at the moment when its defining inwardness is most secret, most withheld from writing—with the equally paradoxical consequence that autobiography is most successful only where *it has been abandoned for the Novel*. The paradoxes determine not only David, who intimates his subjectivity only to displace it into various modes of experiencing the Novel, but also Dickens, who, just as he abandoned what thus remained an autobiographical fragment to write *David Copperfield* in the first place, strikes, and then strikes out, the personal note in his preface. And what had been, it seemed, my own personal note would now prove no less impersonal than a faithful reproduction of these same paradoxes. Even at the moment of its annunciation, my subjectivity had already been annulled as a mere effect of its object. Or alternatively: I have been able to be a subject in the only way this object-text allows: by pointing to the Novel, where one's own secret will be kept because somebody else's will be revealed. In the knowledge, then, that at least where *David Copperfield* is concerned autobiography can *only* be an "autobiographical fragment," let us again change the subject.

II

Characters in *David Copperfield* are frequently coupled with boxes: bags, parcels, luggage. Betsey Trotwood can be accu-

3. For several obvious reasons, it cannot here be a question of undertaking David's psychoanalysis. But for a psychoanalytic account of the "crypt" as a "false unconscious," see Nicolas Abraham and Maria Torok, *Cryptomanie: Le verbier de l'homme aux loups* (Paris: Flammarion, 1976); and for a more-or-less psychoanalytic account of the account, Jacques Derrida, "Fors," the introductory essay to the same volume, pp. 7–73.

rately identified by David, who has never seen her, through the fact that she "carries a bag . . . with a great deal of room in it," and which seems a ready accessory to her "coming down upon you, sharp" (245). Miss Murdstone, who embellishes herself in numerous steel fetters, brings with her to the Rookery "two uncompromising hard black boxes, with her initials on the lids in hard brass nails," and the boxes "were never seen open or known to be left unlocked" (97, 98). Mr. Barkis, himself a carrier of boxes, also has his own, full of money and hidden under his bed, "which he pretended was only full of coats and trousers" (205). So close is the connection between the miser and his box that on his deathbed Barkis becomes "as mute and senseless as the box, from which his form derived the only expression it had" (506). As these examples suggest, characters come with boxes because characters come in boxes, as boxes. Some characters in *David Copperfield* run the risk of being put away, in the asylum with which Mr. Dick is threatened or the prison in which Uriah Heep and Littimer are actually incarcerated, and others encounter the fate of being sent away, like David to his room or to school, or even like Jack Maldon, Mr. Mell, the Micawber family, Mr. Peggotty, and Emily, to the colonies, but a far greater number—anticipating and attempting to avert these fates—have simply put themselves away, in boxes that safeguard their precious subjectivity within. Familiar to us as their eccentricities seem to make them, the characters in *David Copperfield* (as though the real function of eccentricity were to render the eccentric a private person, inaccessible to the general) typically manage to be *arcane*—even when they do not literally inhabit, like Daniel Peggotty, an ark.

How do they box themselves in, seal themselves off? At the molecular level of gesture, they may stop up their ears like Betsey Trotwood and Dora, or suck in their cheeks like Uriah Heep, or, like Betsey Trotwood again and Mrs. Markleham, retire behind their fans. At the molar level of deportment, they may take refuge in a militant bearing. The "firmness" recommended and practiced by the Murdstones is not confined to them: it shows up as well in Betsey's "fell rigidity of figure and composure of countenance" (52), in the "atmosphere of respectability" with which Littimer surrounds himself (356), and in "the outward restraints" that Uriah Heep "puts upon himself" (848). Alternatively, they may pursue a thoroughgoing self-effacement, like Mr. Chillip, who sidles in and out of a room, to take up the less space (58), or Ham with his "sheepish look" (78), or the "mild" Mr. Mell (147). Even their dress participates in their self-sequestration. Betsey ties her head up in a handkerchief, and Peggotty throws her apron over her face. Ham wears a pair of such very stiff trousers that they would have stood quite as well alone (78), and Traddles wears a tight sky-blue suit that makes his arms and legs like German sausages (143). Uriah Heep, like Mr. Spenlow, is "buttoned up to the throat" (275). And when these characters speak, they rarely speak their mind, but more often only its screen: Littimer's composed courtesy, Uriah Heep's hypocritical humility, Betsey's gruff understatement. At the extreme, they protect their subjectivity by refusing to assume it even grammatically: by refusing to say "I," like Markham, who says "a man" instead (419), or Barkis, who designates himself and his desires in the third person—what, more simply and strictly, Emile Benveniste calls the "nonperson."[4]

---

4. That the third person is not a person at all, but rather the form whose function is to express the nonperson, Benveniste argues in "Relationships of Person in the Verb" and "The Nature of Pronouns," both collected in his *Problems in General Linguistics*, trans. Mary Elizabeth Meek (Coral Gables, Florida: University of Miami Press, 1971). Even apter are Roland Barthes's reflections on the "possible affinity of paranoia and distancing" in the use of the third person: "'he' is wicked: the nastiest word in the language: pronoun of the non-person, it annuls and mortifies its referent; it cannot be applied without uneasiness to someone one loves; saying 'he' about someone, I always envision a kind of murder by

Thoroughly encased in such diverse armor, the characters in *David Copperfield* prepare to do battle with the outside world. But the battle, fundamentally dubious, has already been lost in the very preparations for it. It is as though the ravages feared from the others have been assumed by the self in its own name, and that the costs of social discipline have been averted only in an equally expensive self-discipline. Part of the expense, surely, is paid out of the moral category that, though frequently and often hysterically invoked by Dickens to differentiate his characters into good ones and bad, proves absolutely irrelevant to the structural uniformity of their self-concealment. No doubt, Uriah Heep's "umbleness" hides only a vaulting ambition and cankering resentment, while Ham's "sheepishness" masks a heroically good nature; and Betsey Trotwood with her bag and her fell rigidity of figure is a quite different moral type from Miss Murdstone with her two black boxes and her firmness. But the obvious moral distinctions here simply overlay a formal similarity of character that they have not determined and are powerless to affect. It is as if Heep and Ham, Betsey Trotwood and Jane Murdstone, however much the ethical content of their inwardness might differ, agreed on the paranoid perception that the social world is a dangerous place to exhibit the inner self and on the aggressive precautions that must be taken to protect it from exposure. To be good, to be bad are merely variants of the primordial condition that either presupposes: to be *in camera*. Thus, the practical social consequences of goodness, on which Dickens puts strong ideological pressure, are of necessity extremely limited, since the good can only be good, do good, in secret. And the text holds a worse irony in store for good people: that in defending themselves against the outrages of socialization, they unwittingly beat them to the punch. Either, to protect themselves against "outside" aggressions, they need

---

language" (*Roland Barthes by Roland Barthes*, trans. Richard Howard [New York: Hill and Wang, 1977], p. 169).

to commit them, like Betsey Trotwood stuffing cotton in her ears and then stuffing Ham's ears as well, "as if she confounded them with her own" (59), or later with the donkeys. Or else, fearful of the consequences of their aggression, they take it out on themselves, like Mr. Mell, who "would talk to himself sometimes, and grin, and clench his fist, and grind his teeth, and pull his hair in an unaccountable manner" (133). Despite the thin skins in which they are all enveloped (even Murdstone's firm hand can be humiliatingly bitten), characters add to the rough-and-tumble social buffetting from which they would withdraw. Still, if their elaborate defenses finally amount to no more than the fact that they have made their social necessity into their personal choice, this perhaps suffices for a subject who can thus continue to affirm his subjectivity *as a form* even where it no longer has a content of its own.

This is not, of course, the whole story. Such defenses may be indistinguishable from that which they defend against, and thus reduce the subjectivity that mobilizes them to a purely formal category. But they can surely continue to be opposed to that which they defend: the hidden innerness that like the miser's hoard must never see the light of day. Just as we can say of this hoard in a capitalist economy that it is *worth nothing* as soon as it has been removed from circulation and exchange, so we might wonder what value can be put upon an innerness that is never recognized in intersubjectivity. And the epistemological questions inevitably brought forward in such cases are not far away: if the secret subjective content is so well concealed, how do we know it is there? How does the concealing subject know it is there? What could the content of a subjectivity that is never substantiated possibly be? Accordingly, at the same time that the characters in *David Copperfield* embox their subjectivity, they find oblique means and occasions to take the lid off. Peggotty's tendency to burst her buttons (66), Mr. Mell's pouring what seems like "his whole being" into his doleful flute-playing (132), the wasting fire within Rosa Dartle finding vent in her gaunt eyes (350): these are only a few examples of the odd compromises that characters strike, like Freudian hysterics, between expression and repression. In some sense, therefore, the secret subject is always an open secret.

Sometimes, certainly, this open secret is actively *opened*. The dramatic heights of Dickens's fiction are customarily reached when a secret is explosively let out, as at Uriah Heep's unmasking, or when two boxed-in, buttoned-up subjects find release in one another, like David and Peggotty whispering and kissing through the keyhole of his locked room on the last night of his "restraint." Yet even such moments as these only explicate as information what had been previously available to characters as intuition. Though David seems to know Betsey Trotwood only as a legendary dragon, if he nonetheless risks throwing himself on her mercy, sight unseen, it is because he has always known more than this: hadn't his mother told him that "she had a fancy that she felt Miss Betsey touch her hair, and that with no ungentle hand" (53)? Far more often, however, dramatic revelation even of this order is superfluous. Barkis's box might be taken for an emblem of those many secrets in the novel to which everyone is privy: David's "secret" attachment to Dora, which even the drunken dimness of Mrs. Crupp is capable of penetrating; the "secret" of Uriah Heep's interest in Agnes, which he asks others to keep so as to keep them from interfering; Mr. Wickfield's alcoholism, the secret that everyone hides because everyone holds; Miss Murdstone's fetters, "suggesting on the outside, to all beholders, what was to be expected within" (453); and so on. The radical emptiness of secrecy in the novel is most forcefully (if all unconsciously) argued by Miss Mills, whose "love of the romantic and mysterious" (619) fabricates trivial secrets on the same popular romance principles that make them so easily divined.

Even when a character's subjectivity may be successfully concealed from other characters, for us, readers of the novel, the secret is always out. Like David, we have suspected the good nature that underlies Betsey Trotwood's decided and inflexible exterior, and, long before him, we have detected the "secret" of Agnes's attachment. Similarly, we never doubt that Mr. Mell, mild or unmelodious as a social presence, has the milk of human kindness within; that the Murdstones, despite their firmness, are ultimately purposeless creatures; that Uriah Heep lies through his professions of humility; or that Peggotty is dear and loving for all her comic inarticulateness. The hermeneutic problem put to characters by the discrepancy between outside and inside (such that the former can never be counted on to represent the latter, which it is rather constituted to disguise) is never a problem for us, for whom the outside, riven with expressive vents, quite adequately designates the nature of the subject it thus fails to conceal. For us, all the camouflage that characters devise to deceive one another gives way to readerly transparency, as, no less immediately, their secrets become our sure knowledge.

Yet, curiously enough, the fact the secret is always known—and, in some obscure sense, known to be known—never interferes with the incessant activity of keeping it. The contradiction does not merely affect characters. We too inevitably surrender our privileged position as readers to whom all secrets are open by "forgetting" our knowledge for the pleasures of suspense and surprise. (Even a first reading, if there is one, is shaped by this obliviscence, which a second makes impossible to doubt.) In this light, it becomes clear that the social function of secrecy—isomorphic with its novelistic function—is not to conceal knowledge, so much as to conceal the knowledge of the knowledge. No doubt an analysis of the kinds of knowledge that it is felt needful to cover in secrecy would tell us much about a given culture or historical period—though in the case of *David Copperfield* the results of such an analysis would be banal in the extreme: sex, drink, and (for the middle-class subject) work are the taboo categories they more or less remain today. But when the game of secrecy is played beyond those contexts that obviously call for suppression, it is evident that the need to "keep secret" takes precedence over whatever social exigencies exist for keeping one or another secret in particular. Instead of the question "What does secrecy cover?" we had better ask "What covers secrecy?" What, that is, takes secrecy for its field of operations? In a world where the explicit exposure of the subject would manifest how thoroughly he has been inscribed within a socially given totality, secrecy would be the spiritual exercise by which the subject is allowed to conceive of himself as a resistance: a friction in the smooth functioning of the social order, a margin to which its far-reaching discourse does not reach. Secrecy would thus be the subjective practice in which the oppositions of private/public, inside/outside, subject/object are established, and the sanctity of their first term kept inviolate. And the phenomenon of the "open secret" does not, as one might think, bring about the collapse of these binarisms and their ideological effects, but rather attests to their fantasmatic recovery. In a mechanism reminiscent of Freudian disavowal, we know perfectly well that the secret is known, but nonetheless we must persist, however ineptly, in guarding it. The paradox of the open secret registers the subject's accommodation to a totalizing system that has obliterated the difference he would make—the difference he does make, in the imaginary denial of this system "even so."

III

It remains, therefore, an odd fact that readers have traditionally found the Dickens character, particularly in *David Copperfield*, a source of great "charm." What charm, we may ask, is there in the spectacle of such pathetically reduced beings, maimed by their own defense mechanisms, and whose undoubtedly immense energy can only be expended to fix them all the more irremovably in a total social system? How is it that such grotesques are not perceived as the appalling evidence of what T. W. Adorno, speaking of the fate of the subject in such a system, calls "damaged life," but instead as the complacently enjoyed proof of our own unimpaired ability to love them? The charm we allow to Dickens's characters, I submit, is ultimately no more than the debt of gratitude we pay to their fixity for giving us, in contrast, our freedom. We condescend to praise these characters as "inimitable" because they make manifest how safe we are from the possibility of actually imitating them. The reduced model of the subject that they exemplify is refuted or transcended automatically in any reader's experience. For one thing, the consciousness of this reader, effortlessly capable of disarming their self-betraying defenses and penetrating their well-known secrets, must always thereby exceed that of the characters, both individually and severally. Indeed, this "inclusive" consciousness is part of what contributes to the sense that the characters are boxed in. For another, the novel-reading subject can never resemble Dickens's characters, conspicuously encased yet so transparent that they are always inside-out, because the novel-reading subject as such has no outside. However much this subject inclusively sees, he is never seen in turn, invisible both to himself (he is reading a novel) and to others (he is reading it in private). The boxed-in characters, already so reified that they are easily and frequently likened to things (boxes great, like rooms and houses, as well as small), thus come to play object to the (faceless, solitary, secreted) reading subject, whose structural position and the comparison that reinforces it both release *him* from the conditions that determine *them*.

The reader's comparative freedom vis-à-vis the constraints of character is, of course, a general effect in the nineteenth-century novel. For if the Novel is the genre of "secret singularity,"[5] it becomes so less by providing us with an intimate

---

5. "And if from the early Middle Ages to the present day the 'adventure' is an account of individuality, the passage from the epic to the novel, from

glimpse of a character's inner life than by determining this life in such a way that its limitations must forcibly contrast with our own less specified, less violated inwardness. The contrast is inscribed within the nineteenth-century novel as one between the character and the narrator, our readerly surrogate and point of view, who is in general so shadowy and indeterminate a figure that it scarcely seems right to call him a person at all. But Dickens's fiction is particularly relevant to the problematics of modern subjectivity, because his novels pose such a sharp contrast in the extreme difference and distance between the character, who is so thoroughly extroverted that his inner life seems exiguous, and the narrator, who is so completely defaced that, even when he bears a name like David Copperfield, Phiz hardly knows what "phiz" to give him.

As early as the *Sketches by Boz*, these problematics are already rehearsed, though in ways that *David Copperfield* will modify substantially. Formally speaking, the narrative in the *Sketches* is skimpy, fragmentary, never more than anecdotal: stories either never get off the ground, or if they do, terminate in the arrested development characteristic of the "short story." Thematically speaking, the deficiency of narrative in the text corresponds to the lack of adventure, even as a possibility, in the world the text represents. On one hand, a viable agent of adventure cannot really emerge from among the dwarfed and emaciated subjects (typically too small or too thin) who populate the metropolis and who are far too much like the objects that overwhelm them there. And like the diverse articles inventoried in the various junkshops Boz visits—human products divorced from human production or use—these short, foreshort-

---

the noble deed to the secret singularity, from long exiles to the internal search for childhood, from combats to phantasies, is also inscribed in the formation of a disciplinary society" (Michel Foucault, *Discipline and Punish*, trans. Alan Sheridan [New York: Pantheon, 1977], p. 193 [translation modified]).

ened subjects are serially juxtaposed to one another without ever forming a cohesive "community." On the other hand, even if a properly qualified agent of adventure did appear—and several characters at least attempt to qualify for the role—his adventure could only be played out as parody in a world that has routinized even the opportunities for breaking routine. (In "Making a Night of It," for example, the carnivalesque release from clerical chores is as regular as the quarterly pay for doing them.) And should routine fail to meet the case, there would always be the police to close it: the police who appear to stand on every London streetcorner and whose function, like that of their many surrogates in the *Sketches*, is to return adventure to the confinement from which it all too briefly emerged.

Yet every dreary characteristic of the world that Boz represents has been overcome in his representation. Though this world is bound in stasis, Boz is demonstrably the free-ranging flaneur, and to him, in his casual meanderings, befall the adventurous possibilities denied to the characters. Though the world of objects is mute, Boz has wit enough to overcome its alienation and make it speak once more to and of human subjects. And though the faces Boz gazes upon are horribly precise in the deformations by which they reveal class, profession, and the general scars of city dwelling, Boz himself, faceless, shows none of them. Even the characters' lack of community is negated by Boz's confident use of the plural first-person pronoun, as though here were a subject who could count on allies. Altogether, it is as if the problems or constraints arising from the dull urbanism of the *Sketches* found their solution or release in the lively urbanity of the sketching.

The very disparity between problem and solution, however, means that the latter must engender certain problems of its own. Insofar as the subject (Boz) and the object (the world he sketches, including its reified subjects) are merely juxtaposed, each pole retaining its own distinctness, the "solution" borne in the narration has no bearing on the "problem" it would solve—except, no doubt, to offer further evidence of it in the mere contiguity of terms that otherwise remain mutually unrecognizable and unrelated. The lack of any interactive or dialectical connection between subject and object thus becomes registered as the fragmentary form of the sketches themselves, which not only bespeaks the inability of the subject to master his materials, whose abiding heterogeneity can be grasped only in bits and pieces, but also casts into the shadow of a doubt the continuity of that very subject, whose freedom is purchased at the price of his intermittence, his utter ungroundedness. The interest of *David Copperfield* in this light is that the two models of subjectivity that the *Sketches* never reconcile—the one objectified in the character, the other abstracted in the narrator—are here linked and mediated in the actual story, in which a character becomes his own narrator. As Copperfield the narrator recounts the life (really, the death) of David the character, we witness an abstracted, all-embracing subjectivity telling the story of its own genesis, of how, and against what odds and with what at stake, it came to be. Implicitly, the process submits the whole category of the "social" to radical revision. The phenomenology that (as in the *Sketches*) locates the social outside the subject is not ever abandoned, but instead of being taken for granted, it now has to be produced. No longer a mere content whose oppressions or determinations are confined to the second term of a rigid opposition between self and other (or between subject and object, or narrator and character), the social now appears as the very field in which these oppositions are strategically constituted.

IV

We need, then, to consider the story of this autobiography, whose essential drama stems from David's desperate attempt not to be boxed in, or confounded with a box, like the other characters. "Master Copperfield's box there!" says Miss Murdstone, as the wheels of Barkis's cart are heard at the Rookery gates (112). Her words, as always, are ominous, and at the coaching inn not long afterward, David has the anxious experience of being abandoned among boxes, as he waits on the luggage scale for someone from Salem House to claim him:

Here, as I sat looking at the parcels, packages, and books . . . a procession of most tremendous considerations began to march through my mind. Supposing nobody should ever fetch me, how long would they consent to keep me there? Would they keep me long enough to spend seven shillings? Should I sleep at night in one of those wooden bins, with the other luggage, and wash myself at the pump in the yard in the morning; or should I be turned out every night, and expected to come again to be left till called for, when the office opened next day? Supposing there was no mistake in the case, and Mr Murdstone had devised this plan to get rid of me, what should I do? . . . These thoughts, and a hundred other such thoughts, turned me burning hot, and made me giddy with apprehension and dismay. I was in the height of my fever when a man entered and whispered to the clerk, who presently slanted me off the scale, and pushed me over to him, as if I were weighed, bought, delivered, and paid for. (124)

David has more grounds for panic than he knows. Already Mr. Murdstone has locked him up for five days in his room, where, at once starting to internalize his confinement, he has been "ashamed" to show himself at the window, lest the boys playing in the churchyard should know that he was "a prisoner" (109). Even when he is no longer in prison, but down in the parlor, he has retained "a sensitive consciousness of always appearing constrained" (170). But a more awful fate awaits him at Salem House—"a square brick building with wings" (129)—where Murdstone's discipline will be institutionalized. The placard David is there made to carry—"*Take care of him. He bites*" (130)—imposes on him the forfeiture of even linguistic subjectivity, its reduction to the pronoun of the nonperson. (Indicatively, when David inquires about the dog, Mr. Mell replies, "That's not a dog—that's a boy," not "that's you.") David is thus linked to the closed, "close" character in the novel par excellence: "Barkis is willin'" is no worse than "he bites." It is, in fact, rather better, for Barkis has at least taken charge of his self-annulment, whereas David, obliged to wear the placard on his back, where he can't see it, must submit to his.

What I suffered from that placard, nobody can imagine. Whether it was possible for people to see me or not, I always fancied that somebody was reading it. It was no relief to turn around and find nobody; for wherever my back was, there I imagined somebody always to be. . . . I knew that the servants read it, and the butcher read it, and the baker read it; that everybody, in a word, who came backwards and forwards to the house, of a morning when I was ordered to walk there, read that I was to be taken care of, for I bit. (130–31)

As the subject of readerly perusal unable to *look back*, David assumes the very ontology of a character in fiction. This dog's life is only trivially metamorphosed when, again under Murdstone's compulsion, he becomes "a little labouring hind in the service of Murdstone and Grinby" (208). There his confinement is symbolized daily and in detail by the tasks he must perform. "When the empty bottles [to be rinsed, washed, examined for flaws] ran short, there were labels to be pasted on full ones, or corks to be fitted to them, or seals to be put upon the corks, or finished bottles to be packed in casks. All this work was my work" (209). And, as though these operations were being simultaneously practiced on himself: "I mingled my tears with the water in which I was washing the bottles; and sobbed as if there were a flaw in my own breast, and it were in danger of bursting" (210). Finally, when David forms his "great resolution" to run away to Dover, even his own box threatens to turn him into one—the kind the long-legged man calls "a pollis case" (234). If David has "hardly breath enough to cry for the loss of [his] box" (235), this is because, quite apart from the fact that he is exhausted from running, the box ultimately doesn't deserve his tears. All things considered, it is not a bad thing that he takes "very little more out of the world, towards the retreat of [his] aunt, than [he] had brought into it" (235).[6]

We have already glanced at what David calls "my only and my constant comfort" (106) throughout all this: the experience of the Novel. It begins when he happens to read the small collection of novels left by his father and impersonates his favorite characters in them, and is resumed when he recounts these novels to Steerforth at Salem House and to the other boys at Murdstone and Grinby's. It takes a still more active turn when, dejectedly lounging in obscure London streets, David fits the old books to his altered life, and makes stories for himself, out of the streets, and out of men and women. "Some points in the character I shall unconsciously develop, I suppose, in writing my life, were gradually forming all this while" (224). From here it is an orderly progression: first to the fearful and tremulous novice who writes a little something "in secret" and sends it to a magazine (692); then to the writer who, Dora rightly fears, forgets her, "full of silent fancies" (715); and finally, to "the eminent author," as Micawber calls him, who, though "familiar to the imaginations of a considerable portion of the civilized world" (945), nevertheless modestly occults himself in the same gesture that we saw Dickens make in the preface: "I do not enter on the aspirations, the delights, anxieties and triumphs of my art. That I truly devoted myself to it with my

6. For the ultimate mortifying box, of course, is the oblong kind made at Mr. Omer's establishment. It is from Mr. Omer's that David is conveyed to his mother's funeral along with her coffin. Though he is accompanied in the "half chaise-cart, half pianoforte-van" by Omer, Minnie, and Joram, he seems almost grieved to note that "there was plenty of room for us all" (183).

strongest earnestness, I have already said. If the books I have written be of any worth, they will supply the rest. I shall otherwise have written to poor purpose, and the rest will be of interest to no one" (917).

To the last, the experience of the novel provides David's subjectivity with a secret refuge: a free, liberalizing space in which he comes into his own, a critical space in which he takes his distance from the world's carceral oppressions. Yet if, more than anything else, this secret refuge is responsible for forming David into the liberal subject, this is paradoxically because, in a sense, *he is not there*. Certainly, as Miss Murdstone might well have complained, David hides behind his books—but as Clara might have fondly observed, he loses himself in them as well. What has often been considered an artistic flaw in Dickens's novel—David's rather matte and colorless personality—is rather what makes the novel possible, as David's own artistic performance. Far from an aesthetic defect, the vacuity is the psychological desideratum of one whose ambition, from the time he first impersonated his favorite characters in his father's books, has always been *to be vicarious*. It is as though the only way to underwrite the self, in the sense of insuring it, were to under-write the self, in the sense of merely implying it. The Novel protects subjectivity not by locking it in, in the manner of a box, but by locking it out, since the story always determines the destiny of *somebody else*. And what goes for the subject of *David Copperfield* goes in a different dimension for the subject who reads it. He too defines his subjectivity in absentia. Entirely given over to the inner life and its meditations, constantly made to exceed the readerly determinations he both receives and practices, this subject finds himself not where he reads, but—between the lines, in the margins, outside the covers—where he does not. (Another open secret that everyone knows and no one wants to: the immense amount of daydreaming that accompanies the ordinary reading of a novel.) In this sense, the novel would be the very genre of the liberal subject, both as cause and effect: the genre that produces him, the genre to which, as its effect, he returns for "recreation."

What, then, are we to make of the fact that the experience of the Novel, alleged to take its subject out of a box, takes place in one (the "little room" at the Rookery, the "little closet" in Mr. Chillip's surgery, and so on)? The connection between the book and the box is always far closer than their effective polarity suggests. At the coaching inn, for instance, David looks at "parcels, packages, and books," and this reminds us that the book, read in a box, has the visible, palpable shape of one too. But perhaps what best "betrays" the secret consubstantiality of box and book—better than their phonetic alliteration, better than their etymological affinity (both, in a sense, coming from branches of the same *tree*)[7]—is the article of furniture combining a chest of drawers and a writing desk that we call a bureau. At Peggotty's new home, really Barkis's old one, David is "impressed" by "a certain old bureau of dark wood in the parlour . . . with a retreating top which opened, let down, and became a desk, within which was a large quarto edition of Foxe's *Book of Martyrs*" (203). Instead of straightforwardly ascending from box to book, the image suggests rather that one descends *en abîme* within the box through a smaller box to reach the smallest box of all, the book, where the subject at last finds himself, but only in a martyred state. What Barkis's bureau thus opens is the possibility that the book quite simply belongs to the box, as its "property" or one of its "effects."

All this is to say, in other terms, that the story of David's liberation runs parallel to the story of his submission: the chastening of what, with an ambiguous wistfulness, he calls an "undisciplined heart." The discipline from which he has escaped to become the "subject of the Novel" reappears as his own self-discipline. "What I had to do," he says of the time he la-

7. "Book" from OE *bōc*, beech; "box" from Gk *pyxos*, boxtree.

bored to win Dora, "was to turn the painful discipline of my early years to account, by going to work with a steady and resolute heart" (582). Mr. Murdstone's firmness and Mr. Creakle's unspared rod were not, it would appear, total losses. They stand behind David's victories in a succession of trials (Betsey Trotwood's "ruin," the winning of Dora, the losing of Dora) concluded and rewarded by the marriage to Agnes, the woman whom Micawber aptly calls an "appealing monitor" (820). But what seems to ensure this self-discipline most of all is writing itself. "I could never have done what I have done, without the habits of punctuality, order, and diligence, without the determination to concentrate myself on one object at a time, no matter how quickly its successor should come upon its heels, which I then formed" (671). Though David is not recalling here his service at Murdstone and Grinby's, but rather his apprenticeship in shorthand, he might as well be: minus the value judgments, the habits required are quite the same. It is clear too that the discipline of writing does not lie in merely technical skills. As David's apology on the next page for the importance of being earnest confirms, these skills are immediately raised to high moral values—and these values, though differently valorized, are the very ones that help the characters to box themselves in. Paradoxically, writing is thus offered to us in *David Copperfield* as a socializing order from which the written self, always subject to omission, is separated, but with which the writing self, inevitably the agent of such omission, comes to be entirely identified.

What difference, then, finally is there between this book-loving subject and the boxlike characters he would transcend? We see how ambiguous and complicated an answer to this question must be if, by way of conclusion, we consider the rather unmotivated visit that David pays to a prison at the end of the novel. With Mr. Creakle as administrator, and Uriah Heep and Mr. Littimer as model prisoners up to their old tricks, the prison scene makes some familiar points in Dickens's representation of the carceral. That the former Master of Salem House is now the magistrate in charge of a prison, as though he had merely been transferred, bears out the systemic coherence of an institutional network that fabricates the very subjects who then require its discipline. It is true that Uriah Heep's incorrigible hypocrisy would seem to be a manner of resisting the institution that seeks to restrain him and thus of saving from discipline the subject who "puts restraints upon himself." But this secret resistance only perfects the thoroughgoing accommodation that it camouflages. Small wonder the prison has no effect in reforming Uriah, when in another, earlier version (as the "foundation school" where he and his father were raised) it has formed him in the first place. In this sense, Uriah's extravagant encomia on the prison system—"It would be better for everybody, if they got took up, and was brought here" (928)—belie their obvious resentment to bespeak truly the weird erotic attraction between a subject and an institution "made for each other."

The spurious opposition between Uriah and the prison is no sooner displayed, however, than it is displaced into the more authentic-seeming opposition between David and the prison. If the carceral is abruptly brought on stage at the end of the novel, when David is a respected, "untouchable" author, this is to dramatize and celebrate his distance from it: a distance that can be measured in the detached tones—and even the critical ones—of his response. David can afford irony and indignation here because, as the pure observer, he is as free to go as he was curious to come: "We left them to their system and themselves, and went home wondering" (930). Still, much as Uriah, the carceral subject, was fated to be matched with the prison, so David, the liberal subject, must also ensure his status with an institutional match. Not by accident is the prison scene framed, on one side, by David's realization that he loves Agnes with more than a brotherly affection, and on the other, by the actual declaration of his love to her, which prompts her to reveal her well-guarded, well-known "secret." Uriah humbly kowtows to the prison authorities; David modestly asks to be "guided" (916) by the "appealing monitor without" (to use Micawber's distinction) who will reinforce "the silent monitor within." We can't even say that the discipline that merely befalls Uriah is David's voluntary choice, since Uriah too has chosen self-discipline, just as David has turned to account the painful discipline of his early years. Faced with the abundance of resemblances between the liberal subject and his carceral double, the home and the prison-house, how can we significantly differentiate them?

Only, I think, according to the logic of their effects, by looking at how the two modes of discipline are played off against one another in a single system of social control. If only from the *roman noir* (but not only from it),[8] we know that the police interrogate in teams of two. While one agent brutally attacks the suspect's body, the other more humanely appeals to his soul. The suspect is so afraid that the one will beat the guts out of him that he spills them anyway to the other. Likewise, one withdraws from the discipline of stepfathers and their institutional extensions only by turning that discipline to account,

8. In the *Miranda* decision, the U.S. Supreme Court cites actual manuals of police interrogation to describe the ploy known as the "friendly-unfriendly" or the "Mutt and Jeff" act: "In this technique, two agents are employed. Mutt, the relentless investigator . . . knows the subject is guilty and is not going to waste any time. He's sent a dozen men away for this crime and he's going to send the subject away for the full term. Jeff, on the other hand, is obviously a kindhearted man. He has a family himself. He has a brother who was involved in a little scrape like this. He disapproves of Mutt and his tactics and will arrange to get him off the case if the subject will cooperate. He can't hold Mutt off for very long. The subject would be wise to make a quick decision. The technique is applied by having both investigators present while Mutt acts out his role. Jeff may stand by quietly and demur at some of Mutt's tactics. When Jeff makes his plea for cooperation, Mutt is not present in the room" (*Miranda v. Arizona*, 384 U.S. 436, 452 [1966]).

"by going to work with a steady and resolute heart." Though David is ultimately no different from the boxed-in characters he seeks to transcend, just as they are ultimately no different from the processes of disciplinary socialization they seek to avoid, yet in both cases, one becomes no different from the others only by, like them, assuming the effect of a difference which thus continues to operate. *David Copperfield* everywhere intimates a dreary pattern in which the subject constitutes himself "against" discipline by assuming that discipline in his own name. The pattern can hardly be broadcast in the novel, which requires the functioning of the difference to structure its own plot. But neither does the pattern go unbroached in the novel, whose discreet analogies remove the bar of the difference on which its very *Bildung* depends. The fact that the difference between liberal and carceral camps is not substantive, but only effective, has thus the status of a secret—that is to say, inevitably, an open secret. Accordingly, the novel must both keep this secret and give it away. Keep it, because the liberal/carceral opposition is the foundation of the liberal subject as well as the basis of the novel's own role in producing him. Give it away, because this opposition is effectively maintained by seeming always in need of maintenance: as though an impending "deconstruction" were required to inspire the anxious and incessant work of reconstructing a social order that thus keeps everyone on his toes, including the figure of the novelist who writes "far into the night" (950). Can the game of secrecy ever be thrown in? It is not likely so long as the play remains profitable: not just to the subject whom the play allows to establish his subjectivity, but also to the social order that, playing on the play, establishes his subjection. Listen to the different voices of the police, as David does them: "That I suffered in secret, and that I suffered exquisitely, no one ever knew but I. How much I suffered, it is . . . utterly beyond my power to tell. But I kept my counsel, and I did my work" (218).

Index

Abraham, Nicolas, 200n
Adorno, T. W., 208
Althusser, Louis, 65–66n6

Bakhtin, Mikhail, 25, 54
Balzac, Honoré de, vii, ix, 2, 25,
26, 29, 30, 31, 111, 142; *Une
ténébreuse affaire*, 21–24, 28–29,
31
Barthes, Roland, 29n, 89, 177–78,
202–3n
Bentham, Jeremy, 18
Benveniste, Emile, 202
Bersani, Leo, 27
Braddon, Mary Elizabeth, 30; *Lady
Audley's Secret*, 169–71
Brantlinger, Patrick, 147n
Brimley, George, 63n
Brontë, Charlotte, 133, 168
Brooks, Peter, 163–64
Buisson, Henry, 74n

Caillois, Roger, 1, 21n
Carpenter, Edward, 154–55n6
Christie, Agatha, 51, 53
Clausewitz, Karl von, 112
Collins, Philip, 65n5
Collins, Wilkie, ix, 2, 28, 30, 33–
57, 146–91. TEXTS: *Armadale*,
43; *The Moonstone*, 28, 33–57,
156; *The Woman in White*, 146–
91
Culler, Jonathan, 29n

De Man, Paul, 145n
Derrida, Jacques, 200n
Dickens, Charles, ix, xii–xiiin, 2,
4–10, 11, 15, 18–19, 20, 26,
31, 43, 58–106, 127–28, 133,
134, 157, 167, 192–220.
TEXTS: *Bleak House*, xii–xiiin,
58–106, 157; *David Copperfield*,
133, 192–220; *Hard Times*, 100;
Household Words, 94; *Little Dorrit*,
67, 100; *The Mystery of Edwin
Drood*, 43; *Nicholas Nickleby*, 61;
The Old Curiosity Shop, 87; *Oliver
Twist*, 4–10, 11, 15, 18–19, 26,
31, 59–60; *Sketches by Boz*, 209–
211
Donzelot, Jacques, 102–103
Dostoevsky, Fyodor, xiv
Doyle, Arthur Conan, 28, 34, 35,
41, 51
Droit, Roger-Pol, viiin
Dumas, Alexandre (*fils*), 142
du Terrail, Ponson, ix, 30

Eagleton, Terry, 65–66n6, 84–85n
Eliot, George (Mary Ann Evans), 2,
56, 57, 116; *Middlemarch*, 19–
20, 24–25, 26, 30–31, 133

Flaubert, Gustave, ix, 24, 30
Fleming, Ian, 182–83
Forster, John, 61

Foucault, Michel, viii, 17–18, 21, 75n, 112, 208–9n
Fouché, Joseph, 21, 74n
Freud, Sigmund, 100n, 161n, 190

Gaboriau, Emile, 24, 35
Gide, André, 1
Gilbert, Sandra M., 167–68
Grossvogel, David I., 97n
Gubar, Susan, 167–68

Hegel, Georg Wilhelm Friedrich, 87, 99n
Helsinger, Elizabeth K., 146n
Hitchcock, Alfred, 115
Hocquengham, Guy, 160
Hutter, A. D., 52, 53

Kafka, Franz, 97n
Krafft-Ebing, Richard von, 154n6
Kurosawa, Akira, 52

Leroux, Gaston, 51

Macherey, Pierre, 65–66n6
Mannoni, Octave, 16
Marcuse, Herbert, 110n
Maupassant, Guy de, ix, 30
Messac, Regis, 50n
Miller, D. A., back pain of, 191; bored, 145; as child in public library, 168; David Copperfield and, 192–93; heart of, broken by cardiologist, 146–91 *passim*; has "secret" 194–95; working out, 191
Miller, J. Hillis, 67n7, 84–85n, 99n
Moretti, Franco, 115
Mozart, Wolfgang Amadeus, 49, 176

Oliphant, Mrs. (Margaret), 153, 158
Ousby, Ian, 43, 52, 53

Parry-Jones, William Ll., 157n
Pascal, Blaise, 31–32
"Phiz" (Hablot Knight Browne), 209
Poe, Edgar Allan, 35, 41, 50n, 51, 82

Radzinowicz, Leon, 21n
Ray, W. Fraser, 171n
Roberts, David, 64n

Schreber, Daniel Paul, 160–61
Sedgwick, Eve Kosofsky, 140n, 186, 187
Sheets, Robin Lauterbach, 146n
Stendhal (Marie-Henri Beyle), 2, 14, 19, 114
Sue, Eugène, ix, 30, 77n, 142
Symons, Julian, 148n, 182n

Torok, Maria, 200n
Trollope, Anthony, ix, 2, 11–16, 19, 20, 27, 31, 56, 57, 68n, 107–5, 157, 166, 167–68. TEXTS: *An Autobiography*, 123–24, 132, 135; *Barchester Towers*, 107–45, 157, 166; *The Eustace Diamonds*, 11–16, 27, 31; the Palliser novels, 116, 118; *The Three Clerks*, 68; *The Warden*, 127–28

Ulrichs, Karl, 154, 155

Veeder, William, 146n, 154n5
Victoria (Alexandrina Victoria), 105

Weber, Max, 100n
Weeks, Jeffrey, 154n6
Wilde, Oscar, 189, 195

Zola, Emile, ix, 2, 25; *Nana*, 20–21

Printed in the United States
206449BV00001B/33/A

9 780520 067462